DISCARD

THE TROUBLED REIGN
OF
KING STEPHEN

THE TROUBLED REIGN
OF
KING STEPHEN

by

JOHN T. APPLEBY

BARNES & NOBLE INC.
NEW YORK
1970

Printed in Great Britain

For Georgina and V. H. Galbraith,
to mark a golden evening

CONTENTS

Chapter		page
I	1096–1135	1
II	1135–1137	19
III	1137–1139	43
IV	1139	64
V	1140–1141	79
VI	1141	97
VII	1142–1143	123
VIII	1143–1145	134
IX	1145–1147	148
X	1147–1148	156
XI	1149–1152	172
XII	1153–1154	186
	Bibliography	208
	Index	212

GENEALOGICAL TABLES

I Kings of England, 1066-1189 . . . 3

II Parentage of Matilda, Stephen's Queen . 8

III Earls of Northumbria and of Huntingdon . 27

IV Earls of Leicester, of Worcester, and of Warwick 44

V Earls of York and of Derby . . . 56

VI Earls of Pembroke and of Hertford . . 58

VII Earls of Chester 86

ACKNOWLEDGMENTS

I am grateful to the staff of the Library of Congress for having made their facilities available to me and for having treated me with their usual courtesy and helpfulness.

The publication of R. H. C. Davis's *King Stephen* and of his and H. A. Cronne's edition of the charters of the period in Volume III of the *Regesta Regum Anglo-Normannorum, 1066–1154*, has been of great assistance to me, and my debt to them is evident throughout this book.

Finally, I should like to pay a tribute to the memory of my dog Fritz, whose companionship cheered me whilst I was writing this book and who died in July 1968 at the age of sixteen.

J.T.A.

Washington, D.C.

ABBREVIATIONS AND SHORT TITLES

Davis—R. H. C. Davis: *King Stephen* (London, 1967)

G. de M.—John Horace Round: *Geoffrey de Mandeville* (London, 1892)

G.S.—*Gesta Stephani*, ed. K. R. Potter (Edinburgh, 1955)

H.N.—William of Malmesbury: *Historia Novella*, ed. K. R. Potter (Edinburgh, 1955)

Orderic—Orderic Vitalis: *Historia Ecclesiastica*, ed. A. Le Prévost and L. Delisle (5 vols., Paris, 1838–1855)

Regesta—*Regesta Regum Anglo-Normannorum, 1066–1154*, Vol. III, ed. H. A. Cronne and R. H. C. Davis (Oxford, 1968)

R.H.C.—*Receuil des Historiens des Croisades: Historiens Occidentaux* (5 vols., Paris, 1844–1895)

I

1096–1135

S TEPHEN became king of England in such an unexpected
fashion that the chroniclers of the time paid less attention to
his early life than they no doubt would have done if he had
been the recognised heir to the throne during the lifetime of his
uncle, King Henry I. He was the third son of Stephen, count of
Blois and Chartres, and Adela, a daughter of William the Conqueror, the first Norman king of England, and some of the contradictory qualities in his character may perhaps be explained by
his parentage, for Count Stephen and his wife seem to have been
quite different from each other in temperament. The count was
of a happy, cheerful disposition, generous and open-handed and
on good terms with everyone, clerk and lay, in his lands. In
October 1096 he set out for the Holy Land with his brother-in-
law, Robert Curthose, duke of Normandy, his cousin Robert,
count of Flanders, and their followers, the last major contingent
to join the First Crusade. He was probably able to muster a force
of between 250 and 300 knights.[1]

After spending the winter in Calabria, Count Stephen reached
Constantinople in May 1097 and was received with great honour
by the Emperor Alexis. Some of his letters to his wife have
survived, and his account of his reception by the emperor tells us
a great deal about the count. 'The emperor', he wrote, 'worthily
and fittingly received me most considerately as his son and enriched
me with most generous and precious gifts. In all God's army
and ours there is no duke or count or any other leader whom he
trusts and favours more than me. Truly, my dear, his imperial
dignity often begs and admonishes me to entrust one of our sons
to him.' One suspects that Count Stephen had been accustomed

[1] Fulcher of Chartres: *Gesta Francorum Iherusalem Peregrinantium* in *Recueil des
Historiens des Croisades: Historiens Occidentaux* [hereafter referred to as *R.H.C.*]
(5 vols., Paris, 1844–1895), Vol. III, p. 328; Sir Steven Runciman: *A History of the
Crusades* (3 vols., Cambridge, 1951–4), Vol. I, p. 339.

to hearing a great deal about what an extraordinary man his father-in-law had been, for he cannot refrain from adding, 'Your father, my dear, gave many great gifts, but compared with this man he was almost nothing.'

He and his party joined the main body of the crusaders and helped in the capture of Nicea, which surrendered to the Emperor Alexis on 19 June 1097. His crucial test came at Antioch. After crossing Asia Minor, the crusaders arrived there in October 1097 and laid siege to the city, which was so strongly defended that there seemed little hope of its surrendering as Nicea had done. With the winter came rain and bitter cold, and Count Stephen assured his wife that those who said that the heat of the sun was unbearable in Syria were badly mistaken, 'for the winter here is like our winter in the West'.[1] To the misery caused by the elements was soon joined that of hunger. The Christians early exhausted their stock of provisions and could find no more. Men lived on scraps of food; boiled leather was counted a delicacy, and some knights drank their horses' blood. Many died of starvation; some lost heart and deserted, and many more were killed in the frequent encounters with the Turks. In these encounters Stephen played a notable part and distinguished himself by his courage.[2]

As the siege dragged on interminably, he wrote again to 'Adela, his sweetest and dearest wife, and all his faithful men, both great and small', on 29 March 1098. He informed them that he was safe and sound and prospering in this the twenty-third week of the siege, and that 'all our princes, by the common counsel of the whole army, made me, unwilling though I was, their lord and the provider and governor of all their acts'. This might pass for a bit of boasting if it were not corroborated by the contemporary chroniclers of the Crusade. Peter Tudebod refers to him as 'our lord, whom all our great men elected as our leader', and Raymond of Aguilers says that the other princes elected him 'dictator'.[3] The fact remains, however, that he was

[1] H. Hagenmeyer: *Die Kreuzzugsbriefe aus den Jahren 1088–1100* (Innsbruck, 1902), pp. 138–40, 150.

[2] Radulf Cadomensi: *Gesta Tancredi in Expeditione Hierosolymitica*, in *R.H.C.*, Vol. III, pp. 646–7.

[3] Hagenmeyer, op. cit., p. 49; Peter Tudebod: *De Hierosolymitano Itinere*, in *R.H.C.*, Vol. III, p. 74; Raymond of Aguilers: *Historia Francorum Qui Ceperunt Ierusalem*, in *R.H.C.*, Vol. III, p. 258.

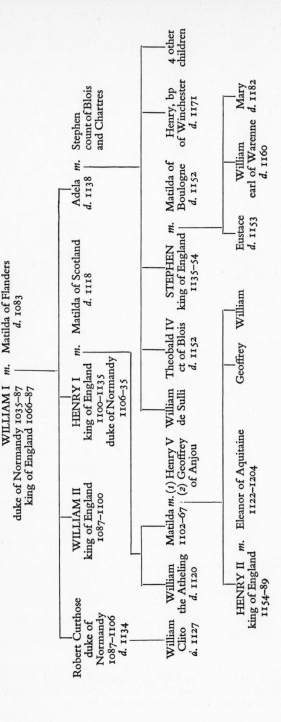

I: Kings of England, 1066–1189

not elected commander-in-chief by his fellow crusaders; one of their many difficulties, indeed, was the fact that the crusading army was made up of a number of independent armies, each under its own leader, and all the leaders were jealous and suspicious of each other. It soon became apparent that most of them were intent on establishing principalities of their own, and none was more openly ambitious than Bohemond, who was already trying to assert a claim to Antioch.

Although Stephen was obviously not commander-in-chief, he evidently was assigned a position of considerable honour and responsibility by the other leaders. Sir Steven Runciman conjectures that 'Stephen was put in charge of the administrative side of the army and was responsible for the organisation of supplies', which, in view of the prevailing famine amongst the crusaders, was certainly the most difficult job they could have found for him. William B. Stevenson says: 'More probably he acted as an executive officer, and saw that certain decisions of the leaders were carried out.' Stephen closed his letter with the promise, 'You will certainly see me as soon as possible.'[1]

It is evident from the despondent tone of this letter, as well as from its conclusion, that Stephen was discouraged and disillusioned. The glorious crusade seemed to have ground to a halt before the impregnable walls of Antioch and to have degenerated into a squabble amongst its leaders as to who could most enrich himself out of their common efforts. One may doubt that Stephen had ever had a great deal of enthusiasm for the Crusade; he had perhaps joined it only because he could not very well stay at home and bear his wife's reproaches when almost everyone else of his rank had gone.

After a winter of bitter privation and hard fighting that apparently brought the crusaders no nearer to their goal, he made up his mind, at the end of May 1098, to desert the Crusade. Pleading illness, he withdrew with his followers to Alexandretta on 2 June. Bohemond meanwhile had been in secret communication with a captain of the besieged garrison who agreed to admit the Christians into the city, and he had persuaded the other leaders of the Crusade to promise that if they succeeded in taking

[1] Runciman, op. cit., Vol. I, p. 232, note 1; William B. Stevenson, 'The First Crusade,' Chapter VIII of *The Cambridge Medieval History* (8 vols., Cambridge, 1911–36), Vol. V, p. 292, note 1; Hagenmeyer, op. cit., p. 152.

Antioch before help arrived from the Emperor Alexis the city should belong to him.

The crusaders entered Antioch on the night of 3 June, and on the following day they were in control of the city, except for the citadel. Two armies meanwhile were marching towards Antioch. The Emir Karbogha reached the city on 8 June and immediately laid siege to the crusaders; the Emperor Alexis, coming from Constantinople to the relief of the crusaders, was about half-way there when Count Stephen and the other deserters met him at Philomelium. They told him an alarming tale of the size of the Moslem army and assured him that the Christians were now beyond help. Alexis turned back, and Stephen started for home. He could hardly have chosen a worse time for his desertion, for on 28 June the crusaders, under Bohemond's leadership, defeated the Turks and put them to flight.[1]

Although Stephen was accused of cowardice and worse, he had fought bravely in the previous engagements. It appears more likely that he was suffering from an attack of common sense, combined with the constant homesickness evidenced by his affectionate letters to his wife and children. Unlike many of the other crusaders, he was not attempting to gain lands and a position of honour in the Holy Land. Everything he loved was back in Chartres, and when he became convinced that the crusaders were in a hopeless position, back to Chartres he went.

When he reached home, however, he found that the news of his desertion had preceded him; Orderic Vitalis says that almost everyone despised and reproached him. Worse still, Pope Paschal II pronounced a sentence of excommunication upon all who had deserted the Crusade and announced that they could be absolved only on condition that they returned to the Holy Land. Worst of all, no doubt, were the reproaches of his wife, who made life unbearable for him. 'But he, well aware of the perils and difficulties, feared to undergo these heavy labours again.' At last he decided that nothing could be worse than his present situation. In 1101, together with Stephen, count of Burgundy, he set out again for the Holy Land.[2]

After a difficult and dangerous passage through Asia Minor,

[1] Peter Tudebod, pp. 74–83; Fulcher of Chartres, pp. 342–50.
[2] Orderic Vitalis: *Historia Ecclesiastica*, ed. A. Le Prévost and L. Delisle [hereafter referred to as 'Orderic'] (5 vols., Paris, 1838–1855), Vol. IV, pp. 117–19.

they reached Jerusalem, which the crusaders had captured on 15 July 1099, in time to celebrate the Easter of 1102. His pilgrimage completed and his good name restored, Stephen and the count of Burgundy then went to Joppa to sail for home. They were waiting for a favourable wind when Baldwin, king of Jerusalem, summoned them to help him repulse a Saracen army that was reported to be coming up from Egypt. The Christians, greatly outnumbered, met the Moslems near Ramleh and were utterly defeated. King Baldwin, the two Count Stephens, and a few knights succeeded in fighting their way into the city and took refuge in the tower. During the night King Baldwin made his escape.

Rather than face being besieged in the tower, the Christians preferred to die fighting. On the next morning they charged into the Moslem army and were all either captured or killed. Both Count Stephens perished gloriously on 19 May 1102.[1]

Countess Adela was left a widow with five sons and three daughters. Although the monastic chroniclers ascribe to her the virtue, beauty, and learning that were conventionally attributed to all the high-born women of the time, she does not seem to have been an attractive character. She was arrogant, self-willed, and proud, and after her husband's death she governed her lands, as regent for her son, with an iron hand and embarked on a series of quarrels with Ivo, bishop of Chartres, that arose from her persistent interference in the affairs of the Church.

In 1106 she entertained Bohemond, now prince of Antioch, who was making a triumphal tour of Europe, and insisted that his marriage to Constance, the daughter of King Philip I of France, be celebrated in the cathedral at Chartres. In the following year she received an even more exalted guest. Pope Paschal II, who was visiting in France, came to Chartres in an effort to settle the quarrel between Adela and Bishop Ivo. Although the pope upheld the bishop, she nevertheless entertained him magnificently and received his blessing.

Adela decided that her eldest son was not worthy to succeed his father. William, 'a good and peaceful man', married Agnes, the daughter and heiress of Gilon de Sulli, took his wife's family name, and made no attempt to claim his inheritance. Adela designated her second son, Theobald, as the future count and

[1] Fulcher of Chartres, pp. 398 and following.

began to associate his name with hers in her official acts. Her
third son, Stephen, she sent to be educated by her brother Henry,
king of England. The fourth son, Henry, she sent to Cluny
while he was still a child, to be made a monk, and the fifth,
Philip, also dedicated to the Church, eventually became bishop
of Châlons. With her sons thus launched into the world, she
retired to the convent of Marcigny-sur-Loire about 1122 and
died there in 1138.[1]

The date of Stephen's birth is unknown, but R. H. C. Davis
thinks that it may have been about 1096.[2] His father and mother
married in 1080 or 1081, and his father was on crusade from 1096
to 1098 and again from 1101 to the end of his life. They had at
least eight children, of whom Stephen was the third of five
sons, and it may well be that he was born considerably earlier
than 1096. Neither do we know when his mother sent him to
her brother. The first date in his life that we can fix with any
certainty is 1113, when he is mentioned as being with King
Henry in Normandy. At an unknown date his uncle conferred
knighthood on him and gave him the county of Mortain, which
had been forfeited in 1106.

That year was a decisive one in King Henry's life, for it was
then that he defeated his elder brother, Robert Curthose, duke of
Normandy, at the Battle of Tinchebrai on 28 September 1106.
William the Conqueror had divided his realms between his two
elder sons, giving Robert, the eldest, the duchy of Normandy,
which belonged to the Conqueror by right of inheritance, whilst
the kingdom of England, which he had gained by conquest,
went to the second son, William Rufus. When William Rufus
died in 1100, Count Robert was on his way back from the First
Crusade, and Henry, the youngest brother, to whom the Conqueror had left only a sum of money, immediately seized the
royal treasury and had himself crowned king of England, without
any reference to the eldest brother's claims.

When Robert returned from the Holy Land, Henry set to
work to take Normandy away from him, on the grounds,
specious although true, that Robert was the centre around whom

[1] Orderic, Vol. II, p. 394; Vol. IV, pp. 188–9, 213; H. d'Arbois de Jubainville:
Histoire des ducs et des comtes de Champagne (7 vols., Paris, 1859–66), Vol. II, pp.
254–5.
[2] R. H. C. Davis: *King Stephen* [hereafter referred to as 'Davis'] (London, 1967),
p. 1.

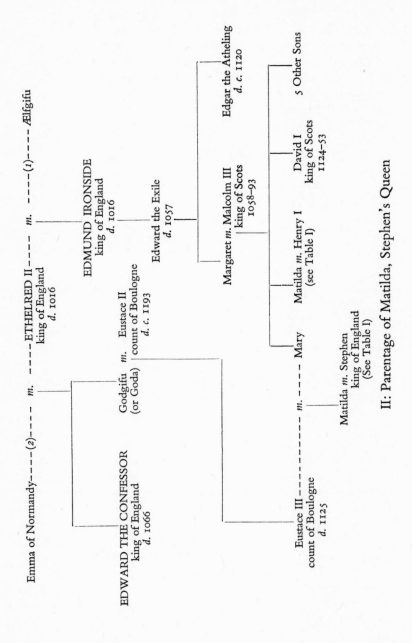

II: Parentage of Matilda, Stephen's Queen

all the discontented nobles of both England and Normandy
rallied and that in any case he was incapable of ruling his duchy.
At Tinchebrai Henry defeated his brother, captured him, and
put him in prison in England, where he remained for the rest of
his long life. William, count of Mortain, the son of the Conqueror's half-brother, was likewise captured, imprisoned for life,
and blinded for good measure. Henry later bestowed the county
of Mortain, forfeited for treason, as he regarded it, on his young
nephew, as we have seen.[1]

By this it will be seen that Stephen had already won the regard
and affection of his uncle, who treated him as if he were a member
of his immediate family. Henry also gave him the extensive
honours of Eye and Lancaster, which embraced respectively
'over 200 manors' and 'about 400 manors'. In 1125 the king
arranged for his marriage to Matilda, the daughter and heiress of
Count Eustace III of Boulogne and his wife Mary, who was the
daughter of Malcolm III, king of Scots, and the sister of Henry's
own queen, also named Matilda. A more brilliant marriage
could hardly have been arranged for Stephen if he had been the
king's own son. His wife was not only the granddaughter of the
king of Scots; she was also the great-great-granddaughter of
Edmund Ironside, king of the English. She brought Stephen
both the county of Boulogne, which was of great strategic
importance to England, since it was the continental land nearest
the island, and the great estates in England that William the
Conqueror had conferred on Count Eustace II in return for his
help during the conquest of England. Apart from the king
himself, Stephen was in all probability the greatest landowner in
England.[2]

Almost nothing is recorded of Stephen's youth at his uncle's
court beyond occasional references to his being with the king in
Normandy. These were active and anxious years in Henry's
life, for he was almost constantly engaged in resisting the efforts
of various rebellious Norman nobles, Count Fulk of Anjou, and
King Louis VI of France, who acted either alone or in various
combinations, as the occasion arose, to try to take the duchy

---

[1] Orderic, Vol. IV, pp. 189, 231, 234, 401-2; Charles Wendell David: *Robert
Curthose, Duke of Normandy* (Cambridge, Mass., 1920), pp. 171-6, 179-80.
[2] John Horace Round: *Studies in Peerage and Family History* (London, 1901),
p.168; Davis, pp. 8-10.

away from him and install as rightful duke of Normandy William
Clito, the only son of Robert Curthose, who was born in 1101
and whom Henry had seized when he captured Falaise in 1106.
Henry, however, did not dare to treat the child as he had the
father, but turned him over to Hélias of Saint-Saëns, the husband
of Count Robert's illegitimate daughter.[1]

The only mention of Stephen that gives any clue to his character
is Orderic Vitalis's account of the rebellion of the inhabitants of
Alençon against him in 1118.   King Henry had taken the town
away from the rebellious Robert of Bellême and given it to
Theobald of Blois in partial payment for Theobald's help in
Normandy.   Theobald in turn had given it to his brother Stephen
in exchange for Stephen's share of their father's land in France.

Stephen's rule was harsh and his exactions almost intolerable,
which suggests that he may have been trying to imitate his
uncle's sternness.   When the inhabitants complained, Stephen
forced them to give him hostages, whom he treated so cruelly
that the inhabitants rebelled and called in Count Fulk of Anjou to
help them.   It was only with the greatest difficulty that King
Henry, coming to his nephew's aid, was able to quench this
rebellion.[2]

During these years of Stephen's youth and early manhood,
while he was being treated with the greatest kindness and favour
by his uncle, Henry's acknowledged heir was his only legitimate
son, William the Atheling, born in 1103, to whom all the free
men of England and Normandy had sworn fealty in 1115.   When
the lad was ten years old Henry had arranged for his marriage to
Matilda, the elder daughter of his old enemy, Count Fulk of
Anjou.   At first sight it seems surprising that Henry should have
sought an alliance with a man who devoted a great part of his
energy to almost ceaseless attacks on the Norman frontier and
who wanted to take away as much of the duchy as he could from
Henry and to foment discord between the duke and the more
rebellious of his subjects.   Henry, however, could ill afford to
have such a dangerous enemy to the south of his duchy,
and he probably hoped by this alliance to win him over as a
friend and ally.   The young couple were married at Lisieux in

[1] Orderic, Vol. II, p. 390; Vol. III, p. 228; Vol. IV, p. 232; David, *Robert Curthose*, pp. 180-1.
[2] Orderic, Vol. IV, pp. 322-4, 331-5.

June 1119, and the future of the succession seemed secured.[1]
All this was drastically changed on the night of 25 November
1120. King Henry and his court had assembled at the port of
Barfleur in Normandy and prepared to return to England.
William the Atheling and about 300 of the younger nobles
embarked in the White Ship, and before they set sail the Atheling
had three barrels of wine distributed amongst the crew. According to Orderic Vitalis, both the crew and the passengers were
thoroughly drunk when they set sail that evening. Stephen
was not amongst the passengers, and Orderic gives two contradictory reasons for his absence from the group in which both his
rank and his age would have placed him. According to the first
account, Stephen boarded the White Ship but was so disgusted
by the drunken and lascivious behaviour of the passengers that
he disembarked and sailed instead with his uncle the king. Later
Orderic says that he had an attack of diarrhoea, left the White
Ship for that reason, and then boarded the king's ship. Henry of
Huntingdon casts further aspersions on the character of the
passengers in the White Ship by remarking that all or nearly all
of them were reputed to be or were in truth 'enmeshed in the
sin of sodomy'.[2]
Some priests came down to the waterside to bless the ship and
her passengers, but they were greeted with jeers by the drunken
young people. After the king's ship had sailed, the White Ship
set sail and was almost immediately driven on to a large rock by
the inebriated pilot. With her port side stove in, the ship
quickly sank. The cries of the drowning passengers could be
heard both on the shore and on board the king's ship, but it was
too dark for the king's party to see what had happened. Only one
passenger, a butcher from Rouen, survived. William the Atheling; two illegitimate children of Henry I, Richard and Matilda,
the wife of Rotrou, count of Perche; Stephen's sister Matilda and
her husband, Richard, earl of Chester; and many others perished.[3]
With the death of the Atheling, the star of William Clito, the
son of Robert Curthose, appeared to be rising. He was generally

[1] William of Malmesbury: *De Gestis Regum Anglorum*, ed. William Stubbs (2
vols., Rolls Series 90, 1887-9), Vol. II, p. 495; Orderic, Vol. IV, pp. 306, 347, 416.
[2] Orderic, Vol. IV, pp. 412, 420; Henry of Huntingdon: *Historia Anglorum*,
ed. Thomas Arnold (Rolls Series 74, 1879), p. 241.
[3] Orderic, Vol. IV, pp. 412-18; William of Malmesbury: *De Gestis Regum
Anglorum*, Vol. II, pp. 496-7.

conceded to be the heir to the throne, for, if one excepts his father, whom King Henry was keeping in prison, he was the last direct descendant of William the Conqueror in the male line. Count Fulk of Anjou returned from a visit to the Holy Land in 1122 to find not only that his son-in-law, upon whom his alliance with King Henry had been founded, was dead, but also that Henry refused to return her dowry to Matilda, who had retired to the cloister at Fontevraud. Fulk therefore went back to his old friends, the rebels amongst the Norman nobles and their chief supporter, King Louis VI of France. Since they were all committed to the cause of the Clito as the natural leader of Henry's opponents, Fulk took the unfortunate young man, who had spent most of his life as an exile and as a puppet in the hands of Henry's enemies, under his wing. He gave William his younger daughter, Sibyl, and conferred upon him the county of Maine, which Fulk had acquired through his wife, Eremburga, the daughter and heiress of Count Élie.[1]

Henry was determined that William should in no circumstances be allowed to succeed him to either Normandy or England, for to allow him to do so would be equivalent to admitting that he had unjustly taken Normandy away from the rightful duke and England from the rightful king, and he strove to check each move that would advance William in any way. In 1124, therefore, he induced Pope Calixtus II to annul William's marriage to Sibyl on the ground of consanguinity within the forbidden degree. Apparently no one was inconsiderate enough to mention the fact that Henry's son William had been related to his bride in exactly the same degree that the Clito was to Sibyl. Henry's enemies were equally fertile in expedients; Louis VI in 1126 called upon his nobles to help the Clito in every way possible, and shortly thereafter Louis arranged for his marriage to Jeanne, the half-sister of his own wife, and gave him the Vexin, the much-disputed land on the border of Normandy and the Ile-de-France on the north of the Seine.[2]

Soon after the disaster of the White Ship, King Henry married Adeliza of Louvain in the hope that she would provide him with

---

[1] William of Malmesbury, op. cit., Vol. II, p. 498; *The Peterborough Chronicle, 1070–1154*, ed. Cecil Clark (Oxford, 1958), p. 45.

[2] William of Malmesbury: *Historia Novella* [hereafter referred to as *H.N.*], ed. K. R. Potter (Edinburgh, 1955), pp. 2–3; Orderic, Vol. IV, p. 474.

an heir.[1]   Although he had had two legitimate children and at
least twenty bastards, his second marriage proved fruitless.   As
William Clito's prospects appeared brighter with each new mark
of King Louis's favour and support, Henry determined upon an
unprecedented step to make sure that the succession remained in
his own family.   His only surviving legitimate child was a
daughter, Matilda, born in 1102, who had been sent to Germany
at the age of eight and betrothed to the emperor, Henry V, a
man thirty years her senior, to whom she was married in 1114.
The emperor had died childless in May 1125, and King Henry
summoned his daughter to return to him.   Matilda did so with
the greatest reluctance, for she had been brought up in Germany,
had many possessions there, and was accustomed to German ways.

Matilda at any rate joined her father in Normandy and went
back with him to England, a country she had not seen for over
fifteen years, in September 1126.   At a great meeting of the
principal members of the clergy and nobility in London at the
following Christmas, Henry demanded that they swear that they
would, 'immediately and without any hesitation, accept his
daughter Matilda, the empress, as their lady if he should die
without a male heir.'[2]

Such an unheard-of demand threw the assembly into conster-
nation.   England had never been ruled by a woman, and this
was not the time to embark on such a rash experiment.   It was
obvious that Henry intended that his heir should rule over both
England and Normandy, and his own experience had shown that
only the strongest and most ruthless of men was equal to such a
task. Furthermore, many of his audience may in their hearts have
sided with William Clito, for there had never been any lack of
rebellious Normans to oppose King Henry.   Finally, although
not many of them could have gained a close acquaintance with
his daughter during the few months that she had been in England,
she was of such a haughty, imperious, and disagreeable temperament that few of them could have welcomed the prospect of
being ruled by such a woman.   If Henry's desperate expedient to secure the succession were to work, Matilda would
have to marry and produce a male heir to carry on the line,
which meant in the last analysis that the English barons were
agreeing to buy a pig in a poke in the shape of Matilda's

[1] Henry of Huntingdon, p. 243.   [2] H.N., p. 3.

future husband, who would of course rule in her name.

Henry had no little difficulty in framing a speech that would set forth his daughter's right to the succession without at the same time making an even stronger case for his brother, Robert Curthose, who was now in prison at Bristol under the care of the king's bastard son, Robert, earl of Gloucester,[1] or for Robert's son, William Clito, since any direct reference to Matilda's descent from William the Conqueror would apply even more strongly to the Conqueror's eldest son and grandson. As reported by William of Malmesbury,[2] then, Henry passed briefly over her right to succeed her grandfather, her uncle, and her father and dwelt instead in glowing terms on her descent on her mother's side from no less than fourteen kings, from Egbert, king of the West Saxons, to Edward the Confessor, who had arranged for the marriage of his great-niece Margaret to Malcolm III of Scotland, whose daughter Matilda was the mother of this same Matilda the Empress whose claims he was now asserting. In his anxiety to leave William the Conqueror out of the picture, Henry may well have caused his hearers to wonder not only how he based his own claim to the throne but also why Matilda's right to the throne was any better than that, say, of her cousin Matilda of Boulogne, Stephen's wife, since her mother and Matilda's were sisters and thus shared the same royal descent that now served to qualify the empress to be Henry's heir.

Whatever their misgivings may have been, the barons had little choice except to take the oath as the king dictated it, for it would have been a brave man indeed who would resist King Henry to his face. As they are reported to have said afterwards, 'With the imperious thunder of his voice, which no one could resist, he compelled rather than ordered the leading men of the whole kingdom to swear to her as his heir.' Bishop Roger of Salisbury later declared that he had taken the oath only on the condition that the king would not give his daughter in marriage to anyone outside the kingdom, which seems a reasonable enough precaution if one is willing to believe that his bishops were brave enough to try to extort a condition from the king as the price of their obedience. In any case, so accomplished an oath-breaker as Henry I must have known that little reliance could be placed on

---

[1] *The Peterborough Chronicle*, p. 48; David: *Robert Curthose*, pp. 186–7.
[2] *H.N.*, pp. 3–4.

an oath exacted under such pressure as he was able to bring.[1]

Archbishop William of Canterbury, as the first subject in the kingdom, took the oath first, followed by Bishop Roger of Salisbury, the king's chief justiciar and most trusted servant, and then all the other bishops and abbots did likewise. After the clergy had taken the oath, David, king of Scots, the king's brother-in-law and the highest-ranking layman present, swore first. A dispute then arose as to who should be next, not so much from eagerness to take the oath as from a jealous concern for dignity and precedence, between the king's bastard son, Robert, earl of Gloucester, and his nephew Stephen. Robert was born before Henry became king and was probably the oldest of his illegitimate children. Henry had recognised him as his child and had given him as his wife Mabel, 'a beautiful and excellent woman, a lady both obedient to her husband and blessed with numerous and most fair offspring'. As the daughter and heiress of Robert son of Hamon she brought her husband extensive lands in Normandy and Wales and the honour of Gloucester in England. Although he was probably married, at the latest, soon after the death of Robert son of Hamon in 1107, his father, who was extremely sparing of earldoms, did not make him earl of Gloucester till 1122. He was not only a brave and resourceful warrior and a natural leader of men; he was a patron of learning and the special friend of William of Malmesbury, who wrote his *Historia Novella* to explain Robert's part in the great events yet to come. Although he was the king's favourite son, he was nevertheless a bastard, and it was probably because of that fact, and not because he favoured Stephen over Robert, that King Henry decided that the count of Boulogne should have precedence over the bastard earl of Gloucester, and Stephen took the oath immediately after King David.[2]

Having thus secured the recognition of Matilda as his heir, Henry next attempted to use her as he had used his son William in an effort to win over the count of Anjou. In the summer of 1127 he sent her back to Normandy, escorted by her brother Robert and Brian fitz Count, with orders to Archbishop Geoffrey

---

[1] *Gesta Stephani* [hereafter referred to as *G.S.*], ed. K. P. Potter (Edinburgh, 1955), p. 7; *H.N.*, p. 5.

[2] *H.N.*, p. 4; John Horace Round: *Geoffrey de Mandeville* [hereafter referred to as *G. de M.*] (London, 1892), p. 420.

of Rouen to arrange for a marriage between her and Count Fulk's only son Geoffrey. No one raised the point that the young couple were related in exactly the same degree as were William Clito and Geoffrey's sister Sibyl, whose marriage the pope had, at King Henry's urging, dissolved on the ground of consanguinity. Count Fulk agreed, and the couple were betrothed that summer. Geoffrey, however, was not yet fourteen years old, and the marriage was consequently delayed.[1]

The fortunes of William Clito were meanwhile rising. When Charles the Good, count of Flanders, was murdered on 2 March 1127, leaving no heirs, Louis VI as overlord bestowed the county on William. In August of that year he launched an attack against Stephen of Boulogne, whose lands bordered on his, presumably in an effort to strengthen his frontiers before turning again to Normandy. Stephen met the attack with such success, however, that the two agreed to a truce to last for three years. Before that period expired, William was wounded at the siege of Alost in a civil war within his county and died in July 1128.[2]

Henry followed his daughter to Normandy in August 1127, and much of his time was spent in coping with the attacks of his enemies on that duchy. He knighted the young Geoffrey of Anjou at Rouen on 10 June 1128, and then the party went to Le Mans, where Geoffrey and Matilda were married on the 17th. By the death of William Clito the most likely contestant to the throne of England was removed, but Henry's scheme for securing the succession to his daughter encountered a fresh obstacle in the incompatibility of the newly married couple.[3]

Count Fulk, a widower, went back to Jerusalem and married Melisende, the daughter of King Baldwin II, whom he was to succeed in 1132 as king of Jerusalem, leaving his counties of Anjou and Maine to Geoffrey. Geoffrey was a high-spirited lad who did not relish being married to a woman eleven years his senior and of such a haughty and disagreeable disposition that life with her was almost impossible. He did not divorce her, as he might well have done. He had succeeded to all his father's designs upon Normandy, and he hoped through his wife, disagreeable though

---

[1] *Historia Gaufridi Ducis Normannorum et Comitis Andegavorum*, ed. Louis Halphen and René Poupardin, in *Collection des textes pour l'étude de l'histoire*, Vol. XLVIII (Paris, 1913), pp. 177–8.

[2] Orderic, Vol. IV, pp. 476–7, 482.

[3] Henry of Huntingdon, p. 247; *Historia Gaufridi*, pp. 178, 180.

she was, eventually to gain control of the duchy. Normandy, however, was the limit of his ambition; he seems never to have shown the slightest interest in England. When he found his wife unbearable he sent her back to her father at Rouen, and Henry took her with him to England in the late summer of 1131. Geoffrey then saved the situation by asking for his wife's return. Henry laid the matter before his council at Northampton on 8 September, and they decided that the only solution was to send her back to her husband, which would indicate that both they and her father took a dim view of the prospects of finding another husband for her. 'After this the king's daughter was sent back to her husband and given a reception fitting for such a virago.'[1]

Matilda may have learned her lesson, at least as regards her behaviour towards her husband; her general character remained unimproved. She went back to her husband and bore him two sons in rapid succession: Henry, born in March 1133, and Geoffrey in May 1134. Her second childbirth was so difficult that her life was despaired of, and she did not have a third child, William, till August 1136.[2]

Robert Curthose died at Cardiff in February 1134, at the age of eighty, having spent the last twenty-eight years of his life as his brother's prisoner. With his death, the infant Henry now appeared to be his grandfather's certain successor, and when King Henry went to Normandy in 1134 it must have seemed to him that his efforts to keep the crown in his family were at last to meet with success. Matilda, who never ceased to style herself the Empress, contrived to poison her father's last years, however, by stirring up trouble between him and her husband. She incited Count Geoffrey to lay claim to various castles in Normandy that he said Henry had promised him at the time of his marriage, and he seems even to have demanded that his father-in-law turn the whole duchy over to him, as his infant son's birthright. These dissensions were seized on joyfully by the rebellious Norman nobles, and the duchy was in such a troubled state that Henry did not dare leave it in order to go back to England.[3]

[1] Henry of Huntingdon, p. 252.
[2] Robert of Torigni: *Chronicle*, ed. Richard Howlett. Vol. IV of *Chronicles of the Reigns of Stephen, Henry II, and Richard I* (Rolls Series 82, 4 vols., 1884–9), pp. 123–4, 129.
[3] Orderic, Vol. IV, p. 486; Vol. V, pp. 18, 42, 45–6; David; *Robert Curthose*, p. 187; Henry of Huntingdon, pp. 253–4; Robert of Torigni, p. 128.

While this matter of the succession to the crown was occupying men's minds, Count Stephen was in the background, and one may suppose that he was occupied largely with his own county of Boulogne and with his estates in England, although he of course was in occasional attendance on his uncle the king, to whom he owed all his good fortune. Brought up largely in England, he had made a good name for himself. The author of the *Gesta Stephani*, who tried to present him in the most favourable light possible, describes him as 'rich and unassuming, munificent and affable, bold and brave, judicious and long-suffering'. William of Malmesbury, writing from the opposite point of view, says: 'He was an energetic man but lacking in prudence, strenuous in war, of extraordinary spirit in beginning any arduous task, lenient to his enemies and easily appeased: though you admired his kindness in promising, still you felt that his words lacked truth and his promises fulfilment.' He tells, too, that Stephen had made many friends by his affable behaviour. 'When he was a count, Stephen had gained such affection as can hardly be imagined by the easiness of his manner and by the way he jested, sat, and ate even with the humblest.' Henry of Huntingdon, a more impartial writer, remarks on his courage and daring, and Orderic Vitalis praises him for being 'humble and gentle to the good and meek'. Richard of Hexham says: 'He was a man of such gentleness and kindness that even his enemies, when they came back to him, found him merciful beyond their hopes.'[1]

There seems to have been much more of his father than of his mother in Stephen's character. From the gallant crusader who ruined his life and reputation by a singularly unfortunate error of judgment and then retrieved his good name by a final act of heroic courage, Stephen inherited a charming and happy disposition, an ability to please and get on well with others, and the daring and bravery that inspired the elder Stephen in the brighter moments of his career. His inheritance from his mother showed only occasionally in ill-inspired fits of sternness, as in his harsh treatment of the inhabitants of Alençon, and most conspicuously in the overwhelming ambition that led him to the greatest gamble of his life.

[1] *G.S.*, p. 3; *H.N.*, pp. 16, 18; Henry of Huntingdon, p. 256; Orderic, Vol. V, p. 129; Richard of Hexham: *Chronicle*, ed. Richard Howlett, in *Chronicles of the Reigns of Stephen, Henry II, and Richard I*, Vol. III, p. 145.

II

1135–1137

KING Henry went to one of his favourite hunting lodges, Lyons-la-Forêt, about eighteen miles east of Rouen, on Monday, 25 November 1135, in order to enjoy his favourite sport. That evening, however, he fell ill. Henry of Huntingdon says that his illness was caused by his eating lampreys, 'which always made him sick, and yet he always loved them. And although his physician had forbidden him this food, the king did not abide by this salutary counsel'. When it became evident that his illness was no mere fit of indigestion, he confessed his sins to his chaplains, and then, as his illness grew more severe, he summoned Hugh, archbishop of Rouen, to his bedside. Hugh arrived on Friday and spent the last three days of the king's life with him. Henry confessed his sins a second and third time and was given absolution; he received Holy Communion and the last anointing. All that the Church could do for him was done. He ordered that his body be buried at Reading in the abbey he had founded, and he directed his son Robert, who had custody of his treasury at Falaise, to withdraw from it £60,000 (this was probably by the Angevin reckoning, equivalent to £15,000 sterling) with which to pay the wages of his servants and hired soldiers and distribute gifts amongst them; the remainder was to be given to the poor for the good of his soul. 'Would that those who held and now hold his treasures had done so!' remarked Archbishop Hugh in his report to Pope Innocent II.[1]

Henry died on the evening of Sunday, 1 December 1135, at the age of sixty-seven. In addition to the clergy, five earls were present at his deathbed: his son, Robert of Gloucester; William of Warenne, earl of Surrey; Rotrou, count of Perche; Waleran, count of Meulan, and Robert, earl of Leicester. The question that exercised the minds of all of them was the disposition the

[1] Henry of Huntingdon, p. 254; Orderic, Vol. V, pp. 49–50; *H.N.*, pp. 13–14.

king would make of his realm. Neither Orderic Vitalis nor Henry of Huntingdon, the two reasonably impartial chroniclers, mentions the succession in their accounts of Henry's death. According to William of Malmesbury, who favoured the empress or, rather, her brother the earl of Gloucester, 'When he was asked about his successor he assigned all his land on both sides of the sea to his daughter in lawful and perpetual succession,' purposely omitting the names both of Count Geoffrey, who was almost at open war with him, and of his grandson Henry, lest Geoffrey make any claims as acting on his son's behalf.

According to the author of the *Gesta Stephani*, some of Stephen's supporters who were present at Henry's death declared: 'So that we should clearly know that it did not please him that what he had for a certain reason approved in his lifetime should be unalterable after his death, when many men were standing by and hearing the truthful confession of his errors, he very openly repented of having forcibly imposed the oath upon his barons.'[1]

When the legitimacy of Stephen's claim to the throne was argued before Pope Innocent II in April 1139, John of Salisbury reports that Arnulf, archdeacon of Séez, one of the king's representatives, stated that 'King Henry changed his mind and on his deathbed designated Stephen, his sister's son, as his heir. And he stated that this had been proved by the oath of Earl Hugh [Bigod of Norfolk] and two knights before the English Church to William, archbishop of Canterbury and legate of the Apostolic See.'[2]

The oath taken by Hugh Bigod is mentioned by Ralph of Diceto, who says: 'Hugh Bigod, the king's seneschal, coming to England, proved by an oath before the archbishop of Canterbury that when King Henry was on his deathbed, because of certain enmities between him and the empress, he disinherited her and made Stephen, count of Boulogne, his heir'. Gervase of Canterbury says: 'One of the greatest men in England was present and swore and said that he was present when King Henry in good faith and of his own free will released [men from] that oath.'[3]

[1] *H.N.*, p. 13; *G.S.*, p. 7.

[2] John of Salisbury: *Historia Pontificalis*, ed. Reginald L. Poole (Oxford, 1927), pp. 85–6, 108.

[3] Ralph of Diceto: *Opera Historia*, ed. William Stubbs (2 vols., Rolls Series 68, 1876), Vol. I, p. 248; Gervase of Canterbury: *Historical Works*, ed. William Stubbs (2 vols., Rolls Series 73, 1879–80), Vol. I, p. 94.

The value of Hugh's oath, however, was challenged before the pope by Ulgar, bishop of Angers, who declared that Hugh had not been present at Henry's death and therefore was not in a position to swear as to what the king had said on that occasion. Earl Robert of Gloucester, who on the other hand had undeniably been present, declared, at the Battle of Lincoln in 1141, that Hugh was a perjurer on two counts, because he had betrayed his oath to support Matilda and because he had falsely sworn that King Henry had granted the realm to Stephen.[1]

It is possible that King Henry, when he felt death approaching, was so bitter against his daughter and her husband for their attempts to take over Normandy that he released his nobles from their oath of fealty to her. It is equally possible that he intended to hold them to their oath but that they so disliked Matilda and Geoffrey that they refused to be bound by an oath that had been extorted from them almost by force. With such contradictory reports as to what happened at Henry's deathbed such speculations are mere guesswork. The significant fact is that soon after Henry's death the Norman nobles, with Robert, earl of Gloucester, amongst them, assembled either at Neufbourg or at Lisieux and offered the duchy to Count Theobald as the eldest of the king's nephews. No mention, apparently, was made on this occasion of the Empress Matilda and her claim, which would indicate that the nobles considered her as quite out of the running.

Whilst they were debating the matter, a monk arrived on 20 December to inform them that Count Stephen had already landed in England and claimed the crown and 'that all the English had received Stephen and chosen to obey him and to make him their king'. Since most of the nobles had estates in both Normandy and England, with Count Theobald's permission they decided to accept Stephen as both king of England and duke of Normandy. Count Theobald, however, as the elder brother was much annoyed by Stephen's temerity.[2]

Count Stephen, as soon as he heard the news of his uncle's death, had immediately set out for England with only a few followers. The speed with which he acted would perhaps indicate that he had already made his plans in advance. He sailed from Wissant and landed at Dover, where he was repulsed

[1] John of Salisbury, op. cit., p. 88; Henry of Huntingdon, p. 270.
[2] Orderic, Vol. V, p. 56; Robert of Torigni, pp. 128-9.

by the castellan. He then went on to Canterbury and was denied entry into the town. Both of these places belonged to Earl Robert of Gloucester, and it was only natural that the men he had placed in charge there should refuse to receive Stephen without specific orders from their master.[1]

When he reached London, however, he was given a reception that made up for the earlier rebuffs. The leading citizens greeted him enthusiastically and at a general assembly unanimously elected him their king. As a condition of this election, Stephen made a treaty with the Londoners, swearing 'that he would gird himself with all his might to pacify the kingdom for the benefit of them all'; whilst the Londoners in turn swore that 'as long as he lived they would uphold him with their resources and guard him with their strength'. Although one may dismiss as extravagant their claim to have the right and special privilege of electing the king, their support was certainly essential for any claimant to the crown, and Stephen gained it without any difficulty.

He went next to Winchester to meet his brother Henry, 'on whom his enterprise wholly depended'. Henry, the fourth son of Stephen of Blois and Adela, had received an excellent education as a monk at Cluny. His uncle, King Henry, invited him to England in 1126 and secured his election as abbot of Glastonbury. The abbey had fallen on evil days, but Henry, who had a notable gift for administration, ruled it so wisely and so well that its fortunes quickly improved, discipline was restored, and its reputation increased. He was consecrated bishop of Winchester in 1129, and by special permission of both the king and the pope he remained abbot of Glastonbury as well, to the great joy of his monks, who refused to part with him.[2]

A further indication that Stephen had formed his plans thoroughly is to be found in the statement in the *Gesta Stephani* that Bishop Henry had often implored the treasurer, William of Pont de l'Arche, with the added inducement of a reward, to turn over both Winchester Castle and the royal treasury to him as soon as the news of the king's death reached them. Bishop Henry could have wanted to secure these only for his brother, whose plans he must have known. The leading citizens of Winchester,

[1] *H.N.*, p. 15; Gervase of Canterbury, Vol. I, p. 94; Orderic, Vol. V, p. 110.
[2] *G.S.*, pp. 3–5; Dom David Knowles: *The Monastic Order in England* (2nd edn., Cambridge, 1963), pp. 282–3, 287.

with the bishop at their head, went out to meet Stephen, greeted him warmly, and escorted him into the city.

Although William of Pont de l'Arche had, properly enough, refused Bishop Henry's request, when he learned of Stephen's arrival he turned over both the castle and the treasury to him. King Henry is said to have amassed nearly a hundred thousand pounds, as well as 'gold and silver vessels of great weight and inestimable value'. The next man to come over to Stephen's side was Bishop Roger of Salisbury, King Henry's chief justiciar and most trusted servant and probably the most powerful man in the kingdom. He, if anyone, should have known King Henry's mind, and the fact that he was one of the first to accept Stephen as Henry's successor was of great importance. Men might have expected Bishop Henry to support his brother merely out of family loyalty, but the adherence of the chief justiciar, to whom King Henry had entrusted the governance of the country when he was in Normandy, certainly convinced many men of the justice of Stephen's claim.[1]

Stephen's successes up to this point meant nothing unless he could succeed in having himself crowned, and only the archbishop of Canterbury could crown the king of England. William of Corbeil had been the first one to take the oath of fealty to the Empress Matilda, and he immediately brought up that oath when Stephen's supporters urged him to anoint the count as king. Then followed a long debate in which Stephen's supporters urged first that the oath was not binding because it had been sworn to under duress and next that King Henry himself had released them from it on his deathbed.[2]

The archbishop was at last convinced by these arguments and particularly, one suspects, by the fact that Stephen was present in England and received by the Londoners, the late king's chief justiciar and his treasurer, and the bishop of Winchester, whereas the empress was across the Channel and taking no steps, as far as he knew, to secure the crown for herself or her infant son. To recognise Stephen must have seemed to the archbishop the surest way to secure a peaceful succession and the tranquillity of the realm. He seized the occasion, however, to wring from Stephen an oath to restore and preserve the liberty of the Church, and Bishop Henry stood as guarantor and pledge for his brother's oath.

[1] *G.S.*, p. 5; *H.N.*, p. 17.   [2] *G.S.*, pp. 6–8.

Stephen was anointed and crowned king of the English in Westminster Abbey by the archbishop of Canterbury on Sunday, 22 December 1135. The fact that William of Corbeil, archbishop of Canterbury and papal legate, the head of the Church in England, crowned Stephen was of particular importance because it showed that he regarded the oath he had taken concerning the succession of Matilda to be no longer binding. All the others who had taken the oath could now follow the archbishop's example in good conscience. William was rather weak and pliable, but he was neither cynical nor vicious, and it is hard to believe that he would perjure himself in his old age.

Only three bishops—the archbishop himself and those of Winchester and Salisbury—no abbots, and few nobles were present. It could not have been an impressive occasion, but the essential rite was performed. Since the death of King Edward almost seventy years before, the succession to the crown had been so irregular that it is almost useless to debate whether it had been by election, by hereditary right, or by seizure. Stephen's contemporaries, at any rate, thought that his claim was as good as anyone else's, and the deciding factor was the quickness and vigour with which he asserted that claim. King Stephen held his Christmas court 'in royal fashion', but it is not likely that the attendance was much larger than it had been at his coronation.[1]

King Henry's body meanwhile had been crudely embalmed[2] at Rouen and then brought to Caen, where it rested for four weeks whilst his servants waited for a favourable wind. Then, as he had ordered, his body was brought to be buried in Reading Abbey, a Cluniac house that he had founded in 1121. Stephen went to Reading for his uncle's funeral on 4 January 1136. Although Henry of Huntingdon says that 'many bishops and nobleman' were present, the list of witnesses to a charter that Stephen granted whilst he was there names only a few more than those who had been present at his coronation. Of the eight, three are the same bishops; Hugh Bigod and William of Pont de l'Arche we have met before, and the only new names are those of Payne son of John and Ingelram of Sai, who Round conjectures had come with Payne. The names of Payne son of John

---

[1] H.N., pp. 15-16; Gervase of Canterbury, Vol. I, p. 95.
[2] Readers with a strong stomach and a taste for the macabre will find the revolting details in Henry of Huntingdon, pp. 256-7.

and Miles of Gloucester, to whom the charter was granted, represent important accessions to Stephen's side from that part of the country in which, later on, he was most to need friends. Miles of Gloucester was sheriff of Gloucestershire and constable of Gloucester Castle, and Stephen's charter confirms him in the possession of his lands and honours; his friend Payne was sheriff of Herefordshire and Shropshire. Between the two they controlled 'all the border between England and Wales from the Severn to the sea'. A second charter on the same subject, which is probably of the same date, gives only three additional names.[1]

From Reading the king went to Oxford, and there he repeated and confirmed the promises that he had made 'to God and the people and Holy Church' on the day of his coronation. The fact that he did this probably indicates that he was met by an assembly of barons larger at any rate than the one at his coronation. Whilst this repetition was of course a bid for their support, it was in no way different from the promises made by Henry I at the beginning of his reign. It had become a well-established custom for the new king to renounce the evil customs of his predecessors and to promise good government to his subjects.[2]

Stephen promised first that when a bishop died he would not keep the temporal possessions of the bishopric in his hands in order to enjoy the income from them but that he would immediately permit a canonical election and confer the temporalities upon the bishop thus elected. He promised secondly that he would not keep private forests belonging to someone else in his own hands, treating them as parts of the royal forest, as King Henry had done, and prosecuting the owners for hunting their own game or cutting their own timber. The extension of the forest laws by Henry I to cover privately-owned forests was bitterly resented, as Stephen's renunciation of it shows. His third promise was to abolish the Danegeld, a tax of two shillings on every hide of land, which his predecessors had levied every year.

While Stephen was at Oxford he learned that his uncle, King

[1] Regesta Regum Anglo-Normannorum, 1066–1154. Vol. III, Regesta Regis Staphani ac Mathildis Imperatricis ac Gaufridi et Henrici Ducum Normannorum, 1135–1154 [hereafter referred to as Regesta], ed. H. A. Cronne and R. H. C. Davis, in continuation of the work of the late H. W. C. Davis (Oxford, 1968), pp. 148–9; G. de M., pp. 10–14, 16.

[2] Henry of Huntingdon, p. 258; Richard of Hexham, pp. 142–4.

David, had invaded England near Christmas and seized five of the most important castles near the border, those of Carlisle, Wark, Alnwick, Norham, and Newcastle-upon-Tyne. David was acting ostensibly on behalf of his niece, the Empress Matilda, for he exacted oaths of fealty to her and took hostages from the leading men of the North, but it is obvious that his main interest was to seize as much territory as he could. Stephen gathered 'such an army as no one in England could remember'. William of Malmesbury tells us that 'knights of all kinds and men in light armour flocked to him, especially from Flanders and Brittany'. They were joined by English mercenaries, who had had lean pickings during the peace and tranquillity of the latter years of King Henry's reign.[1] It is an impressive tribute to Stephen's skill and efficiency as a military leader that he was able to raise such a large army and bring it to Durham in less than a month.

When Stephen arrived in Durham with this great force on 5 February, David, realising the futility of trying to resist such an army, came to meet him and made his submission. He surrendered the castles he had seized, but Stephen graciously allowed him to keep Carlisle. Out of respect for the oath that he had sworn on Matilda's behalf, however, the king of Scots would not swear fealty to the English king. Stephen stayed at Durham for a fortnight, and it is probable that during that time he received the fealty of the leading men of that part of the country. David's son Henry accompanied Stephen to York and there became Stephen's man. The king gave him the earldom of Huntingdon, which David, who had held it by virtue of his marriage to Matilda, the widow of Simon of Senlis, earl of Huntingdon, resigned in his son's favour. Stephen also promised him that if he should decide to revive the earldom of Northumbria, which had been in abeyance since Roger of Mowbray had forfeited it by his treason in 1095, he would give first consideration to Henry. Henry's claim to the earldom was based on the fact that his mother was also the daughter of Waltheof, earl of Northumbria, whom the Conqueror had executed for treason on 31 May 1067.[2]

---

[1] Richard of Hexham, p. 145; Henry of Huntingdon, pp. 258-9; *H.N.*, p. 17; William John Corbett: 'England, 1087-1154', in Vol. V of *The Cambridge Medieval History*, p. 543.

[2] Richard of Hexham, pp. 145-6; Henry of Huntingdon, pp. 258-9; Davis, pp. 134, 137.

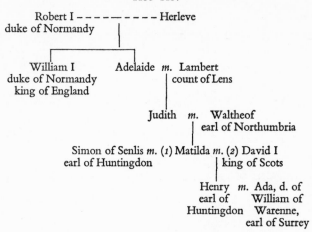

```
        Robert I – – – – – – – – – Herleve
      duke of Normandy            |
                                  |
      ┌───────────────────────────┐
   William I            Adelaide  m.  Lambert
 duke of Normandy                 |   count of Lens
  king of England                 |
                                  |
                        Judith   m.   Waltheof
                                  |    earl of Northumbria
                                  |
         Simon of Senlis m. (1) Matilda m. (2) David I
         earl of Huntingdon            |   king of Scots
                                       |
                              Henry   m.  Ada, d. of
                              earl of     William of
                              Huntingdon  Warenne,
                                          earl of Surrey
```

III: Earls of Northumbria and of Huntingdon

Stephen's return from the North, accompanied by his imposing army, probably constituted the royal progress described by the author of the *Gesta Stephani*. 'The king, therefore,' he says, 'accompanied by a large body of knights, made a progress through England with the splendour befitting the royal majesty. Those who bowed to his authority he received with kindness and respect. In all the churches, towns, and castles he was received by festive throngs. To all who implored him for their own needs he listened with humility and kindness. He made great efforts to re-establish peace in the realm and distributed bountiful gifts in order to restore harmony amongst his subjects.'

By the promptness and vigour of his dealings with King David, Stephen met the first serious challenge to his authority with firmness and decision. He had of course noted the fact that the leading barons of the realm had been holding back, waiting cautiously to see how events would turn out before they committed themselves to the new king. Stephen had been in too great a hurry to be crowned to risk compelling their adhesion, but now he was in a position to demand it. He determined to hold a great ceremonial court at Easter, particularly since his wife had joined him, and he sent urgent summons to the bishops and barons to attend.[1]

Easter was one of the three great feasts of the year when the

[1] *G.S.*, pp. 9, 16.

first two Williams had been accustomed to hold their courts with the greatest possible magnificence and splendour. Henry I, largely because he begrudged the expense, had allowed the custom to lapse, but Stephen determined, on the first opportunity of his reign, to revive it to show that he was indeed king of England and, no doubt, to exact on that occasion the oaths of fealty that had not yet been made to him.

In describing Stephen's Easter court at Westminster on 22 March 1136, Henry of Huntingdon says that 'there had never been a more splendid one in England with regard to the multitudes who attended it, the greatness of those present, the gold, the silver, the gems, the garments, the lavishness in every respect'. The chief event of the day was the coronation of Queen Matilda in Westminster Abbey.[1]

The only incident to mar the splendid festivities occurred at the banquet following the queen's coronation. Henry, King David's son, had probably accompanied Stephen on his way back from the North; at any rate, he was present at the banquet and in such high favour with the king that Stephen seated him at his right hand, a post that belonged to the archbishop of Canterbury, who took precedence over all others. Archbishop William was so offended by this slight to his dignity that he withdrew from the court, and a number of Stephen's nobles were also offended by his partiality to his young cousin. David, in turn, when he learned of the complaints about his son's treatment was so angry that he ordered Henry to return to Scotland.[2]

The list of witnesses to two charters that King Stephen granted on this occasion shows that his acceptance by the bishops and barons as king of England was almost complete. The archbishops of Canterbury and York and twelve of their suffragans were present, as were Hugh, archbishop of Rouen, and four Norman bishops. Five earls were present: William of Warenne, earl of Surrey; Ranulf, earl of Chester; Henry, earl of Huntingdon; Roger of Beaumont, earl of Warwick, and Waleran, count of Meulan. Henry of Sulli, the son of the king's eldest brother, was there, as was Reginald, a bastard son of King Henry. Amongst the barons we have already met Miles of Gloucester, his friend Payne son of John, and Brian fitz Count, the cousin

[1] Henry of Huntingdon, p. 259; Gervase of Canterbury, Vol. I, p. 96.
[2] Richard of Hexham, p. 146.

and particular friend of the Empress Matilda. Many of the others we are to meet later, particularly Geoffrey de Mandeville. One of the charters grants the bishopric of Bath to Robert of Lewes, who owed his election, the first to be held in the new reign, to Bishop Henry of Winchester.[1]

Apart from the ceremonial aspect, the chief function of this gathering, in Stephen's eyes, was to secure the fealty and allegiance of all those present who had not already made their profession, and we may be sure that the king now exacted the oath of fealty from them. The court also served as the Great Council of the realm, and the author of the *Gesta Stephani* tells us that 'the pillars of the Church sat according to their rank, and the common people also, as usual, thrust themselves in everywhere and mingled in a disorderly fashion with the others. Many things to the profit of the realm and of the Church were helpfully put forward and beneficially discussed'. What the secular matters were we are not told; the author reports a long string of complaints about the way in which King Henry had oppressed and persecuted the Church. The new king heard all these complaints patiently and then gave orders, echoing his promises at his coronation, that the freedom of the Church should be kept inviolate, its laws observed, and its ministers respected.[2]

The council was then adjourned, to meet at Oxford early in April.[3] Between the two meetings two events of great importance occurred: Stephen received a letter from Pope Innocent II, recognising him as king, and Earl Robert of Gloucester returned to England.

Immediately after his coronation, one gathers from this letter, Stephen had despatched messengers to the pope to inform him of his coronation by the archbishop of Canterbury. The messengers bore with them letters from the English clergy requesting the pope to confirm his legate's action, and they evidently picked up letters, on their way to the pope, to the same effect from Count Theobald of Blois and King Louis VI of France. There is nothing in the pope's letter to indicate that the Empress Matilda had presented her claim at the same time, that the pope was attempting to judge between two rival claimants, or even

---

[1] *Regesta*, pp. 16–17, 347–8; *G. de M.*, pp. 18–20, 262–6; Knowles, *The Monastic Order in England*, pp. 282–3.

[2] *G.S.*, pp. 16–18.   [3] *G. de M.*, pp. 22–4.

that he was aware that Stephen's claim might be disputed. Innocent simply says that he is informed by all this testimony that Stephen has been elected king by the common wish and unanimous consent of both the nobles and the people and has been crowned by the prelates of the realm. 'And because we learn,' the pope continues, 'that on the very day of your consecration you promised obedience and respect to Blessed Peter and that you are closely related to the late King, pleased by what has been done in your respect, we receive you with paternal affection as the special son of Blessed Peter and the Holy Roman Church, and we particularly wish to retain you in the same prerogatives of honour and friendship with which your predecessor Henry, of outstanding memory, was crowned by us.'[1]

R. L. Poole says that although the genuineness of Richard of Hexham's copy of the pope's letter is 'open to suspicion, . . . I see no reason to question the statements about the credentials with which the king's messengers were furnished'.[2] It is, moreover, the only copy of the letter that we have, and since Stephen obviously received such a letter we must assume that in spite of its deficiencies of style it at any rate preserves the substance of the papal rescript.

The general tenor of the letter, in any case, is clear. The pope has been informed that Stephen has been crowned king, and he concurs in the action of his legate, the archbishop of Canterbury. As J. H. Round observes: 'Though the king was pleased to describe the papal letter which followed as a "confirmation" of his right to the throne, it was, strictly, nothing of the kind. It was simply, in the language of modern diplomacy, his "recognition" by the pope as king.'[3] The letter was, nevertheless, a most important weapon in the hands of those who argued that the oath to the empress was not binding in conscience. Their first and greatest victory was the fact that the archbishop had consented to crown Stephen; that the pope confirmed this action reinforced it.

The arrival of Earl Robert of Gloucester in England shortly after Easter put the crowning touch on Stephen's triumph. Robert, as we have seen, took part in the deliberations of the council that led to the proffer of the duchy of Normandy to

[1] Richard of Hexham, pp. 147–8.
[2] John of Salisbury: *Historia Pontificalis*, pp. 107–8.
[3] G. *de M.*, p. 9.

Count Theobald and that concluded with the acceptance of Stephen as both king of England and duke of Normandy. If he brought forward his sister's claim on her son's behalf at that time no chronicler mentions it; the author of the *Gesta Stephani*, on the other hand, says that Robert himself, on his father's death, was advised to claim the throne in his own right but that, deterred by wiser counsel, he declined to do so, 'saying that it was fairer to yield to his sister's son, to whom it more justly belonged, than presumptuously to usurp it for himself'.[1]

While he was keeping quiet about his sister's claim, his brother-in-law, the young Count Geoffrey, was asserting it as best he could. Knowing how the Normans hated him, he prudently stayed behind and sent his wife into Normandy to see what she could accomplish. Her only support, apparently, came from Guignan Algaso, viscount of Exmes, who turned Argentan, Exmes, and Domfront over to her. Count Geoffrey then followed up his wife's limited success by leading an army to Séez, where his soldiers laid waste the countryside and perpetrated such atrocities that the outraged inhabitants slew over 700 of them and drove the whole army back into Maine. After this defeat, Geoffrey and Matilda seem to have abandoned for the time being any further efforts to claim Normandy. At Christmas 1135 Count Theobald, acting on his brother's behalf, arranged a truce with Geoffrey.[2]

William of Malmesbury, Earl Robert's spokesman, says that the earl, 'while he was in Normandy, had wearied his mind with much thought on what he should do in this matter, for he saw that if he submitted to King Stephen it could be contrary to the oath he had taken to his sister, but he understood that if he resisted it would profit neither his sister nor his nephew and would certainly do him enormous harm'. Since all the leading men of England had already gone over to Stephen with willing hearts, William of Malmesbury says that Robert decided to come to England and attempt to win them over to his sister's side. He could not embark on this treasonable course openly, and he therefore 'concealed his secret purpose for a time by pretending to share in their defection'. These are amongst the most important pages in William's work, for they present Robert's excuse and justification for his future conduct.

[1] *G.S.*, p. 8.   [2] Orderic, Vol. V, pp. 56–9.

The author of the *Gesta Stephani* says that King Stephen had sent repeated messages and letters to Earl Robert, summoning him to his presence, and eventually the earl would have to choose between doing homage to the king or forfeiting his estates. William of Malmesbury, then, attempts to excuse what Earl Robert regarded as a violation of his oath to his sister, although no one else except King David appeared to consider the oath binding, by saying that under the cover of an oath of fealty to Stephen that he did not intend to keep he was preparing to stir up a revolt against the king.

When Stephen and his court reassembled at Oxford early in April, Earl Robert 'was received with favour and distinction and obtained all he asked for according to his wish, on paying homage to the king'. According to William of Malmesbury, however, he did homage 'under a certain condition, that is to say, for as long as the king maintained Robert's condition unimpaired and kept the agreement with him'.[1] It must be remembered, however, that William is writing an apologia for Earl Robert and is in the difficult position of having to explain Robert's submission to Stephen in such a way as to clear him both of breaking his oath to his sister and of swearing an oath to Stephen that he did not intend to keep. The apologist solves the problem by making Robert's oath to Stephen a conditional one, but since this is the keystone of his defence of the earl one may wonder if Robert's oath of fealty was in truth and explicitly conditional. As every king since the Norman Conquest had been at great pains to make clear, every tenant-in-chief held his lands of the king in return for his fealty and service. The tenant was not the absolute owner of the land he held; all the land of England belonged ultimately to the king, and the tenant held only at the king's pleasure. Earl Robert took the oath in order to retain his lands, which he held of the king, and the oath of fealty was an explicit recognition of that dependence.

Stephen was now at the height of his power. He had been crowned king and had received the homage of the bishops and barons of England at his Easter court; he had been recognised by the pope, and he had recently subdued, with great success, an attempted incursion by the king of Scots. In such circumstances, surrounded by his court at Oxford and secure in his possession of

[1] *H.N.*, pp. 17–18; *G.S.*, pp. 8–9.

the crown, one may well doubt that he would accept a mere conditional act of homage from the man who he knew would be most likely to dispute his right.

The chief function of the court that he had assembled at Oxford was to debate the issues that were treated in his charter and to witness that charter. The principal provisions are his promises to amend those abuses in the treatment of the Church about which the bishops had complained at the meeting at Easter.

The preamble of the charter gave him an opportunity to make clear the impregnability of his position. 'I, Stephen,' it begins, 'by the grace of God elected king of England by the consent of the clergy and people, and consecrated by William, archbishop of Canterbury and legate of the Holy Roman Church, and confirmed by Innocent, the pontiff of the Holy Roman See, out of respect and love of God concede that Holy Church shall be free and confirm my due reverence for her.'

He then promises that he will neither be guilty of simony himself nor tolerate it in others and that he will respect the persons, possessions, and dignities of the clergy. He admits that 'jurisdiction and power over churchmen and all their clerks and property and the distribution of the goods of the Church are in the bishops' hands'. He confirms the Church in all the possessions and tenures that it had at the death of William the Conqueror, which implies a promise to restore everything that William Rufus and Henry I had taken from it. He lays particular emphasis upon his promise to respect the last wills and testaments of the clergy and to allow their possessions to be disposed of according to their directions, rather than, it is implied, to seize them into his own hands as his last two predecessors had often done. A notable concession to the clergy is his promise to put all the possessions of a vacant see in the custody of the officials of the Church until a new bishop should be elected.[1]

In marked contrast to the specific assurances to the clergy are the sketchy promises made to the laity. Stephen announces that he will retain all the forests that had been designated as such by the first two Williams but that he relinquishes those that had been created by Henry. He promises to stamp out all exactions and

[1] See Z. N. Brooke: *The English Church and the Papacy from the Conquest to the Reign of John* (Cambridge, 1932), pp. 176–7; Margaret Howell: *Regalian Right in Medieval England* (London, 1962), pp. 29–32.

injustices and evil-doings on the part of sheriffs or any others, and
he ends with a vague promise to observe and cause to be observed
'good laws and ancient and just customs' in legal processes.[1]

The detailed nature of Stephen's promises to the Church are
evidence, not of his desire to strike a bargain with the bishops in
order to secure their support, for he had already received their
fealty, but of the influence of his brother Henry, bishop of
Winchester. Henry was the chief exponent in England of the
ideas that are associated with the reforms of Gregory VII and his
successors, and he took every occasion to assert the independence
of the Church, the leading article in the Hildebrandine programme. William of Malmesbury points out that all of
Stephen's efforts to secure the crown would have been in vain if
his brother had not supported him, and Stephen was now repay-
ing his debt to his brother by allowing him to dictate the terms
of his promises to the Church.[2]

In the list of witnesses to the charter, Bishop Henry's name
appears next after those of the archbishops of Canterbury and
Rouen, and Robert, earl of Gloucester, is the first layman to
subscribe.

At Rogation-tide, 26–29 April, Stephen apparently fell ill, for
the rumour that the king was dead spread through the country.
Hugh Bigod seized Norwich Castle in preparation for the
anarchy that would be inevitable if the king were dead, and he
refused to surrender it till Stephen appeared in person and forced
him to do so.[3] This can hardly be considered a rebellion, for
Hugh, whose part in securing Stephen's coronation had already
been noted and who witnessed the charter at Oxford, did not
attempt to resist the king's authority but merely took prudent
steps for his own safety in case of trouble.

The first recorded rebellion is that of Robert of Bampton in
Oxfordshire, whom the author of the *Gesta Stephani* describes as
'a voracious consumer of wine and food who in peace-time gave
up his days to gluttony and drunkenness'. Although he did
homage to the king, he filled his castle with knights and archers
and plundered the surrounding countryside. He was tried by
the king's court on a charge of having stirred up rebellion in the
kingdom, found guilty, and sentenced to forfeit his castle and all

---

[1] *Regesta*, pp. 96–7; G. de M., pp. 22–3.
[2] H.N., p. 15.   [3] Henry of Huntingdon, p. 259.

his property. Robert escaped from the knights who were sent
to take possession of his castle, and the garrison renewed their
depredations. Stephen himself then led an army to Bampton,
captured the castle, and sent the garrison into exile.

Robert of Bampton was small fry; the next rebel with whom
Stephen had to deal was 'a man of eminent rank and birth',
Baldwin of Redvers. Richard of Hexham says that the king
refused him 'a certain honour', which was probably the castle
of Exeter. Baldwin seized the castle, 'which had always been a
royal possession', stocked it with provisions, and behaved in such
a warlike way that the citizens sent messengers to Stephen, who
was then at Bampton, to complain that Baldwin was threatening
the king's peace.[1]

Stephen sent an advance guard of 200 cavalry to Exeter and
followed with his army. The author of the *Gesta Stephani*
describes the castle as 'raised on a very high mound, surrounded
by an impregnable wall, fortified with towers of hewn limestone
built by the emperors'. Baldwin had installed a strong force,
'bound by fealty and an oath never to yield to the king', and
although he himself was not there, his wife Adelise and their
children were in the castle. At this stage in the evolution of the
art of war, the only way to reduce such a castle was to starve the
garrison into submission, and Stephen and his army settled down
to do so, enlivening their stay by subjecting the castle to a constant
hail of arrows and stones and attempting to undermine the walls.
Stephen also sent a force of 200 knights to Baldwin's castle at
Plympton, about five miles east of Plymouth. The garrison
there soon surrendered, and Stephen's men demolished the castle,
ravaged Baldwin's land, and returned to the king at Exeter 'with
many thousands of sheep and cattle'.

After Stephen had spent almost three months and £10,000
on the siege, the wells within the castle, 'by the operation of the
divine power', dried up, and the garrison were reduced to using
wine for their cooking and baking and even for putting out the
fires that the besiegers started by flinging lighted torches into the
precincts. When their wine gave out, the garrison sent their
two highest-ranking members to treat with the king concerning
the terms of surrender. Bishop Henry of Winchester, a crafty

---

[1] G.S., pp. 18–21; Richard of Hexham, p. 146; Sir Frank Stenton: *The First
Century of English Feudalism, 1066–1166* (2nd edn., Oxford, 1961), p. 239

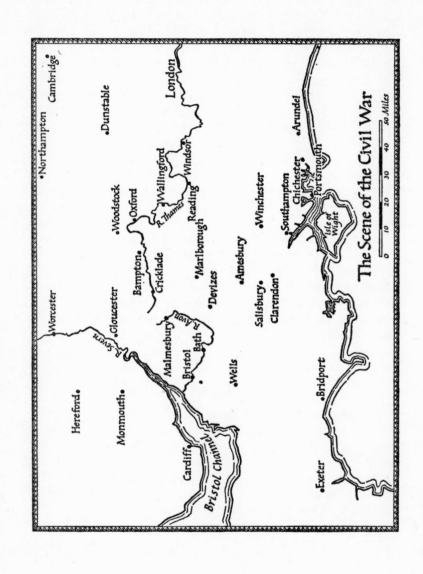

The Scene of the Civil War

0 10 20 30 40 50 Miles

warrior, observing their 'sagging and wasted skin', realised that they were in the last extremities of thirst and advised his brother not to treat with them but to force them to an unconditional surrender, which implied the possibility of being put to death for their rebellion.

Adelise, Baldwin's wife, then came to the king, 'barefoot, with her hair hanging loose on her shoulders, shedding floods of tears', to beg for mercy, but Stephen sent her back to the castle with the same reply that he had given the others. Some of Stephen's barons, however, sympathised with Baldwin's men, and others, says the author of the *Gesta Stephani*, were accomplices and helpers in his rebellion. Earl Robert of Gloucester, who was present with the king's army, may probably be included in the latter group. None of the barons, in any case, wanted to see one of their number completely vanquished and humiliated by the king. The growth and consolidation of the royal power under Henry I had been accomplished at the barons' expense, and they had no desire to see the diminution of their powers continued under Henry's successor.

They therefore came to Stephen and begged him to treat the garrison leniently. They appealed first to his good nature by telling him that 'it was more consonant with his dignity and more befitting the royal clemency to grant life to the suppliant prisoners than mercilessly to deprive them of the little life they had left' by punishing them with death. They then advanced the extraordinary argument that since the garrison had not sworn allegiance to the royal majesty and had taken up arms only in fealty to their lord, Baldwin, they should not be held responsible for their rebellion. This argument struck at the very foundation of the king's authority and power. His barons paid him homage in person and swore fealty to him as their lord, but every free man in England, no matter what his rank and regardless of whether or not he had sworn an oath, owed allegiance to the king, and that allegiance overrode any ties that might bind a man to an intermediate lord. By even listening to such an argument, Stephen was throwing away his most powerful resource, his claim to the allegiance of all Englishmen. If he accepted this argument it would be equivalent to admitting that he could claim the allegiance only of the narrow circle of barons who had in person sworn fealty to him as their lord and that the vast body of rear-tenants, knights, and free men owed primary allegiance to the lords of whom they held their land and not to the king.

Stephen allowed the besieged 'not only to go forth in freedom but also to take away their possessions and adhere to any lord they wanted to'. He did this, his apologist tells us, 'in order to win their attachment and have them more devoted to his service', but it was probably the worst mistake he could have made, for his contemporaries saw it not as an indication of a merciful and kindly disposition but as evidence of a weakness of character. As Henry of Huntingdon remarks: 'Following the worst of advice, he did not punish these traitors: for if he had punished them, so many castles would not afterwards have been held against him.'[1]

When Baldwin learned that his garrison at Exeter had surrendered and were treated with such surprising leniency, he withdrew to the Isle of Wight, almost the whole of which belonged to him by inheritance, and stocked his castle of Carisbrooke in preparation for a second rebellion. He had also assembled 'a huge fleet of pirates' and was preying on the traders between England and Normandy. Stephen left his brother Henry in charge of Exeter and went to Southampton to collect a fleet. The king, as we have seen, was weak in his treatment of rebels after he had defeated them, but he was brave and energetic in quelling their rebellions. Whilst the fleet was assembling and fitting out in preparation for an attack on the Isle of Wight, Baldwin suddenly came to the king, made his submission, and sued for pardon. The author of the *Gesta Stephani* explains his surrender as due to the urging of his friends and to the failure of the supply of water in his castle because of a sudden drought. The drying-up of the wells in both Exeter Castle and Baldwin's island stronghold leads one to believe that the spring and summer of 1136 must have been unusually dry, although the author of the *Gesta Stephani* sees the hand of God in both failures.

Stephen's determination in capturing Exeter Castle after a siege of three months must have convinced Baldwin that the king was preparing to reduce his island stronghold in the same fashion. When he submitted, he begged the king to restore his former possession to him, but Stephen, although he had been unduly merciful to Baldwin's followers, would not listen to their

[1] *G.S.*, pp. 22–8; Henry of Huntingdon, p. 259; Davis, p. 25.

ring-leader. His second attempt at rebellion was enough to convince Stephen that mercy would be wasted on him. He stripped
him of all his possessions and sent him into exile. Baldwin
promptly took refuge with Geoffrey of Anjou, received a cordial
welcome at his court, and turned his talents to stirring up trouble
in Normandy.[1]

Stephen had thus met the first serious challenge to his authority,
and he had acted with energy and despatch. He punished the
perpetrator of the rebellion by confiscating his lands and sending
him into exile, which constituted the harshest penalty, short of
death, that a king could lay on one of his barons. Stephen's
mistake lay not in his treatment of Baldwin of Redvers but in his
failure to hold Baldwin's men accountable for their share in his
rebellion.

With this major disturbance quelled, England was now at
peace and the king's authority unchallenged. Stephen therefore
prepared to go to Normandy. His brother, Count Theobald,
seems occasionally at least to have been acting on Stephen's
behalf, for he had negotiated the truce with Count Geoffrey, and
many of the barons who had done homage to Stephen in England
were amongst the principal men in Normandy. It was now
incumbent upon Stephen to go there, assert his authority, and
provide for the governance of the duchy.

As he was preparing to embark, however, he heard that Roger,
bishop of Salisbury, was dead. Roger had acted as chief justiciar
under Henry I, and Stephen had confirmed him in that office.
The chief justiciar, an office created by Henry I to provide for the
governance of England during his frequent absences in Normandy,
was the head of the judicial and financial administration, and
during the king's absence he governed the country in the king's
name.[2] If Bishop Roger were dead, Stephen would be faced
with the difficult task of finding a replacement for the man who
had been second only to the king for almost thirty years. He
therefore hastened to Salisbury and found that the report was
untrue and the bishop in good health. The fact that he then
gave up his plan of going to Normandy for the time being

[1] G.S., pp. 29–30; John Beeler: *Warfare in England, 1066–1189* (Ithaca, N.Y.,
1966), p. 83.
[2] H. G. Richardson and G. O. Sayles: *The Governance of Medieval England from
the Conquest to Magna Carta* (Edinburgh, 1963), pp. 158–65.

D

indicates that the duchy was not in an unusually disturbed state and that Count Geoffrey was observing the truce.[1]

During the course of the summer Stephen went to Brampton, near Huntingdon, to enjoy the hunting, and while he was there he held a forest court 'concerning the forests of his noblemen, that is, concerning the woods and the game, and broke his oath and promise to God and the people'. It will be remembered that in his charter at Oxford he reserved his rights over the forests that the first two Williams had created but renounced his rights over those that Henry I had added. Even though the land was outside the royal demesne, that is, the lands held immediately by the king, William the Conqueror and his successors had designated as royal forests some areas held by their barons. In those forests the king alone had rights of 'vert and venison', that is, of felling timber and of hunting. This caused a hardship on the nominal owners of the land, for it deprived them both of the sport of hunting to supply game for their tables and of the right to fell their own timber for building and for firewood. That Stephen was applying the forest law to areas that had not been made forests by either of the two Williams is evident from Henry of Huntingdon's comment.

Stephen held his second Christmas court at Dunstable. He had now been king of England for a year, and he had overcome every obstacle with boldness and courage. After his success in putting down the rebellions of Robert of Bampton and Baldwin of Redvers, his authority seemed to be unchallenged. Count Geoffrey meanwhile had broken the truce, led a raid into Normandy in September, and burned Lisieux. The Normans had put up a stout resistance and driven him and his army back into Maine in less than a fortnight. Geoffrey had behaved with such barbarity that his chances of gaining a foothold in a country that he had treated with such cruelty seemed remote indeed.'[2]

Accompanied by Bishop Alexander of Lincoln and many of his barons, Stephen crossed over to Normandy in the third week of March 1137 and landed at La Hougue. He met his brother Theobald, who seems to have been exercising a sort of general supervision over Normandy for him, at Évreux and promised to give him 2,000 marks of silver every year. In May he had a

[1] Orderic, Vol. V., p. 63.
[2] Henry of Huntingdon, pp. 259-60; Orderic, Vol. V, pp. 67-75.

conference with King Louis VI, did homage to him for Normandy, and made a treaty of friendship with him. Although Louis did not furnish him with any material aid, his recognition of Stephen as duke of Normandy was a further confirmation of the legality of his claim.[1]

Count Geoffrey now invaded Normandy with an army of 400 knights and laid waste the country about Exmes, burning and plundering with his usual barbarity. Earl Robert of Gloucester, who had crossed over to Normandy on Easter Sunday, was suspected of favouring Geoffrey, and William of Ypres urged the king to take action against him. William was the son of Philip, count of Ypres, and when Charles the Good, count of Flanders, was murdered in 1127 William claimed Flanders. King Louis decided in favour of William Clito, as we have seen, and the Clito's successor, Thierry of Alsace, drove William of Ypres out of Flanders. He took refuge in England and attached himself to Stephen. They became fast friends, and when Stephen gained the crown he put William in command of his force of Flemish mercenaries.

On William's advice Stephen 'tried to catch Robert in an ambush', but Robert had been forewarned by his friends and avoided the trap. According to William of Malmesbury, when Earl Robert accused the king of having set a trap for him, Stephen confessed his fault and swore 'that he would never again take part in such a crime', with Archbishop Hugh of Rouen as guarantor of his oath. Stephen and Robert seem never to have been on especially friendly terms, and this obscure incident is used by William of Malmesbury as the beginning of their enmity. Although Robert did not side openly with Count Geoffrey during his invasion of Normandy, it was obvious on which side his sympathies lay, and Orderic Vitalis also says that he was suspected of having gone over to the enemy.[2]

Stephen collected a large army at Lisieux in June and prepared to lay siege to Argentan and the other castles near the border that Geoffrey had seized, but trouble broke out between the Normans and the king's Flemish mercenaries. Orderic Vitalis says that the Norman barons were angry because Stephen placed all his

---

[1] Henry of Huntingdon, p. 260; Orderic, Vol. V, p. 81; Robert of Torigni, p. 132.
[2] H.N., p. 21; Orderic, Vol. V, p. 82.

trust in William of Ypres, and they refused to fight under William's command. Robert of Torigni, who seems to have known the ways of soldiers, says that fighting broke out between the Normans and the Flemings over a cask of wine. The lower ranks were reflecting the attitude of their leaders, and Stephen found it impossible to mount an offensive against Geoffrey with such troops.

Geoffrey excelled at raids in which he met little opposition; he had no desire to confront Stephen's army, regardless of its disunity. Towards the end of June Stephen and Geoffrey arranged for a truce to last either two or three years, on condition that Stephen pay Geoffrey 2,000 marks of silver every year. Geoffrey demanded and received the first year's payment in advance.[1]

By the beginning of July Stephen had restored peace throughout Normandy, and the remainder of his stay was uneventful. Henry of Huntingdon, who says that Stephen 'carried through brilliantly everything that he began', sums up the beginning of his reign: 'These two years were most prosperous for King Stephen, but the third, as we shall tell, was mediocre and confused.'[2]

[1] Orderic, Vol. V, pp. 83-5; Robert of Torigni, p. 132.
[2] Henry of Huntingdon, p. 260.

III

1137–1139

KING Stephen returned to England in Advent 1137, which began that year on 28 November, and immediately brought trouble on himself by his effort to provide for Hugh 'the Poor', the brother of his close friends Waleran, count of Meulan, and Robert, earl of Leicester. Their father, Robert of Beaumont, count of Meulan and earl of Leicester, who had been the trusted friend of Henry I and probably the most powerful layman in England, had died in 1118, leaving three sons, Waleran and Robert, who were twins, and Hugh. After their father's death the twins were brought up by Henry I, because of the love he bore their father. Waleran, as the elder of the twins, succeeded to his father's estates in France and Normandy and the title of count of Meulan; Robert became earl of Leicester and inherited his father's vast holdings in England. Hugh, the third son, was called 'the Poor' because he did not share in the division of lands, having been born after the settlement had been confirmed by the king.[1]

In order to hold the support of this extremely powerful family, Stephen had betrothed his infant daughter Matilda to Count Waleran in 1136. He now arranged for Hugh's marriage to the daughter of Simon of Beauchamp, hereditary constable of Bedford Castle and the owner of extensive estates in Bedfordshire, who had died without male issue at some time after April 1136, when he had witnessed King Stephen's charter at Oxford.[2] Stephen also proposed to bestow on Hugh both Bedford Castle and Simon's 'honour', or barony. The only flaw in this arrangement was that the castle and honour were in the possession of

[1] Richard of Hexham, p. 151; Orderic, Vol. IV, p. 438; Geoffrey N. White: 'King Stephen's Earldoms', in *Transactions of the Royal Historical Society*, 4th ser., Vol. XIII (1930), p. 78; *id.*, 'The Career of Waleran, Count of Meulan and Earl of Worcester (1104–1166)', *T.R.H.S.*, 4th ser., Vol. XVII (1934), pp. 19–48.
[2] *G. de M.*, pp. 171, 263.

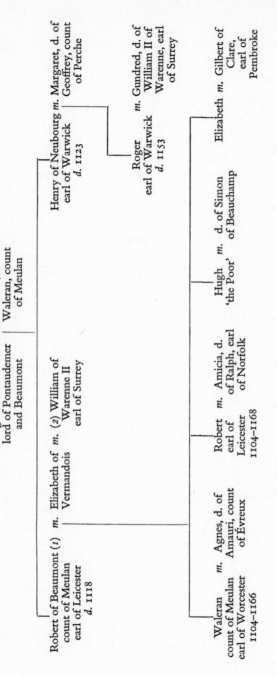

IV: Earls of Leicester, of Worcester, and of Warwick

Miles of Beauchamp, the elder son of Simon's younger brother Robert, and the king had already confirmed him as constable of Bedford Castle.

Stephen sent messengers to Miles, ordering him to turn the castle over to Hugh. 'He promised that if Miles willingly acceded to his order he would grant him honours and many gifts, but that if he showed any kind of opposition he would very soon have to bear the weight of complete disaster. On receiving the delegation from the king, Miles finally said that he would gladly be the king's knight and obey his commands, provided that the king did not try to remove him from what was the hereditary possession of himself and his family, but that if the king was in earnest and really determined to do him this wrong he would endure his anger with what patience he could, but the king would never get the castle until Miles was reduced to the last extremity.'[1]

As Sir Frank Stenton observes: 'In theory the custody of a royal castle must always have been revokable at the king's pleasure.' Miles had only recently been confirmed in his possession of the castle, however, and it seems clear that the king had designated him, rather than Simon's daughter, as Simon's heir. Orderic Vitalis, moreover, says that Miles 'was afraid of losing his whole inheritance', and rightly so, for Stephen evidently intended to transfer the whole Beauchamp honour to Hugh. This was not a mere question of deciding a fine point of feudal law as to whether a daughter or a brother's son inherited the estate of a man who died without sons; the king had already confirmed Miles as the heir, and he now proposed to take his inheritance away from him.[2]

The author of the Gesta Stephani says that Stephen held his Christmas court of 1137 'with magnificence and solemnity' and then sent his messengers to Miles. Orderic Vitalis says that Stephen went to Bedford at Christmas, which may mean during the Christmas season rather than on the day itself, 'with the winter rains beating upon him'. Henry of Huntingdon says that the king besieged Bedford on Christmas Eve and all through the Christmas season, which scandalised many people, for he paid little or no attention to the great solemnity.[3]

[1] G.S., pp. 31–2.
[2] Stenton: The First Century of English Feudalism, p. 238; Orderic, Vol. V, p. 104.
[3] G.S., p. 31; Orderic, Vol. V, pp. 103–4; Henry of Huntingdon, p. 260.

Stephen at any rate, about Christmas 1137, against the advice of his brother Henry, went to Bedford 'with an army collected from the whole of England' and laid siege to the castle, which was stoutly held by Miles and his brother Payne. One siege is pretty much like another, and there is no need to dwell on the measures that Stephen took to seize the castle or that Miles and his garrison devised to resist them.

Stephen was called away to deal with a fresh incursion of the Scots, but he left the greater part of the army to continue operations at Bedford. After the siege had been going on for five weeks and the garrison were on the verge of starvation, Bishop Henry of Winchester arrived and persuaded Miles to surrender. Although the author of the *Gesta Stephani* implies that Stephen intended to create Hugh the Poor earl of Bedford, it does not seem likely that he did so. He at any rate entrusted Bedford Castle to Hugh, although, as the author of the *Gesta Stephani* points out, Hugh was not to enjoy it for long.[1]

While Stephen was in Normandy in the spring of 1137, David, king of Scots, had collected an army and threatened to invade Northumberland. At Stephens's order an English army had assembled at Newcastle-upon-Tyne to resist him, and a truce had been agreed upon, to last till Advent. Shortly after Stephen returned to England in December, David and his son Henry sent messengers to him, renewing their demand for the earldom of Northumbria and threatening to invade England unless he granted their requests. Stephen sent the messengers back with a refusal, and the Scots prepared for war.

They invaded Northumberland on 10 January 1138, perpetrating frightful cruelties on the inhabitants. The author of the *Gesta Stephani* describes them as 'barbarous and filthy, neither overcome by excess of cold nor enfeebled by severe hunger, putting their trust in swiftness of foot and light equipment; in their own country they care nothing for the awful moment of the bitterness of death; amongst foreigners they surpass all in cruelty'. Richard of Hexham, who witnessed their depredations, says that they were 'more atrocious than any pagans, respecting neither God nor man'. They slew the inhabitants without regard for sex, age, or condition, and they

[1] Orderic, Vol. V, pp. 103, 106; G.S., p. 33; White, 'King Stephen's Earldoms', pp. 79–82. See, however, Davis, p. 135.

destroyed, plundered, and burned towns, churches, and houses.
Stephen reached Northumberland with his army about 2
February. The Scots withdrew into Roxburgh, and Stephen,
keeping apparently to the coast, crossed the Tweed and ravaged
the greater part of the Lowlands. The two armies did not meet,
however, and Stephen turned back after a fortnight without
having defeated the Scots. Richard of Hexham gives three
reasons for his withdrawal: it was the beginning of Lent, a holy
season during which many of his barons did not want to bear
arms or wage war; the Scots would not meet him in battle, and
his provisions were running low. The Scots had stripped the
country so bare that it would obviously have been impossible
for his army to live off the countryside. He had at any rate
driven the Scots back across the border.[1]

When Stephen returned to the south he held a meeting of the
Great Council at Northampton at Eastertide, 3 April, but we
are told nothing about the proceedings except that Robert
Warelwast was elected bishop of Exeter and that two abbots were
also elected. One of them, Robert, a monk of Cluny, who was
elected abbot of Winchcombe, was said to be related to the king.[2]

From Northampton Stephen went to Gloucester, probably
because of reports of disaffection along the Welsh border. There
he learned that Geoffrey Talbot, who had witnessed one of his
charters at Easter 1136, had seized Hereford Castle and was
fortifying it. Stephen went to Hereford, where he was welcomed by the townspeople as 'their natural lord'. He
summoned his army and devoted four or five weeks to reducing
the castle. Again he made the mistake of allowing the garrison
to depart unpunished, 'for he was a king of gentleness and peace'.
Geoffrey had fled to his castle at Weobley, about ten miles to the
north-west, when Stephen appeared before Hereford, and the
king now took Weobley, but did not succeed in capturing
Geoffrey. Stephen installed garrisons in the two castles, pronounced a sentence of banishment on Geoffrey, and then set out
for London. Geoffrey meanwhile returned to Hereford and
burned the town on 15 June. He then took refuge in Bristol,
the chief stronghold of Earl Robert of Gloucester.[3]

[1] Richard of Hexham, pp. 150-2, 155; G.S., p. 36.
[2] The Chronicle of John of Worcester, ed. J. R. H. Weaver (Oxford, 1908), p. 48.
[3] G. de M., p. 263; John of Worcester, pp. 48-9; G.S., p. 38; Orderic, Vol. V,
p. 110.

It was probably on his way to London that Stephen met Earl Robert's messengers. According to William of Malmesbury, the earl 'immediately after Pentecost [22 May] sent representatives and abandoned friendship and faith with the king in the traditional way, also renouncing homage, giving the reason that he did it justly because the king had unlawfully claimed the throne and disregarded, not to say belied, all the faith he had sworn to him; and that he himself likewise had acted contrary to law in that he, after taking the oath to his sister, had not been ashamed to give his hands to another in his lifetime'. William of Malmesbury also says that Robert 'produced the terms of a bull from the pope, bidding him obey the oath he had taken in his father's presence', which the chronicler promises to insert later on in his book. He does not do so, and it would be surprising if Robert could have produced such a bull, since it would contradict both the pope's decision handed down shortly after Stephen's coronation and the judgment that was to be pronounced in 1139.[1]

Robert was acting, as J. H. Round points out, on the assumption that his 'allegiance to the king was a purely feudal relation, and, as such, could be thrown off at any moment by performing the famous *diffidatio*'. But, as Round continues, 'this essential feature of continental feudalism had been rigidly excluded by the Conqueror', and Richardson and Sayles say that '*diffidatio*, the renunciation of allegiance, had never been recognised in England as a means of releasing a subject from his duty to the king or regularising a state of war between a lord and his vassals'.[2] There is nothing in the course of English history up to this time to indicate that a subject, no matter how powerful he might be, could withdraw his allegiance without laying himself open to the charge of rebellion and treason. So it was with Earl Robert's renunciation of his allegiance; no matter how William of Malmesbury, the earl's apologist, presents it, Robert's message was nothing less than a declaration of war on his king by a subject.

Robert had not, until this time, given any evidence of asserting that his sister had a claim to the throne; if he thought so, he had certainly kept quiet about the matter, and by rendering fealty to Stephen in April 1136 he had accepted him as king. He had

[1] H.N., p. 23.
[2] G. de M., pp. 27–8; Richardson and Sayles, *The Governance of Medieval England*, p. 148.

been in Normandy since the spring of 1137, and at some time
during the spring of 1138 he came over openly to his sister's side,
allied himself with her and her husband, and set to work to
deprive Stephen of his crown. Robert of Torigni says that Earl
Robert made an agreement with Count Geoffrey about Easter,
3 April, and Orderic Vitalis recounts that 'Geoffrey of Anjou, in
the month of June [1138], came to Normandy with an army and
by prayers and promises won Robert, earl of Gloucester, over
to his side'.[1] It is noteworthy that in both these cases it is Count
Geoffrey and not his wife who is mentioned, and in the first
stages of the plot the empress is in the background, except when
the matter of the oath is brought up.

There had been a number of violations of the truce that Count
Geoffrey had agreed to, and a party of rebels was forming in
Normandy. In addition to Earl Robert, Reginald of Dunstanville, another bastard son of Henry I, was ravaging the Cotentin,
and the exiled Baldwin of Redvers and other enemies of the king
had joined him.[2]

When he received Robert's declaration of war, Stephen went
on to London, no doubt to take counsel with his friends, and it
was probably at this time that he sent two of the men in whom he
had the greatest trust, Waleran, count of Meulan, and William
of Ypres, to deal with the situation in Normandy. Instead of
hanging Earl Robert's messengers or throwing them into prison,
Stephen, with that affability at which his subjects never ceased to
wonder, allowed them to go on to Bristol to deliver Robert's
instructions to his followers there, 'namely, that they should fill
their camp at Bristol with abundance of provisions, should
accept as allies all who came in to them, and should at once
commit against the king and his supporters, as opponents of the
earl, the harshest and most hostile acts they could'.[3]

With Earl Robert's declaration of war, Bristol now became
the rallying point for all the disaffected in the kingdom and the
centre from which they plundered the countryside. The
garrison at Bristol cast covetous eyes on the town of Bath, ten
miles to the south-east, and sent a detachment equipped with
scaling ladders 'and other devices for climbing a wall', to see if

[1] Robert of Torigni, p. 136; Orderic, Vol. V, p. 108.
[2] Orderic, Vol. V, pp. 104–5.
[3] G.S., p. 37; Orderic, Vol. V, p. 108.

they could take the town. They hid in a valley at early dawn and sent three of their number, Geoffrey Talbot, his relation Gilbert of Lacy, and William Hoset, as scouts to discover the best way of attacking the town. Robert, bishop of Bath, was responsible for the defences, and his men, seeing the spies, rushed out and captured Geoffrey Talbot, whilst his two companions escaped. They fettered Geoffrey's feet and put him in a dungeon under a strong guard.

The detachment from Bristol, having lost their leader, went back and reported to Geoffrey's companions what had befallen him. A group of them went to Bath, stood outside the walls, which were guarded by the bishop's soldiers, and begged Bishop Robert to come out and parley with them, promising him 'a free and unmolested exit and a safe return'. Bishop Robert, a simple soul, went out to talk with them, whereupon they seized him and threatened to hang him before the walls of Bath unless he handed Geoffrey back to them. The bishop then had no choice but to order Geoffrey's release.[1]

The reduction of Bristol was obviously the most important task facing the king, but he was curiously dilatory in undertaking it. He collected an army and went to Bath, which he seems to have chosen as the base of operations nearest Bristol, but he did not arrive there till well after the middle of June, for, as we have seen, Geoffrey Talbot burned Hereford on 15 June, took refuge at Bristol, and was captured at Bath and released before Stephen arrived there.

From Bath the king and his army went to reconnoitre Bristol and were greatly discouraged by their observations. The city lies at the confluence of the Rivers Avon and Frome, and although it would have been easy enough to blockade it by land, it could still be supplied by water. Stephen asked his barons for advice as to how he could bring the city to submission. Some of them advised him to build a huge dam below the town, thus cutting off access by water and at the same time flooding the city. Others, of a more practical turn of mind, said that he should build castles on each side of the town to cut off traffic over the bridges and should station his army before Bristol Castle in order to starve the garrison into submission.

Knowing the use to which Earl Robert later put Bristol, we

[1] G.S., pp. 38–41; John of Worcester, pp. 49–50.

are of course wiser than King Stephen, and we find it almost
incredible that he did not take the advice of his wiser barons,
settle down to the siege of Bristol, and stay there till he had
captured the city.   Sieges were long and boring operations that
had to be persisted in till the garrison was on the point of starvation, but, given enough time and men, even the stoutest castle
could eventually be captured.   Stephen never lacked for men,
apparently, and he certainly had with him at this time a force
large enough to invest the castle.

   The king, however, may not have realised the strategic importance of Bristol; it may have seemed to him to be merely one of a
number of centres of disaffection, all of which were calling for
immediate attention, and it must be remembered that Earl Robert
had not followed up his *diffidatio* by any overt act of rebellion.
The author of the *Gesta Stephani* says that Stephen was misled
by the advice of some of his barons, 'who only pretended to serve
the king and rather favoured the earl'.   At any rate, instead of
besieging Bristol he left a strong garrison at Bath to hold the city
in check and marched some twenty-five miles to the south, to
Castle Cary, which was held by Ralph Lovel, a firm friend and
supporter of Earl Robert.   When Castle Cary surrendered
Stephen turned north again, marched to Harptree, about ten
miles south of Bristol, held by William son of John, and captured
the castle.[1]

   Leaving garrisons at these castles, he went next to Shropshire,
where William son of Alan, who was constable of Shrewsbury
Castle and sheriff of the county and was married to a niece of
Earl Robert, had declared for Robert and was filling the castle
with the king's enemies.   On the way, Stephen captured Dudley
Castle, thirty miles south-east of Shrewsbury, from Ralph Painel.

   When William son of Alan learned of the king's approach, he
fled with his wife and children, leaving his uncle, Ernulf of Hesding, in charge of the castle.   Ernulf and his companions swore
faithfully that they would never surrender.   Stephen and his
army, amongst whom was Miles, Constable of Gloucester, at
last filled the moat with wood, set fire to it, and smoked the
garrison out.   For the first time he now treated his enemies as
rebels and traitors.   He hanged Ernulf, four of his more noteworthy companions, and eighty-eight of the garrison.   This

[1] G.S., pp. 44–6.

unwonted severity had a salutary effect on some of Ernulf's accomplices, who came to the king, begged for mercy, and surrendered their castles to him.[1]

While he was thus occupied in the west, we hear of his queen for the first time since her coronation. Queen Matilda summoned help from Boulogne and laid siege to Dover Castle, which was held for Earl Robert by Walkelin Maminot, a son-in-law of Robert of Ferrers. Her friends and relations sent over a fleet to blockade the harbour so that the rebels could get no help from that quarter, whilst the valiant queen was besieging the castle. Robert of Ferrers, one of Stephen's most loyal supporters, exerted his powers of persuasion on his son-in-law, and Walkelin at last surrendered the castle.[2]

The Scots meanwhile were invading the north with renewed fury. King David and his army, which the English estimated at 26,000 men, invaded Northumberland on 8 April and for the first time ravaged the east coast, which had hitherto escaped their depredations. They devastated County Durham and penetrated into the North Riding, working terrible havoc. They burned and plundered like savages; they slaughtered the inhabitants with refinements of cruelty, and they seized the women and held them as captives or sold them as slaves.[3]

King Stephen was too busy to defend his northern border, and the task of organising the north against the invaders fell to the aged Thurstan, archbishop of York. He was an old friend of Stephen's. The king's mother, Countess Adela, had sheltered the archbishop when he was in exile in 1119, and his advice had helped her to decide to enter the convent at Marcigny, where she spent the remainder of her life.[4] He had been present at the Easter court of 1136 and had had no hesitation in accepting Stephen as king.

Thurstan called together the northern barons, and their names make a roster of the great families of the north: William of Aumale, Walter of Gant, Robert of Bruce, Roger of Mowbray, Walter Espec, Ilbert of Lacy, William of Percy, Richard of Curcy, William of Fossard, and Robert of Stuteville. Thurstan

[1] John of Worcester, pp. 50–1; Orderic, Vol. V, pp. 112–13; G. de M., p. 285.
[2] Orderic, Vol. V, p. 112.
[3] Richard of Hexham, pp. 155–9.
[4] Donald Nicholl: Thurstan, Archbishop of York, 1114–1140 (York, 1964), p. 194.

told them that their cause was just and most holy, for they were opposing danger in defence of Holy Church and their fatherland; he organised a veritable holy war. He sent word to all his parish priests to lead their parishioners under their processional crosses and promised the barons all the help in his power, both spiritual and material. They were cheered by the arrival of Bernard of Baliol, one of the greatest of their number, who came with a band of knights sent by the king. The barons went to their estates to collect their forces and then assembled at York. They went to confession, fasted three days, and received absolution and his blessing from the archbishop, who gave them his cross and the banner of St. Peter to carry into battle. Although Thurstan was so infirm that he had to be carried in a litter, he proposed to accompany the army, but the barons dissuaded him. In his place he sent Ralph Nowel, bishop of the Orkneys, one of the archdeacons of York, and other members of his clergy.[1]

They marched to Thirsk, about twenty-three miles north of York, where an army drawn from the whole of Yorkshire was assembling. The parish priests, as Thurstan had ordered, led their parishioners, carrying their crosses and the relics of the saints. Robert of Bruce and Bernard of Baliol, who were friends of King David, went to him to beg him at the last moment to stop the destruction, promising him that if he would withdraw his army they would ask King Stephen to grant the earldom of Northumbria to David's son Henry. David, however, would not listen to them. Robert of Bruce then renounced the homage that he had done to King David for his lands in Scotland, and Bernard of Baliol renounced the fealty that he had sworn when David had captured him in an earlier engagement.[2]

Robert and Bernard returned to the English army and found that another contingent from the south, led by William Peverel and Geoffrey Halsalin of Nottinghamshire and Robert of Ferrers of Derbyshire, had joined them. The leading men of the army then swore an oath that they would be faithful to each other and that they would either win or die. Their pickets brought the news that the Scots had crossed the Tees and were advancing southwards, 'destroying the province after their usual fashion'.

---

[1] Richard of Hexham, pp. 159–61; Henry of Huntingdon, p. 262.
[2] Richard of Hexham, pp. 161–2; Ailred of Rievaulx: *Relatio de Standardo*, ed. Richard Howlett, in *Chronicles of the Reigns of Stephen*, etc., Vol. III, pp. 192–5.

The English marched seven miles to the north, to Northallerton, and on a moor two miles from the town they prepared to meet the Scots. To serve as a rallying-point they erected a ship's mast on a wagon, and at the top of the Standard, from which the battle was to take its name, they placed a silver pyx containing the Blessed Sacrament and affixed the banners under which they were to fight, those of St. Peter of York, St. John of Beverley, and St. Wilfred of Ripon. The knights dismounted. Richard of Hexham says that they had their horses led away so that the animals would not be thrown into a panic by the noise and the shouts of the Scots; Ailred of Rievaulx says that they did so in order that no one might flee.[1]

Before the battle was joined, Walter Espec, sheriff of Yorkshire, harangued the English, ending with the stirring words, 'Who would want to live if the Scots win, to see his wife befouled by the Scots' lust and his little ones spitted on their spears?' Bishop Ralph Nowel, acting for the absent archbishop, addressed them and gave the army absolution: 'We absolve you from all burden of sin in the name of the Father, Whose creatures they have foully and horribly destroyed, and of the Son, Whose altars they have defiled, and of the Holy Spirit, Whose elect they have killed like madmen.'[2]

The Battle of the Standard began at six on the morning of 22 August, with the Galwegians leading the assault on the English line. The English formed a wall of shields, from behind which their archers, 'the bulk of whom appear to have been commoners from Yorkshire', poured their hail into the Scots. The Galwegians broke and fled, the panic spread to the rest of the army, and by midmorning the Scots were in wild flight. The doughty men of Yorkshire pursued them across the moors, cutting them down by hundreds; Richard of Hexham says that more than 10,000 of them were killed or captured. Henry of Huntingdon says that 11,000 were killed, not counting those who fled the field and were later slain in the moors and forest. Although the Scots outnumbered the English by far, they were an undisciplined rabble, whereas the English were led by experienced knights.[3]

[1] Richard of Hexham, pp. 162-3; Ailred of Rievaulx, p. 189.
[2] Ailred of Rievaulx, pp. 185-9; Henry of Huntingdon, pp. 262-3.
[3] C. Warren Hollister: *The Military Organization of Norman England* (Oxford, 1965), p. 230; Richard of Hexham, p. 164; Henry of Huntingdon, p. 264; Beeler: *Warfare in England, 1066-1189*, pp. 85-93.

King David did not stop in his flight till he had reached the safety of Carlisle, seventy miles to the north-west, and his son Henry did not rejoin him with the tattered remnants of his army till three days later.[1]

The Battle of the Standard was fought at the same time that King Stephen was reducing Shrewsbury Castle. These victories, together with Queen Matilda's capture of Dover Castle, greatly strengthened his position. In gratitude for their leadership in the north, he made William of Aumale earl of York and Robert of Ferrers earl of Derby.[2] These were Stephen's first creations, and they were bestowed on men of wealth and standing. Robert of Ferrers was the most substantial landowner in Derbyshire and among the richest men in England. His wife, Hawise, was a granddaughter of Robert, count of Mortain, the Conqueror's half-brother.

William of Aumale, too, was descended from Herleve, the Conqueror's mother, for his grandmother, Adelaide, was a full sister of the Conqueror, and he and King Stephen were thus second cousins. William had made his sister countess of Aumale, and the title descended to her son Stephen by her third husband, Eudes, the exiled count of Champagne, and then to Stephen's son William, whom the king now made earl of York.

William of Malmesbury accuses Stephen of making earls of men so poor that he had to endow them with estates and revenues that had belonged directly to him, but this was certainly not the case with regard to these two men and to Gilbert of Clare, one of the greatest lords of the Welsh marches, whom Stephen made earl of Pembroke in this year. Gilbert was married to Elizabeth, the sister of Robert, earl of Leicester, and Waleran, count of Meulan, and was thus allied to one of the most powerful families in England. Stephen also made Count Waleran, to whom he had given the city of Worcester, earl of Worcester, but Waleran seems never to have used the title, styling himself instead count of Meulan.[3]

The traditional view has been that under the Conqueror and his sons the earl had lost most of his administrative and military

---

[1] Ailred of Rievaulx, p. 198.
[2] Richard of Hexham, p. 165.
[3] *H.N.*, p. 23; Orderic, Vol. V, p. 112; *G. de M.*, pp. 267–77; Henry of Huntingdon, p. 282; White: 'King Stephen's Earldoms', pp. 56–72.

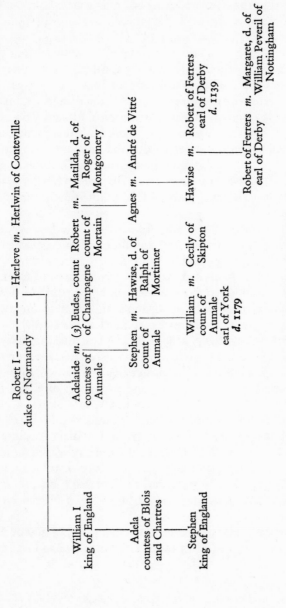

Robert I ------- Herleve m. Herlwin of Conteville
duke of Normandy

William I
king of England

Adela
countess of Blois
and Chartres

Stephen
king of England

Adelaide m. (3) Eudes, count   Robert m. Matilda, d. of
countess of   of Champagne   count of   Roger of
Aumale   Mortain   Montgomery

Agnes m. André de Vitré

Stephen m. Hawise, d. of
count of   Ralph of
Aumale   Mortimer

Hawise m. Robert of Ferrers
earl of Derby
d. 1139

William m. Cecily of
count of   Skipton
Aumale
earl of York
d. 1179

Robert of Ferrers m. Margaret, d. of
earl of Derby   William Peveril of
Nottingham

Robert of Ferrers
earl of Derby

V: Earls of York and of Derby

duties, which with the increasing centralisation of the government had passed to the sheriff, a man more directly responsible to the king. Sir Frank Stenton holds that 'By the beginning of Stephen's reign an earldom gave to its holder little more than a title and the precedence which it implied.' In a society in which rank and its trappings were highly regarded, however, an earldom, conferring on its holder the highest rank a man could attain, next to that of the king himself, was the greatest sign of favour that the king could bestow.

R. H. C. Davis, however, has recently advanced the view that earls, at least in Stephen's reign, were responsible both for the defence of their counties and for their administration. According to Mr. Davis, this reversal of the trend in the administration of the counties that had been initiated by Henry I was due primarily to Stephen's growing distrust of the governmental machinery that he had inherited from his predecessor and that was dominated by Henry's chief minister, Bishop Roger of Salisbury. The king and his friends suspected Roger and his circle of treasonable tendencies, and since most of the sheriffs were under Roger's control he could conceivably use the central administrative machinery to further the treasonable designs that Stephen was beginning to impute to him. It would of course be almost impossible for Stephen, without disrupting the whole government, to replace the sheriffs by men of whose loyalty he could feel certain or to find among his friends men who had the the skills to perform the sheriffs' more menial administrative tasks, but as a check on their powers he began at this time, according to Mr. Davis, to create earls 'to oversee the work of the sheriffs and suppress incipient rebellion', and Mr. Davis points to the significant fact that Stephen created almost all the new earldoms between 1138 and 1140, a period when, as we shall see, his difficulties with Bishop Roger were coming to a head.[1]

Whilst the Scots were licking their wounds at Carlisle, Alberic, bishop of Ostia, whom Pope Innocent II had sent as his legate to England and Scotland, arrived at King David's court on 26 September. The Scots had adhered to the anti-pope Anacletus

[1] Stenton: *The First Century of English Feudalism*, pp. 228–34; William Stubbs: *The Constitutional History of England in Its Origin and Development* (3 vols., 6th edn., Oxford, 1897, reprinted 1967), Vol. I, pp. 389–94; Davis, pp. 32–3, 129–32. I am most grateful to Mr. Davis, who has kindly read this passage in order to make sure that it states his views correctly.

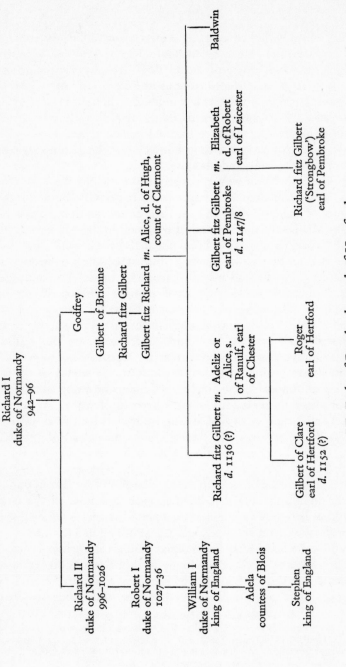

VI: Earls of Pembroke and of Hertford
(De Clare Family)

during the papal schism of 1130, but with his death in 1138 they
now professed allegiance to Innocent. The legate succeeded in
inducing them to agree to a truce till Martinmas, 11 November,
and he made the Galwegians promise to bring all the girls and
women they had captured to Carlisle and set them free before
that date. The Galwegians 'and all the others most firmly
promised him that henceforth they would not in any way violate
churches, and that they would spare children and women and
those who were infirm through sickness or age, and that henceforth they would not kill anyone at all unless he resisted them'.

After staying with David for three days, the legate started
southward on 29 September. When he joined King Stephen he
reported on his mission to the Scots and urged the king to exert
every effort to arrive at a lasting peace with them. His efforts
were opposed by many of the barons whose lands they had
ravaged and who urged the king to proceed against them manfully till he had reduced them to complete submission. Queen
Matilda, however, seconded the legate's pleas, 'for she dearly
loved her uncle David, king of Scotland, and Henry, his son and
her cousin', and bent all her efforts towards inducing her husband
to make peace with them.[1]

Alberic summoned an ecclesiastical council to meet at Westminster on 13 December, at which eighteen bishops and about
thirty abbots were present. After passing a number of canons
relating to the discipline of the Church and the morals of the
clergy, they turned to the matter of electing an archbishop of
Canterbury. William of Corbeil had died on 21 November
1136, and Orderic Vitalis says that Bishop Henry of Winchester
had immediately been elected to succeed him. Because a bishop
could not be transferred from one see to another without the
pope's permission, Henry had gone to Normandy in Advent
1136 and sent messengers to Innocent II to request his consent to
the change, whilst he spent the winter in Normandy.

Although Orderic is usually quite well-informed about affairs
in England, his account is not corroborated by any English writer,
and in all the many and heated controversies surrounding the
bishop of Winchester no mention is made of this election.
Orderic's story has an air of improbability about it, for Bishop
Henry, the busiest and most energetic of men, is hardly likely

[1] Richard of Hexham, pp. 167–71, 176.

merely to have sent messengers to the pope and then settled down to a long and inactive winter of waiting in Normandy. If Henry had indeed been elected archbishop of Canterbury, one may be sure that he would have pressed his suit to the pope in person.[1]

Gervase of Canterbury, who had the traditions and collective memory of the monastery at Canterbury to draw upon, says that although Henry eagerly desired the honour he was frustrated by both the king and the queen. His account of the election, joined to that of Ralph of Diceto, dean of St. Paul's and a reliable reporter of the traditions of his cathedral, makes it clear not only that Henry was not elected but also that some powerful force was working against his election.

Henry was certainly the most able bishop in England and the obvious candidate for the position of archbishop. He was a brilliant success both as abbot of Glastonbury and as a bishop of Winchester; he had received a good education at Cluny; his personal life was above reproach, and the only objection that could be made to him was that his character was as much that of a knight as of a bishop, if not more so.

It is also understandable that the king did not want to see his ambitious younger brother advanced to the headship of the Church in England. Although Henry had been of the greatest service in helping him to secure the crown, he was of such an independent and indeed overweening turn of mind that Stephen may have feared that as archbishop of Canterbury he would be not merely beyond his control but even so arrogant that it would be impossible to work with him in that close cooperation that ideally should exist between the king and the archbishop.

Stephen, however, could hardly support the candidacy of any other English bishop without provoking an open break with Henry, and, furthermore, it would be difficult to find a bishop in England at this time who was of the calibre to make a good archbishop. One solution, then, was to turn to an establishment that had already furnished the English Church with such notable leaders as Lanfranc and Anselm. Theobald, who came of a knightly but not distinguished Norman family, had been prior

---

[1] Richard of Hexham, pp. 172–5; Orderic, Vol. V, pp. 78–9. See also Knowles: *The Monastic Order in England*, p. 288, and Lena Voss: *Heinrich von Blois, Bischof von Winchester (1129–71)* (Berlin, 1932), pp. 16–17. Dr. Voss says: 'Heinrich machte merkwürdigerweise keinerlei Anstalten, selbst an die Kurie zu gehen, um seinen Wünschen den nötigen Nachdruck zu verleihen.'

of Bec since 1127 and had been elected abbot in 1137. He was both pious and learned, but he had ruled his abbey for such a short time that he could hardly have gained much renown, and one may surmise that his election as archbishop was due more to the reputation of the house he headed than to his own fame.

At any rate, on 24 December 1138, Jeremiah, prior of Christ Church, and some of his monks, in the presence of the king, the legate, and the assembled bishops and clergy, elected Theobald, abbot of Bec, as archbishop of Canterbury. The election took place at the end of the council and was carefully engineered so as to be held in the absence of Bishop Henry, who as administrator of the vacant diocese of London was ordaining a deacon at St. Paul's. When he learned what had been done behind his back, he was so enraged that he broke off the ceremony of ordination. All this seems to indicate that Orderic's story of Henry's election and the subsequent quashing by the pope of that election is not be relied upon. The legate consecrated Theobald on 8 January 1139 at Canterbury in the presence of almost all the bishops of England.[1]

In that same month the legate and a number of English clerics set out for Rome to attend the general council that Pope Innocent II had summoned. Only five English bishops attended: the newly consecrated Theobald, Ernulf of Rochester, Simon of Worcester, Roger of Coventry, and Robert of Exeter, together with four abbots, one of whom was Richard, abbot of Fountains, whom the aged and infirm Thurstan had sent in his place. Richard of Hexham says that the king was not willing to allow any more bishops to attend because of the unsettled condition of the kingdom.[2]

While the council was in session, the pope heard the appeal that the Empress Matilda had made against King Stephen, charging him with perjury and with having unlawfully usurped the crown. It is significant that Matilda did not do this till two years had passed and her brother Robert had come out openly on her side. He may well have been the brains behind the appeal, for until he espoused his sister's cause we hear of few actions on her part, and her husband's only contribution was the cruel and

---

[1] Gervase of Canterbury, Vol. I, pp. 99, 109; Ralph of Diceto, Vol. I, p. 252. See also Saltman: *Theobald, Archbishop of Canterbury*, pp. 7–13.

[2] Richard of Hexham, pp. 176–7.

senseless raids into Normandy that served merely to harden the Normans in their hatred of the Angevins. Since the crime alleged against Stephen was that of perjury, which fell within the competence of the spiritual courts, only the pope could hear the case.

Matilda's representative, Bishop Ulgar of Angers, argued that Stephen was guilty of perjury inasmuch as he had violated his oath to receive her as King Henry's heir. Stephen was represented by Roger, bishop of Coventry; Lupel, a clerk of the late William, archbishop of Canterbury, and Arnulf, archdeacon of Séez, who later became bishop of Lisieux. Arnulf, as spokesman for the king's defence, declared that in the first place Matilda was not King Henry's lawful heir, since she was the daughter of an invalid marriage, her mother having been a nun when King Henry carried her away from the convent and tore off her veil, and therefore Stephen's oath was not binding; and secondly that Henry had changed his mind on his deathbed and designated Stephen as his heir, as Hugh Bigod and two knights had sworn to the archbishop of Canterbury.

This startling accusation produced a great uproar and seems to have caught Bishop Ulgar off his guard. He reviled Arnulf for making such a charge against King Henry, 'who raised you and all your family from the dunghill', but he failed, as Gilbert Foliot noted, to cite the most convincing evidence for the validity of Henry's marriage: the fact that Anselm, archbishop of Canterbury, had investigated the matter, satisfied himself that Matilda had not taken a nun's vows, and then performed the ceremony. In defence of the validity of Henry's marriage Ulgar alleged that Pope Paschal II had anointed Henry's daughter Matilda as empress, which he would not have done if she had been illegitimate, whereas there is no evidence that Pashcal II had ever performed such a ceremony; and he challenged the truthfulness of Hugh Bigod's oath by declaring that neither Hugh nor Arnulf had been present at Henry's deathbed.

The most telling argument in favour of Stephen's case was not mentioned, although it was of course in the pope's mind: that the archbishop of Canterbury, the papal legate, had already heard the arguments and had pronounced in Stephen's favour and that the pope had confirmed the decision by his recognition of Stephen in the early part of 1136. It was hardly likely that the pope would now reverse a decision made by his legate and confirmed by himself.

Innocent therefore refused to listen to any further arguments. He accepted Stephen's gifts and sent him a friendly letter confirming him as king of England and duke of Normandy.[1]

The negotiations for peace between the English and Scottish kings that the legate Alberic had set on foot continued after his departure. Queen Matilda apparently took an active part in them, for it was in her presence that the treaty was signed at Durham on 9 April 1139. Stephen gave Henry, whom he had previously made earl of Huntingdon, the county of Northumberland, except for two castles, those of Bamburgh and Newcastle-upon-Tyne, and made him earl of Northumbria. He directed that those of his barons who held land in Northumbria and who wished to do so should do homage to Henry for their lands, saving their fealty to the king. For their part, King David and his son, with all their barons, promised to keep the peace in all things and to be faithful to King Stephen as long as they lived. As pledges of their fidelity they gave the sons of some of the leading Scottish noblemen as hostages.

Henry accompanied his cousin, Queen Matilda, back to the south and met Stephen at Nottingham, where he renewed the promises he had made at Durham. He spent the whole summer in England, and it was probably at this time that he married Ada or Adeline, the daughter of William of Warenne, earl of Surrey, with whom he had fallen in love.[2]

---

[1] John of Salisbury: *Historia Pontificalis*, pp. 85–8, 107–13; *The Letters and Charters of Gilbert Foliot*, ed. Z. N. Brooke, Adrian Morey, and C. N. L. Brooke (Cambridge, 1967), pp. 65–6; G. *de M.*, pp. 250–61.

[2] Richard of Hexham, pp. 177–8; Orderic, Vol. V, p. 114.

IV

1139

KING Stephen had been fortunate in enjoying the support of the Church. The influence of his brother Henry and of the chief justiciar, Bishop Roger of Salisbury, had been important factors in his securing the crown in the first place; Pope Innocent II had twice recognised him as king of England, and he had obtained the election of his nominee, Theobald, as archbishop of Canterbury. His opposition to Henry's election as archbishop had, however, caused his brother to cool off considerably in his support, and in order to strengthen his wavering loyalty Stephen had secured his appointment as papal legate on 1 March 1139.[1] Thus was created an extraordinary situation in which the bishop of Winchester outranked the archbishop of Canterbury, but the newly consecrated Theobald seems to have been too timid to protest against this affront to his dignity.

In the summer of 1139 Stephen took a step that, however necessary it may have been, nevertheless cost him the support of the English bishops. It has already been noted that Roger, bishop of Salisbury, who had been chief justiciar under Henry I, had continued in that position after Stephen's accession and thus was responsible for the conduct of the whole machinery of the government, which he had built up to a degree of efficiency and complexity that was probably unrivalled anywhere in Europe at that time.

Bishop Roger was not only the most powerful man in England, next to the king; he had amassed an enormous fortune, and through his friendship with King Henry he had founded a family dynasty. One of his nephews, Alexander, had been bishop of Lincoln since 1123; another nephew, Nigel, was made bishop of Ely ten years later, and his son Roger was the king's chancellor.

[1] *H.N.*, p. 29.

Bishop Roger was a mighty builder of castles and had erected
fortifications at Sherborne, Salisbury, Malmesbury, where he
built a castle 'actually in the churchyard, hardly a stone's throw
from the abbey', and Devizes, 'than which there was not another
more splendid within the bounds of Europe'. Bishop Alexander,
on a scale hardly less magnificent, had built castles at Sleaford
and Newark 'for the protection, as he said, and glorification of
his diocese'.[1] All three of these bishops loved display and osten-
tation, and even in the best of times the power and prosperity of a
family that King Henry had 'raised from the dust' would be sure
to excite much envy.

The defection of the earl of Gloucester, the revolt of some of
his supporters, and the rumours that he would shortly come to
England and lead a rebellion against the king of course aroused
in the king and his friends a feeling of uneasiness and a tendency
to watch for the slightest signs of treasonable inclinations. Their
suspicions were sharpened when Bishop Roger began stocking
his castles with weapons and food on a lavish scale and going about
with an enormous bodyguard of troops. All three of the bishops
'aroused general astonishment on account of the extraordinary
concourse of knights by which they were surrounded on every
side whenever they attended court'. The author of the *Gesta
Stephani* charges that Bishop Roger was already in secret communication with Earl Robert and his sister and had promised
them his help.

Waleran, count of Meulan, and his friends pointed out all this
to the king, warned him that the three bishops were contemplating treason, and urged him to take steps to curb them before it
was too late. By this time Stephen was suspicious of the loyalty
of almost everyone, as he had good reason to be, but he was
extremely reluctant to proceed against the three bishops on a
mere suspicion when he knew that any hostile action against them
would unite the whole body of bishops against him in defence of
their order, be the offenders never so guilty. He debated the
matter for a long time, but at last he decided to follow Count
Waleran's advice at the first opportunity.[2]

The occasion arose at a meeting of the Great Council at Oxford
about 24 June 1139. Oddly enough, William of Malmesbury,

---

[1] *H.N.*, p. 25; Henry of Huntingdon, p. 265.
[2] *G.S.*, pp. 48–50; *H.N.*, p. 26.

who in general favours the king's opponents, in his account seems to place the major share of the blame for the brawl that arose on the three bishops and their supporters, whilst the author of the *Gesta Stephani*, who usually writes from the royalist point of view, puts the blame on Stephen's party.   According to William of Malmesbury, Bishop Roger was unwilling to attend the council in the first place and remarked in William's hearing: 'By my blessed lady Mary, somehow I am disinclined to this journey. This I know, that I shall be as useful at court as a colt in battle.' When the bishop and his retinue arrived at Oxford, a quarrel arose between his men and those of Alan, count of Brittany and earl of Richmond, over their lodgings.   'The bishop of Salisbury's men, who were sitting at table, leaped up to fight before they had finished their meal.'   Swords were drawn, and in the fight Count Alan's nephew was almost killed, his men were put to flight, many of the bishop's men were wounded, and one knight was slain.

At this breach of his peace the king ordered the bishops into his presence and demanded that they make satisfaction by surrendering the keys of their castles 'as guarantees of their trustworthiness'.   It was not until they hesitated over surrendering the castles that the king 'put them under close arrest to prevent their going away'.

The author of the *Gesta Stephani* says that the brawl was started by the king's knights, 'at the instigation of the crafty count of Meulan and some others'.   Orderic Vitalis, in support of this, says that the brothers Waleran and Robert and Alan of Brittany formed a plot against the bishops' men and that the king's knights attacked the bishops' men, killed some, captured others, put the rest to flight, and then returned to the king, who, it is implied, had sent them on their mission in the first place.

The author of the *Gesta Stephani* says that 'when a general council of the ill-disposed had been held, they hastened in a body to arrest the bishops on the ground that they were offenders against the king's majesty', which implies that the king and his advisors talked the matter over and ordered the arrest of the bishops on trumped-up charges of disturbing the peace, when it was the king's knights who were responsible for the fray in the first place.   The king's supporters then invaded the bishops' lodgings in arms, violently plundered everything they found, and brought Bishops Roger and Alexander to the king.

Whether justly or unjustly, depending upon which account one chooses to believe, Stephen arrested the bishops of Salisbury and Lincoln and Bishop Roger's son, the Chancellor Roger. Bishop Nigel of Ely, who was lodging outside the town, as soon as he heard the news, 'for he had a guilty conscience', fled to his uncle's castle at Devizes and prepared to resist the king. His flight and preparations for resistance were seen as an admission of guilt and confirmed the king in his conviction of the bishops' treasonable designs. Stephen immediately sent William of Ypres to invest Devizes. The king followed him shortly, bringing with him the two bishops under arrest and Roger, the chancellor, in chains. Henry of Huntingdon, however, says that he left Bishop Alexander in prison at Oxford during the expedition, and this seems the more likely, since Alexander is not mentioned in the various accounts of the proceedings at Devizes.

When the king and his captives arrived at Devizes, Bishop Roger entered upon a fast, either voluntarily, according to William of Malmesbury, or because the king was determined to starve him into submission, as the author of the *Gesta Stephani* says. The castle meanwhile was being stoutly defended by Bishop Nigel and Matilda of Ramsbury, Bishop Roger's mistress and the chancellor's mother. Stephen declared that unless they surrendered the castle he would have the chancellor 'hanged on high right before the entrance to the castle', and he had Roger brought out with a halter round his neck to show that he meant to carry out his threat if it became necessary to do so. He allowed Bishop Roger to confer with his nephew, and Roger bitterly upbraided Nigel for having brought all this trouble on him by fleeing to Devizes and preparing for war instead of going back to his diocese, as prudence would have dictated.

Bishop Nigel seems to have been willing to see his uncle starved to death and his cousin hanged before he would surrender the castle, but Matilda of Ramsbury was not made of such stern material. After three days she sent a messenger to the king with the offer to surrender if he would set her lover and her son free. Stephen accepted, and thus easily he secured not only Devizes but Salisbury, Sherborne, and Malmesbury as well, together with all the stocks of food and weapons and the great store of money that had been laid up in them. The treasure that he thus acquired must have been enormous, for he not only replenished his own exchequer, which had been drained by the almost constant warfare upon which he had been engaged, but also gained enough to buy Constance, the sister of King Louis VII, as a wife for his elder son Eustace. The continuator of Florence of Worcester reports that it was said that more than 40,000 marks of silver was found in the castles, as well as many vessels of gold.[1]

Bishops Roger and Nigel then returned to their dioceses, considerably chastened. Stephen took Bishop Alexander with him to Newark, where the bishop had built a castle that was the pride of his heart, and threatened to starve him to death before the gates of the castle unless he surrendered both Newark and Sleaford to him. Alexander complied, and the king thus gained two important fortifications guarding the approaches to Lincoln.

Stephen's actions caused a tremendous uproar amongst the clergy. He had indeed laid violent hands on the Lord's anointed, but whilst one may feel that his methods were unduly violent, he was certainly justified in depriving the bishops of their castles and checking their preparations for rebellion. No one attempted to deny that they were plotting treason, and the king could not well allow them to continue indefinitely on such courses. He had every right to demand the surrender of their castles, which were held at the king's pleasure. R. H. C. Davis has pointed out that the arrest of the bishops was 'an outrageous breach of hospitality, and it was aggravated considerably by the fact that the offence was committed by the king and in the king's court'.[2] One must remember, however, that having demanded the surrender of their castles, as was his right regardless of who started the brawl at Oxford, and having been refused, it would have been the height of folly for Stephen to allow the bishops to flee to their castles and set up their rebellion there, which is exactly what Bishop Nigel attempted to do.

Stephen might have used less spectacular methods to secure the surrender of the castles, but the very violence of his actions shows that his patience was exhausted. The end did not justify the means, of course, but the final result must have been highly gratifying. He foiled four rebels in their intended treason; he

[1] H.N., pp. 26–7; G.S., pp. 51–3; Orderic, Vol. V, pp. 120–1; Henry of Huntingdon, p. 265; Florence of Worcester: Chronicon ex Chronicis and Its Continuations, ed. B. Thorpe (2 vols., London, 1848–9) Vol. II, p. 113.
[2] R. H. C. Davis: 'What Happened in Stephen's Reign, 1135–54', History, Vol. XLIX, no. 165 (February 1964), p. 4.

won six immensely strong and important castles with all their stocks of food and weapons, and he confiscated the great sums of money that were stored in them.

Bishop Stubbs says: 'The arrest of Bishop Roger was perhaps the most important constitutional event that had taken place since the Conquest',[1] but it is difficult to see on what grounds he makes the statement. Stephen was not attempting to establish any new rights or to extend his powers; in fact, he was following established precedents. He was asserting, as his predecessors had done, that his ministers were answerable to him for their actions, that castles could be held only at the king's pleasure and must be surrendered on demand, and that ecclesiastics who held secular offices were accountable for their conduct of those offices. None of this was new, and one can hardly see in his actions anything more than a determination to maintain the well-established rights of the Crown.

The indignation of the chroniclers, who were of course all clerics, at his treatment of members of their order should not blind us to the fact that other clerics thought that the bishops had received their due deserts,[2] and that many laymen, as well as not a few clerics, were gratified to see these three overweening bishops, whose immense riches, great power, and ostentatious arrogance had made enemies on all sides, thus humiliated and stripped of their castles. Some bishops rose to their defence as fellow-bishops; none spoke in their behalf as a friend.

His arrest of the three bishops and his taking over of their castles did not, in the long run, cost him the support of the Church. The bishops concerned and also that stout defender of his order, the bishop of Winchester, did of course take up an openly hostile attitude to the king, but the three bishops were meditating treachery before he acted, and his brother had already become lukewarm in his support because he had been denied the archbishopric of Canterbury. They would doubtless have gone over to the empress even if Stephen had not acted as he did.

It is easy to form an exaggerated idea of the Church's influence at this time, for almost all our information comes from churchmen. The support of the Church was of course of immense importance when Stephen was attempting to gain the crown, for

[1] Stubbs: *The Constitutional History of England*, Vol. I, pp. 352–3.
[2] *H.N.*, p. 28.

only the archbishop could crown the king and only the Church could pronounce on the binding power of the oath to support the empress. Once he had gained the crown, however, he was much more dependent upon the support of the greater barons than he was on that of the Church. Short of outright imposition of the sentences of excommunication and interdict, for which they would have needed the pope's approval, the bishops could not do him a great deal of harm, compared with the material advantages that the greater barons had, and as a matter of fact in the struggle that ensued the bishops did not play a decisive part, although Henry of Winchester no doubt liked to think that he did.

The extent of the influence of the Church may be judged by the decisions of the council that Bishop Henry, as papal legate, summoned to meet at Winchester on 29 August 1139. Almost all the bishops of England attended; the only ones who are mentioned as not being present were Archbishop Thurstan, who excused himself by a letter pleading his poor health, and Alexander of Lincoln. Archbishop Theobald attended, although it was certainly an anomalous position for a metropolitan to be attending a council summoned and presided over by one of his suffragans. He took little part in the proceedings, but he no doubt used the opportunity to form an opinion, and one may be certain that it was not a favourable one, of the state of the Church in England. For one fresh from the monastery of Bec, a house noted for the fidelity of its observance of the Rule, it must have seemed strange to be present at a meeting called to pass judgment on a king who had deprived of his castles a bishop who had openly kept a mistress and promoted his son's career at court.

Bishop Henry opened the council by having the pope's bull, dated 1 March 1139 and appointing him legate in England, read to the assembly. Speaking in Latin, 'for he was addressing educated men', he brought up the matter of the arrest of the three bishops. 'It was a lamentable crime,' he said, 'that the king had been so led astray by those who instigated him to this as to order hands to be laid on his men, especially when they were bishops, in the peace of his court.' The king's confiscation of the supplies and monies in the castles he termed a robbery of Church property. 'The king's outrage upon divine law caused him so much grief that he would sooner suffer great damage to his person and possessions than that the dignity of bishops should be lowered

by such a humiliation.' He then requested the archbishop and
the others to decide what should be done, assuring them that he
would not hesitate to carry out their decision through regard
either for his brother or for his own property and even his life.

He had ordered his brother to attend the council, and the king
had come to Winchester, although he was not present at these
proceedings. Stephen sent some earls to ask why he had been
summoned, and Henry sent them back with the message that
the king should either come before the council and defend his
actions or else submit to its judgment, according to canon law,
for he had advanced the extreme view that the bishops were
answerable only to ecclesiastical courts and could not be judged
by the king.

When the earls returned to the council they were accompanied
by Aubrey de Vere, the king's chamberlain, who acted as his
spokesman. Aubrey declared that almost every time Bishop
Roger came to court his men had raised a brawl and that at
Oxford they had attacked Count Alan's men at the instigation
of Bishop Alexander of Lincoln, through hatred of Alan. Bishop
Roger, Aubrey said, secretly favoured the king's enemies, and the
king had abundant proof of this. 'Everyone was saying that as
soon as the empress came he would take her side, together with
his nephews and his castles.' Aubrey then advanced the classic
defence, used by William the Conqueror in his case against Odo,
bishop of Bayeux and earl of Kent, and by William Rufus
against William of St.-Calais, bishop of Durham and the king's
chief minister, that Roger had been arrested 'not as a bishop but as
a servant of the king, who had both managed his affairs and
received his pay. The king', he continued, 'had not seized the
castles by force, but both the bishops had surrendered them gladly
in order to avoid facing a charge for the brawl they had stirred
up at court'. As for the money that Bishop Henry was claiming
as Church property, it lawfully belonged to the king, for Roger
had taken it out of the royal treasury in King Henry's time and
had willingly given it up to Stephen, as he had many witnesses
to prove. It was the king's will, Aubrey said in concluding, that
the settlement already made between him and the bishops should
remain in force.

Bishop Roger in his defence claimed 'that he had never been
King Stephen's minister or received his pay' and declared that it

F

he did not find justice in the council he would appeal to the pope. Bishop Henry then said that the king's charges against the bishops should have been made before a Church council and tried by canon law, and he directed that the king restore their property to the bishops, pending such a trial. To this piece of presumption the king paid no attention.

Since the archbishop of Canterbury apparently declined to take an active part in these proceedings, Stephen requested that the council be adjourned till the arrival of Archbishop Hugh of Rouen, one of his firm supporters. When Hugh arrived a few days later he quickly disposed of the matter with flawless logic. The bishops might have their castles, he said, if they could prove by canon law that they were entitled to them. Even if they could prove by canon law that they had a right to them, which they certainly could not do, 'they ought to hand over the keys of their fortifications to the disposal of the king, whose duty it is to fight for the peace of all. So the bishops' whole case will fall to the ground', he summed up, 'for either it is unjust, according to the canon law, for them to have castles or, if this is permitted by the king as an act of grace, they ought to yield to the emergencies of the time by delivering up the keys'.

After the archbishop had spoken, Aubrey de Vere delivered a threat to the bishops. The king, he said, had been told that they were murmuring against him and preparing to send some of their number to Rome to complain against him to the pope. 'If anyone went anywhere out of England contrary to his wish and the majesty of the Crown, it might be difficult for him to return,' Aubrey warned them.

Realising, no doubt, the weakness of their arguments, the council broke up without pronouncing any censure upon the king and without the king's having budged in the slightest from his position. Bishop Henry and Archbishop Theobald went to him, fell at his feet, and begged him not to 'suffer a divorce to be made between the monarchy and the clergy'. Stephen rose respectfully before them, and, since he had technically been guilty of having laid violent hands on the clergy, he agreed to perform an unspecified penance for that offence. He kept, however, the castles, the supplies, and the money that he had taken from the three bishops. In spite of Bishop Henry's stirring accusation against the king, the council implicitly admitted that

Stephen was in the right by passing a statute directing that all castles and fortifications in the bishops' hands should be turned over to the king as his own property. The chief effects of the council at Winchester were virtually to confirm the king in his actions against the three bishops and to widen the breach between Stephen and his brother, who, papal legate though he was, saw his accusations against the king disregarded by his fellow bishops.[1]

When the council broke up, on 1 September, the king turned his attention to William of Mohun, who was using his castle, on a conical hill at Dunster in Somerset, as a base for plundering all that part of the country. Stephen went there with a large army, but when he found the castle to be almost impregnable he abandoned the idea of conducting a protracted siege in person, built a fortification to hold the garrison in check, and gave the task of subduing the rebels to Henry of Tracy, to whom he had awarded the lands forfeited by Robert of Bampton. Henry pursued his assignment with enthusiasm and ability, put a stop to the raids, and captured over a hundred of William's knights.[2]

Stephen was drawn away from Dunster by the news that the exiled Baldwin of Redvers had landed at Wareham in Dorset with a large body of troops and had been admitted to Corfe Castle, five miles to the south, 'the most secure of all the English castles'. Stephen hastened there with his army, but again he found that the castle was almost impregnable and could be captured only by a long siege. There were few pitched battles at this time; the Battle of the Standard, whose results were decisive, was one of the chief exceptions. Most warfare consisted of the dreary and time-consuming business of besieging castles, which to the limited methods of offence of the day were usually impregnable except by a long siege. Beyond a certain limit, the size of the besieging force was of little account; more men than were needed to contain the besieged garrison would be of little help and would only be costly to maintain in food and wages. In such circumstances, Stephen did all that he could by taking steps to confine the garrison within the castle, thus stopping their ravages, and then entrusting the continuation of the siege to one of his lieutenants.

[1] H.N., pp. 29–34; G.S., p. 53; Henry of Huntingdon, p. 266; John of Worcester: Chronicle, ed. J. R. H. Weaver (Oxford, 1908), p. 55.
[2] G.S., pp. 54–5; Henry of Huntingdon, p. 261; Davis, p. 76, note 19.

Whilst he was before Corfe Castle he heard the news that he most dreaded: that Earl Robert and his sister had raised an army and would shortly land in England. Up to this time the various rebellions against the king had been sporadic and unorganised. Although most of the rebels had been friends and partisans of Earl Robert, each of them had acted on his own initiative, and there had been no one person directing operations. The arrival of Earl Robert, a skilled warrior, in England would change all that and provide the leadership that the rebels had lacked. Stephen left Corfe and devoted himself to putting all the likely harbours where the invaders might land into a state of defence.[1]

Earl Robert and his sister landed at Arundel on 30 September with a force of only 140 knights and were received into the castle by King Henry's widow, Adeliza of Louvain, who had obtained the castle and honour of Arundel as part of her dower, and her second husband, William of Aubigny, whom Stephen made earl of Lincoln some time before Christmas 1141. Leaving his sister with her step-mother, Robert set out for Bristol with a guard of twelve knights 'by a hidden byway'. When he heard the news of the earl's landing, Bishop Henry of Winchester set guards on all the roads and met Robert on his journey. The author of the *Gesta Stephani* says that although 'it must be doubtful, or rather quite incredible', that he should do so, it was commonly reported that the bishop made 'a compact of peace and friendship' with the earl and let him go unharmed. As K. R. Potter points out, however, the story is not at all improbable, for Bishop Henry's support of his brother was by now lukewarm at best, and his recent defeat at the council at Winchester, when the king had disregarded his authority, had estranged them still further.[2]

Earl Robert was met, half-way to Bristol, by a man who was to prove the most faithful and one of the ablest of his sister's supporters, Brian fitz Count, a son, probably illegitimate, of Alan 'Fergant', duke of Brittany.[3] Brian had been brought up and educated at King Henry's court, and it will be remembered that he and Earl Robert had escorted the empress to Normandy for her betrothal to Count Geoffrey. Through his wife Brian

---

[1] G.S., p. 56.
[2] H.N., p. 34; G. de M., p. 322; G.S., p. 39 and note 1.
[3] Alan IV, 'Fergant', duke of Brittany, who died in 1119, is not to be confused with Alan of Dinant, 'the Black', count of Brittany and earl of Richmond, whom we have met earlier. See *The Complete Peerage*, Vol. X, p. 780.

held the castle of Wallingford,[1] a fact that was to prove of the greatest importance in the events that followed. After they had conferred, Brian went to make Wallingford an impregnable outpost for the rebels, whilst Robert went on to Bristol.

Stephen meanwhile arrived with his army and struck terror into the heart of Countess Adeliza. Although she had been in secret correspondence with the plotters and had pledged fealty to them, she now realised that her treason might easily cost her all her possessions in England. She therefore assured the king that she was not entertaining the empress and her knights as friends, but that they had forced themselves on her.[2]

Bishop Henry arrived on the scene with a large bodyguard of cavalry. When he learned that the king was planning to besiege the castle and capture the empress and her small army, he gave Stephen the astonishing advice that it would be wiser to let Matilda join her brother so that he could more easily capture the two of them together. Stephen had already reconnoitred Bristol and found it impregnable, and it is almost incredible that he should have been taken in by his brother's advice. The events of the last few weeks should have shown Stephen that his brother was not to be relied upon, but the king apparently could not believe that his brother would betray him. At any rate, he allowed Matilda to join her brother at Bristol and gave her as escorts the bishop of Winchester and Waleran, count of Meulan. 'It is not the custom of honourable knights to refuse escort to anyone, even their bitterest enemy', says William of Malmesbury in defence of the king's chivalrous gesture. 'In this permission, indeed,' says Orderic Vitalis, 'the king's great simplicity or stupidity may be seen, and prudent men may lament that he was so heedless of his own welfare and the safety of his realm.'[3]

When Matilda arrived at Bristol she was joined by Miles of Gloucester, the castellan of Gloucester Castle, who, together with her brother and Brian fitz Count, was to be her most faithful supporter. Miles, it will be remembered, was amongst the first barons to recognise Stephen as king, and he had been of great help to him at the siege of Shrewsbury in August 1138. Now, in Matilda's words, 'Miles of Gloucester came to me as quickly as

[1] Stenton: *The First Century of English Feudalism*, p. 235.
[2] *H.N.*, p. 35; John of Worcester, p. 55.
[3] *H.N.*, p. 35; Orderic, Vol. V, p. 121.

he could at Bristol and received me as his lady and recognised
me as the rightful heir to the realm of England, and from there
he took me with him to Gloucester, and there he did his liege
homage to me against all men.'[1]

Thanks in large measure to Stephen's leniency, his enemies
were now in possession of two strongholds, Bristol and Gloucester,
protected by a redoubtable outpost at Wallingford, with two
capable leaders, Earl Robert and Miles of Gloucester, to organise
and direct their efforts to deprive him of his throne. 'But King
Stephen was quite unconquered and unbroken by all the sea of
troubles that pressed on him, and gathering his forces in a large
army he boldly tried to overcome his enemies one by one.'

Since he could not hope to reduce either Bristol or Gloucester
with Wallingford sitting astride his lines of communication, he
turned to that castle as his first objective. When he arrived there
with his army his barons pointed out that 'that castle was most
securely fortified by impregnable walls, that supplies had been
put into it in very great abundance, enough to last for a great
number of years, and that the garrison consisted of a very strong
force of invincible warriors'. They might have added that the
castellan, Brian fitz Count, was a man of the utmost determination and ingenuity.

If Stephen himself did not realise it, however, his friends should
have pointed out to him the strategic importance of the castle
and the impossibility of reducing the rebels' strongholds to the
west until this bastion was taken. We have already noted how
he failed even to attempt to take Bristol, and he now, in the same
way, turned aside from Wallingford after building two castles
(at this time a castle was simply a fortified position) there and
placing in these temporary structures a garrison strong enough to
hold Wallingford in check but by no means strong enough to
reduce it.[2]

Henry of Huntingdon criticises Stephen as being quick enough
at undertaking many designs but slothful in prosecuting them,
and this characteristic was most evident in the ensuing months.
Stephen dashed here and there with his army, as we shall see, but
he remained always on the defensive, rushing from one castle to
another as the danger seemed most acute, but rarely staying long

---

[1] *G. de M.*, pp. 56, 284–5; *Regesta*, p. 150.
[2] *G.S.*, p. 61.

enough to inflict a decisive defeat on his opponents. The author of the *Gesta Stephani* writes of him: 'It was like what we read of the fabled hydra of Hercules; when one head was cut off two or more grew in its place. That is precisely what we must feel about King Stephen's labours, because when one was finished others, more burdensome, kept on taking its place without end, and like another Hercules he always girded himself bravely and unconquerably to endure each.'[1] This description applies quite accurately to the situation prevailing before the landing of Earl Robert and the empress, when one sporadic rebellion followed another without any apparent connexion or organisation. Once the two had reached England, however, the rebellion gained what it had hitherto lacked, a capable leader, and as long as Stephen continued to shy away from the rebels' chief strongholds he could hope for only temporary and sporadic successes.

Leaving a garrison at Wallingford, Stephen undertook what seems to have been a reconnaissance along the edges of the enemy's country. From Wallingford he went some thirty miles to the west to South Cerney, which Humphrey of Bohun, at the direction of Miles of Gloucester, his father-in-law, had fortified, apparently to serve as a link between Gloucester and Wallingford. Stephen stormed the castle and captured it.

From there the king went ten miles south-west to Malmesbury, one of the castles that Roger, bishop of Salisbury, had been forced to surrender. Robert fitz Hubert, 'a cruel and crafty man', related to William of Ypres, the king's chief lieutenant, had captured the castle and burned the town on 7 October. Stephen laid siege to the castle, and after eight days Robert and his garrison surrendered. William of Ypres arranged for the surrender, and it may have been through his influence that his kinsman was allowed to leave unpunished after he had given up the castle. Robert, as might be expected, took refuge with the earl of Gloucester.[2]

After these two successes Stephen went twenty miles to the south to Trowbridge, a castle belonging, like South Cerney, to Humphrey of Bohun. He began the laborious business of building siege-engines to batter the walls, but the task of capturing

---

[1] Henry of Huntingdon, p. 283; G.S., p. 46.
[2] G.S., p. 62; H.N., p. 36; John of Worcester, pp. 56, 61. It seems probable that John of Worcester is referring twice to one and the same siege, but the chronology is so confused that one cannot be sure.

the castle appeared too great for his army. Adopting his usual tactices in such cases, he stationed a garrison at Devizes, ten miles to the east, another of Bishop Roger's castles, and the two forces by their alternate raids made a desert of the surrounding country.

Worse than this check, however, was the news that Miles of Gloucester, 'a man of the greatest spirit and active and very ready for mighty enterprises', had led an army to Wallingford and defeated the garrison that the king had left there in the two makeshift castles. 'After wounding some and killing others and capturing and fettering all the rest, he returned to his own district with the glory of a splendid victory.'

Using Gloucester as his base, Miles brought all the surrounding country 'as far as the depths of Wales' under subjection. On 7 November he captured Worcester, sacked the town, and burned a part of it. In spite of a feeble effort on the king's part to oppose him, he took Hereford with little difficulty, although he did not succeed in capturing the castle. He also took Winchcomb and recaptured South Cerney. By the beginning of Advent, when Stephen arranged for a truce during the holy season, Miles was in control of everything within twenty-five miles of his base at Gloucester, with the outpost at Wallingford still holding out, while Stephen had almost nothing to show for his efforts.[1]

The king held his Christmas court at Salisbury and wore his crown with all the customary pomp. His reason for going there was no doubt the death of Bishop Roger, 'who breathed away what life remained to him and died' on 11 December of a quartan fever. Henry of Huntingdon says that he died as much of shame as of old age; certainly his last days were spent in the deepest disgrace. Even though Stephen had confiscated part of the bishop's treasure when Roger surrendered his castles, he still had a great sum of money, 'likewise a great many vessels of hammered goldsmith's work, some of silver, some of gold, artistically engraved'. When the king reached Salisbury he took possession of all this treasure. The canons of the cathedral also gave him £2,000 to free their lands from all obligation to pay geld, and Stephen in turn gave them 20 marks for their own use and 40 to help pay for a new roof for the cathedral at Old Sarum.[2]

---

[1] G.S., pp. 62–4; H.N., p. 36; John of Worcester, pp. 56–7.
[2] G.S., pp. 64–5; H.N., p. 37; Henry of Huntingdon, p. 266; John of Worcester, pp. 58–9; Regesta, p. 289.

V

1140–1141

A LTHOUGH his enemies had control of Bristol and Gloucester and the surrounding countryside and although
Earl Robert had turned Caen and Bayeux over to Count
Geoffrey of Anjou when he joined his sister's cause, Stephen's
position was far from precarious. Early in 1140 he succeeded
in forming an alliance with King Louis VII. Queen Matilda and
their eldest son, Eustace, went to France, and in February 1140
Eustace was betrothed to Constance, the king's sister. Louis
conferred the duchy of Normandy on him and received his
homage for it. The king of France was an extremely cautious
man, and it is not likely that he would have entered into such an
alliance if he had taken seriously the threats to Stephen's position.[1]

Early in 1140 a rebellion arose in a new quarter. Nigel, bishop
of Ely, smarting from his recent treatment at the king's hands,
hired 'at his own expense knights who were prepared for any
crime, ready in hand and mind', and began attacking such of his
neighbours as supported the king. Stephen collected the usual
large army and marched to their defence. The Isle of Ely was in
those days truly an island, about four miles by seven, amongst
the fens, with only one approach over a narrow causeway
guarded by a castle at Aldreth.

Stephen's army built a bridge of boats over a narrow part of
the water out of reach of the castle, laid hurdles over the boats,
and thus crossed over to the island. Daniel, a monk of Ramsey
Abbey who knew the district well, showed them a shallow ford
over the fens and guided them across it and to Ely. Catching
the bishop and his garrison by surprise, the army captured some
of the knights and a great quantity of treasure that the bishop
had laid up. Approaching the castle at Aldreth from the rear,

[1] Orderic, Vol. V, pp. 108–9; John of Worcester, p. 61; Gervase of Canterbury,
Vol. I, p. 112.

where it was undefended, the army took it easily, and with it the
remainder of the bishop's knights, who had taken refuge there.
The bishop escaped with difficulty and fled to Gloucester, where
all the king's enemies had congregated.[1]

Trouble now arose in Cornwall, a district that hitherto enjoyed
peace. Reginald of Dunstanville, a bastard son of Henry I, had
joined the rebel party in Normandy in 1138. When he came to
England, lured by the promises of lands and honours that the
empress and Earl Robert were making to all who would join
them, Robert arranged a marriage for him with the daughter
of William fitz Richard, the greatest landowner in Cornwall,
and William apparently turned most of his lands over to him.
William of Malmesbury says that Robert made Reginald earl of
Cornwall, and the author of the *Gesta Stephani* says that he had
in his hands 'the earldom of all Cornwall'.[2]

Reginald at any rate 'began to behave with more vigour than
discretion', filling the castles with soldiers and harrying the king's
supporters. Stephen arrived in Cornwall with great despatch
and captured all of the castles that Reginald was holding. He
put Alan, count of Brittany and earl of Richmond, in charge of
the captured fortifications and left him with a sizable body of
troops and instructions to drive Reginald and his men completely out of the county.[3]

Robert, earl of Gloucester, had apparently remained at Bristol
since his arrival and left the fighting to Miles of Gloucester. The
earl seems not to have had much heart for fighting, and there was
probably some truth in the taunt that Henry of Huntingdon puts
into the mouth of Baldwin fitz Gilbert just before the Battle of
Lincoln in 1141: 'He threatens much but does little; he has the
voice of a lion and the heart of a rabbit; he stands out through his
eloquence but sinks into obscurity through his laziness.' William
of Malmesbury explains his inactivity at this time by saying that
he 'behaved with restraint and avoided nothing more carefully
than even a slight loss of men to gain a battle'.[4]

When Robert heard, however, that the king was in Cornwall,
he sent for the main body of rebel troops at Gloucester, their

[1] G.S., pp. 66–7; R. H. C. Davis: 'The Authorship of the *Gesta Stephani*',
English Historical Review, LXXVI (April 1962), pp. 217, 229.
[2] Orderic, Vol. V, p. 104; H.N., p. 42; G.S., p. 67; Davis, pp. 139–40.
[3] G.S., p. 68.
[4] Henry of Huntingdon, p. 272; H.N., p. 41.

headquarters, and set out to intercept the king.   Stephen meanwhile learned of Robert's plans and summoned all the barons of
Devon to help him.   With these reinforcements he hurried to
meet Robert's forces 'as though he meant to fight the earl that
very day'.   When Robert realised that he would have to fight
against a sizable army rather than the small force that Stephen
had taken with him to Cornwall, he fled back to Bristol. Stephen
demolished a great many of the unlicensed castles that had sprung
up over that part of the country, but he again did not feel that
his forces were strong enough to attack either Bristol or Gloucester.

It will be remembered that when Stephen took Malmesbury
he allowed Robert fitz Hubert to go free, probably through the
influence of William of Ypres, Robert's kinsman.   Robert joined
the earl of Gloucester, but in furtherance of his own ends he and
his men stole away from the rebel army and made for Devizes.
On the night of 26 March 1140 he led his men into the castle by
means of leather scaling-ladders that they had contrived to fix
on the parapets of the castle walls.   They surprised and captured
most of the garrison.   The remainder hastily took refuge in one
of the towers, but since they were not prepared for a siege they
were forced to surrender after four days.

Robert and his men then began devastating the countryside.
William of Malmesbury calls him a savage and says that 'he was
the cruellest of all men within the recollection of our age' and that
he was accustomed to boast of having been present when eighty
monks were burnt together with their church.   When the earl
of Gloucester learned of Robert's feat he sent his son, probably
William, the eldest, with a large force to Devizes, ostensibly to
help Robert but actually to make sure of his adhesion to the rebel
party.   Robert informed William that he had seized the castle in
order to occupy it himself and not in order to hand it over to
someone else, and he boasted that he intended to use Devizes as a
base from which he would seize all the country from Winchester
to London and hold it as his own, with the help of some knights
that he proposed to import from Flanders.[1]

Robert's declaration is particularly interesting because it is a
naked statement of that spirit of anarchy that was to manifest
itself throughout England in the troubled years that were to
come.   The ensuing disorders arose not only from the struggle

[1] G.S., pp. 68–70; H.N., pp. 43–4.

between Stephen and his supporters on the one hand and the Empress Matilda and her party on the other; confusion and misery were compounded by the actions of such men as Robert fitz Hubert, who seized the opportunity to grasp whatever they could for their own advantage and from such strongholds as fell into their hands to prey on their neighbours.

Having driven William away, Robert chose Marlborough as the first step in his ambitious plans. The royal castle there was held by John fitz Gilbert, who is described by both William of Malmesbury and the author of the *Gesta Stephani* as a supporter of the empress but by the continuator of Florence of Worcester as loyal to the king: a confusion that was inevitable in times when almost everyone was for himself first of all and then for the king or the empress only as self-interest dictated.

Robert sent word to John that he wanted to make 'a pact of peace and friendship' with him and requested that he be admitted to Marlborough Castle in order to discuss matters with him. John agreed to the proposal, admitted Robert to the castle, and clapped him into a dungeon. He and his men rushed out and captured some of Robert's bodyguard, whom they confined with their leader, and chased the remainder back to Devizes.

Earl Robert and Miles of Gloucester then came to Marlborough and offered John 500 marks, along with hostages for their keeping the promise, if he would turn Robert over to them for a fortnight, at the end of which time his captive was to be returned to John in good condition. When John agreed to this bargain, Earl Robert and Miles took Robert to Gloucester and tried to induce him to surrender Devizes to them, but Robert steadfastly refused, saying that he had sworn to his helpers that he would never surrender the castle to anyone and that all his men had sworn the same oath. Earl Robert and Miles threatened to hang him, and at last he agreed to order his men to surrender the castle in order to save his life.

The earl and Miles, true to their word, brought the captive back to John at the appointed time and proposed a second bargain. If John would let them take Robert to Devizes with them and if they succeeded in gaining the castle, they would allow John to hold it for them. John agreed, and the earl and Miles took the captive to Devizes. John meanwhile wrote to the garrison to assure them that neither he nor the earl meant any

harm to their leader and to exhort them to hold fast to the oath
they had sworn, which would indicate that his allegiance did not
lie with Earl Robert, at any rate.

When they arrived at Devizes, Robert reversed his stand and
refused to order his men to surrender the castle, and the garrison
within, equally faithful to their oath, likewise refused to surrender.
Miles first had two of Robert's nephews hanged before the gates
in order to terrorise Robert and the garrison into submission, and
when that act produced no results he had Robert himself hanged.
The garrison remained steadfast in their refusal, and the earl and
Miles then withdrew in frustration.

King Stephen then purchased the submission of the garrison,
whom Robert's death had left without a leader, with 'very large
sums of money' and turned the castle over to Hervey the Breton,
his son-in-law, 'a man of distinction and soldierly qualities'.   One
assumes that Hervey of Léon had married an illegitimate daughter
of Stephen, for with the death of the infant Matilda the king had
only one legitimate daughter, Mary, who was dedicated to the
religious life in her childhood.[1]

At a meeting of the Great Council at Winchester in 1140 the
king raised the question of a successor to Bishop Roger of
Salisbury, and his brother Henry proposed their nephew, Henry
of Sully, whose presence we have noted at Stephen's Easter court
of 1136 and who witnessed his subsequent charter of liberties at
Oxford.   The council would not agree to this, and Bishop Henry
left the court 'in great wrath'.   The king consoled his nephew
by appointing him abbot of Fécamp.   Count Waleran of Meulan
then proposed the name of his protégé, Philip of Harcourt,
archdeacon of Évreux, who had succeeded Roger as the king's
chancellor.   Stephen and the council welcomed this nomination,
but neither Bishop Henry as papal legate nor the clergy of
Salisbury would agree to it.   Philip's name had to be dropped,
but Stephen later appointed him bishop of Bayeux, a see that
was not under Henry's control.[2]

William of Malmesbury mentions that the king stayed in the
Tower of London at Whitsuntide, 26 May, with only one

[1] G.S., p. 71; H.N., p. 44; Florence of Worcester, Vol. II, pp. 126–7; The
Complete Peerage, Vol. XII, part 2, pp. 727–8.
[2] G. de M., p. 263; Regesta, pp. 17, 96, 348; Orderic, Vol. V, pp. 122–3;
Florence of Worcester, Vol. II, p. 124.

bishop in his company, John of Neuville, bishop of Séez. The
other bishops, he says, either did not want to come to the king's
court or were afraid to do so. This would indicate that Stephen's
rough treatment of Bishop Roger and his family had alienated
most of the English bishops.

William of Malmesbury is likewise our only authority for the
account of the negotiations that took place after Whitsuntide.
According to his account, Bishop Henry arranged for a parley
to be held near Bath between representatives of the two sides.
The empress sent her brother Robert 'and the rest of her advisors';
the king was represented by Queen Matilda, Archbishop Theobald, and Bishop Henry. 'They wasted both words and time
and parted without making peace.' The empress professed to be
ready to submit the matter to the arbitration of the Church, but
the king, quite naturally, maintained that his right to the crown
had already been irrevocably settled and refused to allow the
question to be raised again.

In September 1140 Bishop Henry crossed over to France and
discussed the troubled situation with King Louis, Count Theobald, 'and many ecclesiastics'. He returned near the end of
November, 'bringing instructions that would have benefited the
country had there been anyone to combine words and deeds', but
the chronicler does not tell us what the instructions were; he
merely says that the empress and her brother agreed to them at
once but the king postponed a decision till it was too late.[1]

In spite of these obscure negotiations, the struggle entered into
a more extended sphere and a more destructive phase with Earl
Robert's capture of Nottingham early in September 1140. At
the instigation of Ralph Paganel, the continuator of Florence of
Worcester writes, Earl Robert induced some knights of Roger,
earl of Warwick, who avoided committing himself to either
side, to join him and a company of knights in an attack on
Nottingham, ninety miles from Gloucester, which brought
the war into the heart of the Midlands. When this army,
increased by a great number of mercenaries, arrived at Nottingham the citizens fled in terror to the churches for refuge. The
city apparently fell without a struggle, and the attackers began the
usual looting. They captured one of the wealthier citizens and
ordered him to give them all his money. He led them into the

[1] H.N., pp. 44-5.

cellar of his house, where his valuables were reported to be, and while they were busy breaking open his chests he stole out of the house, locking the doors behind him. Then he set fire to the house, and more than thirty of the looters were burned alive.

The fire spread, and soon the whole town was in flames. Those who escaped from the churches were captured and led away in chains, some as far away as Gloucester; almost all the rest of the population perished in the general conflagration. This was a senseless act of destruction of the sort that was to become more common as the war was prolonged. The capture of Nottingham served no useful purpose, for it was too far from the rebels' strongholds of Gloucester and Bristol to serve as a permanent base for them; the only object of the marauders was to spread devastation and disorder and to seize such plunder as they could.[1]

With the spread of the rebellion Stephen sorely needed all the support he could find, and he turned now to two brothers whose possessions stretched from Chester to Lincoln and who had not committed themselves to either side. Ranulf 'aux Gernons', earl of Chester, held, in addition to the county palatine from which he took his title, lands in twenty-two shires. William of Roumare, later earl of Lincoln, Ranulf's elder half-brother, had inherited the holdings of his father, Roger fitz Gerald of Roumare in Lincolnshire. Their mother, Countess Lucy, had as her dowry considerable estates in that county. The half-brothers, who were devoted to each other and always worked together, had married the relations of two of the foremost rebels: Ranulf was married to Matilda, the daughter of Earl Robert of Gloucester, and William to Hawise, the sister of Baldwin of Redvers.

Although these alliances might have inclined them to side with the rebels, Earl Ranulf had grievances against both sides and had declined to commit himself. At the root of his discontent was the matter of the honour of Carlisle. His father, Ranulf 'le Meschin', had been lord of Carlisle before Henry I made him earl of Chester. When Richard, earl of Chester, perished in the wreck of the White Ship together with his wife, Stephen's sister Matilda, without a direct heir, King Henry had granted the earldom to Richard's cousin, Ranulf 'le Meschin', but the king seems to have made him surrender Carlisle in exchange for the earldom. In view of the enormous extent of the honour of Carlisle, this

[1] Florence of Worcester, Vol. II, pp. 128–9.

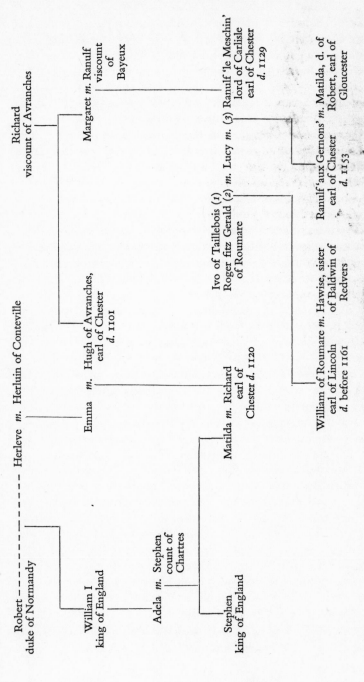

VII: Earls of Chester

Ranulf and William treated the townspeople so harshly that both the citizens and the bishop sent repeated messages to the king to tell him of the seizure of the castle, to complain of the treatment they were receiving, to beg him to come to help them, and to offer to 'see to it that the king got possession of the castle with the greatest secrecy'. As Sir Frank Stenton points out, 'burgesses were helpless against a baronial garrison in the castle of their town. . . . But burgesses must long have remembered the occasions when they had no help but in the king'.[1]

It may seem surprising to find Bishop Alexander siding with the king against the rebels after the treatment he had received at Stephen's hands, but Alexander loved comfort and luxury and magnificent display, and he seems to have been much less committed to the empress than was his brother, the bishop of Ely. His castle-building, which led to his difficulties with the king, was prompted not by a spirit of rebellion but 'for the protection, as he said, and glorification of his diocese',[2] which was now threatened by the activities of these ambitious men.

When he received these reports showing how Ranulf and William had taken advantage of his eagerness to secure their support and had betrayed him, Stephen gathered an army and hastened to Lincoln immediately after Christmas. He was always prompt to take action against anyone who dared to seize a royal castle, and the grave view that he took of the brothers' usurpation is shown by the fact that he proceeded against them 'actually during the Christmas festival'.[3]

The townspeople admitted him to the city, and he found that the two brothers were so confident of the hold they imagined they had over him that they 'had settled unsupiciously in the city's castle' and 'expected nothing less than the king's arrival'. Orderic Vitalis implies that he reached Lincoln at night, for he says that with the help of the townspeople the king captured seventeen knights who were in the city 'at night, unexpectedly'. He then laid siege to the castle immediately. William of Malmesbury, who loses no occasion to criticise him, says that 'This seemed unfair to many because, as I have said, he had left

[1] G.S., p. 73; H.N., p. 46; Orderic, Vol. V, p. 125; Stenton: *The First Century of English Feudalism*, p. 240.

[2] H.N., p. 25.

[3] 'In ipsis natalis Dominici feriis', which probably means during the Twelve Days of Christmas. H.N., p. 47.

them before the festival without any suspicion of ill-will and had not, in the traditional way, renounced his friendship with them, what they call "defiance".[1]   As in the case of the seizure of the bishops, however, Stephen was clearly acting within his rights, and William of Malmesbury is asserting that a king had to 'defy' traitors before taking action against them.   If any of Stephen's predecessors had 'defied' the numerous traitors they had to deal with there is no record of such a proceeding.

Earl Ranulf succeeded in escaping from the castle by night with a few of his men and hastened to his father-in-law, Earl Robert of Gloucester, for help.   He went to the empress and pledged his fealty to her, and then he and Robert set about raising an army.   In addition to his tenants in Cheshire, Ranulf enlisted 'a dreadful and unendurable mass of Welsh', whilst Robert and Miles of Gloucester summoned their adherents, 'most of them disinherited men inflamed to war by grief for what they had lost and by consciousness of valour'.[2]

While the king was besieging Lincoln Castle and his enemies were collecting an army in the west, Stephen's nephew William, formerly treasurer of York and now archbishop-elect, visited him and secured from him his confirmation in the lands and possessions belonging to the see, thus setting in motion one of the strangest ecclesiastical quarrels of the time.   Most of the arch-bishops of York had a difficult time during the twelfth century. Thurstan had undergone exile and humiliation in defence of his claim to be independent of the see of Canterbury; William was to experience prolonged litigation and deprivation before he was finally installed as archbishop, and at the end of the century Geoffrey, the illegitimate son of Henry II, was to be driven out of England by the contumacious chapter of York.

Archbishop Thurstan had died at Pontefract on 6 February 1140, and the chapter of York had spent the remainder of the year in quarrelling over the election of his successor.   Bishop Henry of Winchester, who had been defeated in his scheme to make his nephew, Henry of Sully, bishop of Salisbury, eventually persuaded the chapter to elect him archbishop of York.   Henry was now abbot of Fécamp, and following the example of his uncle, who was both abbot of Glastonbury and bishop of

---

[1] *H.N.*, p. 47.
[2] *H.N.*, pp. 46–7; *G.S.*, p. 73; Orderic, Vol. V, p. 125.

Winchester, he refused to relinquish Fécamp upon his election to
York. Pope Innocent II, however, would not permit him to
hold both offices, and the election was quashed.

At this point the king intervened and sent William of Aumale,
earl of York, to order the chapter to elect his nephew William,
then treasurer of York, as archbishop. William was the son of
Herbert of Winchester, an illegitimate son of Herbert II, count of
Maine, and Emma, an illegitimate daughter of Stephen's father,
Count Stephen of Blois and Chartres. John of Hexham describes
him as 'brought up always amidst pleasure and wealth and rarely
accustomed to work, but loved by the innocent for the kindness
of his heart and by the people for his liberality'.

His election was opposed by Walter of London, the senior
archdeacon of York, and his fellow archdeacons and by the
abbots of the new Cistercian monasteries in the north. As soon
as William was elected, the archdeacons set out for Lincoln to
protest to the king, but Earl William intercepted them on their
way and imprisoned them in his castle at Bytham. William,
the archbishop-elect, meanwhile went to the king and received
the temporalities of his see, as we have noted above.[1]

Having collected their army, Robert of Gloucester and Ranulf
of Chester set out from Gloucester and marched to Lincoln by an
indirect route in order to take the king by surprise, with Robert
in command of the expedition. They arrived on the outskirts of
Lincoln on 1 February 1141, apparently, but the River Witham
was so swollen by the winter rains that they were held up on the
west bank. Stephen's forces were encamped in the city, probably in the area between the cathedral and the castle, which they
were besieging. William of Malmesbury charges that Stephen
had turned the cathedral itself into a castle,[2] which probably
means that he was using it as a base from which to conduct the
siege. Although the height, some 200 feet above the river, gave
him a slight advantage over the approaching rebels, it was not

---

[1] John of Hexham in Simeon of Durham: *Historical Works*, ed. Thomas Arnold
(2 vols., Rolls Series 75, 1882–5), Vol. II, pp. 305–7; Dom David Knowles: 'The
Case of St. William of York', *Cambridge Historical Journal*, V (1936), No. 2,
reprinted in *The Historian and Character* (Cambridge, 1963), to which citations in
these notes refer, p. 80; Reginald L. Poole: 'The Appointment and Deprivation
of St. William, Archbishop of York', *English Historical Review*, XLV (1930), pp.
273–6.
[2] *H.N.*, p. 48.

an easily defended position, for the castle, occupied by hostile troops, was on one edge of it.   Furthermore, he did not want to fight a defensive war, for even if he succeeded in holding out behind the city walls he might be bottled up within the city indefinitely.   For the first time since the rebellion began he had a chance to meet Earl Robert, his chief adversary, in the field, and, confident in his cause, he may have wanted to put it to the test by the ordeal of battle, with the decision, as the men of that time believed, lying in the hands of God.

At earliest dawn on Candlemas Day, 2 February, which was also Sexagesima Sunday, he heard Mass in the cathedral.   During the ceremonies the candle that he was holding broke in his hand and the flame went out, which men were afterwards able to see as a portent.   Henry of Huntingdon adds that the chain broke by which the pyx, in which the Blessed Sacrament was reserved, was suspended over the altar, and the pyx fell upon the altar. 'This was a sign of ruin to the king.'[1]

Stephen and his forces, which included the townspeople, descended to the plain to the west of the city, beside the river. He sent forward a body of knights and foot-soldiers to guard the ford across the river, but Earl Robert and some of his men succeeded in crossing (William of Malmesbury says that they swam across), charged the king's men, and seized the ford.   The remainder of the rebels then crossed the river, and the two armies drew up their lines.

While his army was taking its position, the king called the leaders together for advice as to the conduct of the battle.   Even at this late hour some of them counselled him to leave the defence of the city to the townspeople whilst he withdrew from the scene, raised an army from the whole of England, and then returned to deal with his enemies 'with royal severity'.   Others advised him to seek a truce out of respect for the sacred character of the day. The king disregarded this half-hearted advice and ordered his army to prepare for battle.[2]

Orderic Vitalis says that each of the armies was drawn up in three lines or formations.   At the front of the king's army were the Flemish and Breton mercenaries, commanded respectively by William of Ypres and Alan of Brittany.   Facing them was 'a

---

[1] G.S., p. 74; Orderic, Vol. V, p. 129; Henry of Huntingdon, p. 271.
[2] G.S., p. 74; H.N., p. 48; Orderic, Vol. V, pp. 126-7.

raving mob' of Welshmen led by two brothers, 'Mariadoth and Kaladrius', that is, Cadwaladr ap Gruffydd ap Cynan and his brother-in-law, Madog ap Maredudd. King Stephen led the centre formation, which was dismounted, 'and fought bravely for his life and for the state of his kingdom'. Facing the king's formation were Earl Ranulf and his knights, likewise dismounted, and the foot-soldiers that Ranulf had brought from Cheshire. Robert, earl of Gloucester, who was in general command of the whole rebel army, led the disinherited men he had collected from his part of the country. Orderic does not tell how the third formation on the king's side was made up, but it may have consisted of the townspeople. On the other hand, Henry of Huntingdon may be correct in saying that the royal army was in only two lines.

According to Henry of Huntingdon, the first rebel line was composed of Earl Ranulf and his men, the second of those whom King Stephen had disinherited, and the third of 'the great Duke Robert' and his men, with 'a crowd of Welshmen, armed with daring rather than weapons', on the flanks. King Stephen fought on foot with a multitude of armed and dismounted knights, whilst his earls led two bodies of mounted knights. Oddly enough, neither William of Malmesbury nor the author of the *Gesta Stephani* gives any details about the composition of the two armies.

Stephen had on his side five earls: Alan, count of Brittany and earl of Richmond; Waleran, count of Meulan and earl of Worcester; Waleran's half-brother, William of Warenne, earl of Surrey; Simon, earl of Northampton, and William of Aumale, earl of York, one of the heroes of the Battle of the Standard. Orderic Vitalis also mentions Gilbert of Clare, earl of Hertford, and Henry of Huntingdon names Hugh Bigod, whom he calls earl, although it is not likely that he had been given the title at this time. In addition to the Flemish and Breton mercenaries, Stephen had the army he had brought with him for the siege and the townspeople of Lincoln, who were probably well to the rear, although it might have been better for the king if they had been given the front rank.[1]

[1] Orderic, Vol. V, pp. 126-8; Sir John Edward Lloyd: *A History of Wales* (2 vols., 3rd edn., London, 1939), Vol. II, p. 489; Henry of Huntingdon, pp. 268, 271; *H.N.*, p. 49; *G. de M.*, p. 50; Davis, pp. 141-2.

When the armies were in position, their respective leaders addressed them. The orations that Henry of Huntingdon reports are, of course, his idea of what should have been said, but they probably have some basis in fact and at any rate summarise the arguments that each side used. Ranulf of Chester first made a brief talk, thanking Earl Robert and the others for coming to his aid at the peril of their lives and stating that since he was the cause of their peril it was fitting that he should strike the first blow against 'the most faithless king, who broke the peace after he had given pledges'. Robert of Gloucester then made a much longer speech. He accused Stephen of having broken his oath and usurped the kingdom, of having thrown everything into confusion and caused the deaths of many thousands, and of having taken their lands from the lawful owners and distributed them to those who had no right to them. After pointing out to his followers that their position with the river at their backs left them no chance to flee, he reviled the leaders of the royal forces, each in turn.

Alan of Brittany, he said, was an execrable man, befouled with every sort of sin. Waleran, count of Meulan, was cunning and deceitful, 'slow to fight and quick to flee'. Hugh Bigod was doubly a perjurer, having both broken his oath to the empress and falsely sworn that King Henry on his deathbed had released his barons from their oath and given the kingdom to Stephen. William of Aumale was a man of such filthy life that his wife had run away from him. He accused William of Warenne, earl of Surrey, of living in adultery with the wife of William of Aumale and of being a friend of Bacchus and a stranger to Mars, stinking with wine and unused to battle. As for Earl Simon of Northampton, his deeds were words only, his gifts were promises only. All the rest were cut from the same cloth, hardened robbers, foul plunderers, glutted murderers, all stained by perjury.

Because King Stephen did not have a good speaking voice, Baldwin fitz Gilbert, a younger brother of Gilbert, earl of Hertford, spoke in his stead. Their army, he said, had three advantages: the justice of their cause, their great numbers, and their courage. Their cause was just because they were fighting on behalf of the king, to whom they had sworn fealty before God, against those who had broken their oath to him, and their lord the king, God's anointed, was in their midst. He declared that they had as many horsemen as their opponents and more

foot-soldiers. And as for their courage, who could deny it?
Robert of Gloucester, he said, threatened much but did little;
he was loud in his words but lazy in his deeds. The earl of
Chester was a man of reckless daring, quick in cooking up
conspiracies but fickle in following through with them, rash in
war and heedless of peril, always striving for his own advancement and seeking the impossible. The Welsh that Earl Robert
had brought had no proper arms, and lacking both the knowledge and the habit of war they ran like beasts to throw themselves
upon their opponents' spears.[1]

The knights on the king's side attempted to begin the battle
with a formal joust, as though it were a tournament, but when
they saw that their opponents were in deadly earnest, 'fighting
not with lances at a distance but with swords at close quarters',
they changed their tactics. The accounts of the Battle of Lincoln
differ in distributing the blame, but they all agree that the king
was shamefully deserted by his earls at the very outset of the
fighting. William of Malmesbury says simply that all of them
fled as soon as the battle was joined. The author of the *Gesta
Stephani* says that 'a great many, like the count of Meulan and the
famous William of Ypres, fled shamefully before coming to close
quarters'. According to Orderic Vitalis, William of Ypres with
his Flemings and Alan with his Bretons were the first to turn their
back to the enemy. When they saw the rout of the first division,
Waleran of Meulan, William of Warenne, Gilbert of Clare, 'and
other famous Norman and English knights' were filled with terror
and likewise fled. Baldwin fitz Gilbert, Richard fitz Urse,
Ingelran of Say, and Ilbert of Lacy then gathered round the king.

Henry of Huntingdon says that the division made up of the
disinherited, which was in the rebels' front line, attacked the
wing led by Alan of Brittany, Waleran of Meulan, Simon of
Northampton, and William of Warenne 'with such force that
in the twinkling of an eye it was scattered and broken into three
parts. Some of them were killed, some captured, and some
put to flight'. The wing led by William of Aumale and William
of Ypres attacked the Welsh, who poured in from the sides, and
put them flight. While the Welsh fled, Earl Ranulf and his
troops from Cheshire attacked the pursuers and routed them
immediately. All the king's mounted knights then fled, and

[1] Henry of Huntingdon, pp. 268–73.

William of Ypres, 'although he was most skilled in war, seeing the impossibility of helping the king, delayed his help till better times'.

John of Hexham gives only a brief account of the battle, saying that Alan of Brittany and his troops deserted before the fighting began and that William of Aumale by his flight exposed the king to peril.[1]

Regardless of which wing was the first to break and who led the flight, at the first assault of the enemy the mounted knights and the Flemish and Breton mercenaries fled from the field, leaving the king in the midst of his enemies, with only the men on foot to fight beside him. 'But the the king stood in the ranks like a lion, the bravest of the brave, fearing the assault of no man.' Stephen fought with the utmost bravery, 'remembering the deeds of his ancestors', like his father, Count Stephen, at Ramleh, as those about him were slain or captured. He cut down everyone who attacked him, till his sword broke in his hands. A townsman from Lincoln gave him a Danish battle-axe, and Stephen fought on till he was standing almost alone against his enemies. He succeeded in giving Earl Ranulf such a blow on the head with his axe that he knocked him to his knees. Attacked from all sides, he was at last struck by a stone and fell to the ground; 'it is not known who dealt the blow'.

William of Cahagnes tore off Stephen's helmet and cried, 'Here, all of you, here! I've got the king!' With Stephen were captured Baldwin fitz Gilbert, covered with wounds, and Richard fitz Urse, 'brilliant in giving and receiving blows'. Even after the king was captured, his men fought on till they were all captured or killed. The survivors of the battle, however, estimated that no more than a hundred had been killed.

With the king captured and his army defeated, Earl Ranulf and the other victors entered Lincoln in triumph. In revenge for the help the townspeople had given the king, the victors slaughtered them like cattle and plundered and burned the houses and churches, creating 'a piteous scene of devastation everywhere'.[2]

[1] H.N., p. 49; G.S., pp. 74-5; Orderic, Vol. V, pp. 127-8; Henry of Huntingdon, pp. 273-4; John of Hexham, pp. 307-8.
[2] John of Hexham, p. 308; Orderic, Vol. V, pp. 128-9; G.S., p. 75; Henry of Huntingdon, p. 274. The fullest modern account of the Battle of Lincoln is to be found in Beeler: *Warfare in England*, pp. 108-19.

VI

1141

EARL Robert of Gloucester brought the captive king to his sister at Gloucester on 9 February 1141, a week after the battle, and they decided that he should be imprisoned for life in the castle at Bristol, the strongest fortification in their possession. The king was kept in confinement and was not permitted to leave his quarters, and later on he was fettered with iron rings. Such of the other captives as could do so were allowed to purchase their freedom.

The Empress Matilda was filled with the greatest joy, for she felt that she now had the realm of England within her grasp. Like her predecessor, she had as her first objective the city of Winchester, where the royal crown and treasure were held, and next the city of London, where she planned to be crowned at Westminster. Before she could enter Winchester, however, she had to secure the adhesion of the bishop, and she and her brother sent pressing messages to Henry, urging him 'to receive her immediately in the cathedral as queen'. She set out meanwhile for Cirencester, fifteen miles south-east of Gloucester, on 17 February, accompanied by two bishops, Bernard of St. David's and Nigel of Ely, and Gilbert Foliot, abbot of Gloucester, and received the submission of that city.[1]

The author of the *Gesta Stephani* represents Bishop Henry as being in a quandary because he was not prepared 'to support the king's cause and restore it to its former flourishing condition' and yet 'on the other hand it appeared to him a dreadful thing and unseemly in the sight of men to yield so suddenly to his brother's foes while that brother was still alive'. K. R. Potter observes that 'such loyalty as the bishop felt was loyalty to the Church, not to his brother', but one may perhaps observe that his greatest loyalty was to himself and his own interests.[2]

[1] *H.N.*, p. 50; Florence of Worcester, Vol. II, pp. 129–30; John of Hexham, p. 309.
[2] *G.S.*, p. 78.

97

He agreed to confer with the empress, and they met on an open area at Wherwell, outside Winchester, on 2 March, 'a rainy and cloudy day'. Henry laid down the conditions for his recognition of her, and his price was high. She swore 'that all the matters of chief account in England, especially gifts of bishoprics and abbacies, should be subject to his control if he received her in Holy Church as lady and kept his faith to her unbroken'.

Her brother Robert, Brian fitz Count, Miles of Gloucester, and some others of her leading supporters took the same oath. 'Nor did the bishop hesitate to receive her as lady of England and give her assurance, together with some of her followers, that as long as she did not break the agreement he would keep faith with her himself.'

On the next day, 3 March, the turncoat legate arranged for her reception in Winchester. She was escorted into the city by a procession of barons and knights, the clergy and people of the city, and 'two convents of monks and one of nuns from the same city, with processional songs and praises'. She entered the cathe-dral with Bishop Henry on her right and Bishop Bernard of St. David's on her left. Four bishops, Alexander of Lincoln, Nigel of Ely, Robert of Hereford, and Robert of Bath, were in the procession. Matilda took possession of the castle, where were stored what little was left of the royal treasure and the object that she desired most in the world, the royal crown. At a public meeting in the market-place the people, at Bishop Henry's direction, hailed her as lady and queen.[1]

Queen, of course, she was not and could not be till she had been anointed and crowned, nor could she be lady of England in the sense of 'the territorial lord and head of the feudal state' till she had been so elected by a body that could claim to be repre-sentative of the barons. She did, however, become the lady of those who swore allegiance to her, in this case the bishop and citizens of Winchester and the others who pledged their fealty to her. She was anticipating, in her headstrong fashion, the election and coronation on which she had set her heart and was using titles to which she had no right.[2]

[1] H.N., pp. 50–1; Florence of Worcester, Vol. II, p. 130; G.S., p. 79.
[2] Austin Lane Poole: *From Domesday Book to Magna Carta, 1087–1216* (2nd edn., Oxford, 1956), p. 3; G. de M., pp. 56–80.

She went next to Wilton, twenty miles north of Winchester. Archbishop Theobald, at the legate's invitation, came to meet her, but he declined to swear fealty to her till he had consulted the king. He, together with a number of bishops and laymen, was allowed to visit Stephen in his captivity at Bristol, and the king, in view of the hopelessness of his position, gave them 'a courteous permission to change over as the times required'.[1]

At this point the accounts of Matilda's movements become obscure.[2] William of Malmesbury, who is careful in his dating, says that she spent Easter, 30 March, at Oxford. The continuator of Florence of Worcester implies that she spent Easter at Wilton and then says that she went to Reading at Rogation-tide, 4 May, where she was received with many honours and where Robert of Oilly, castellan of Oxford, did homage and agreed to turn over the castle to her. Only then did she go to Oxford, where 'she received the lordship and homage of all the city and the adjacent region'.[3]

Whilst Matilda was making her progress, the legate had summoned an ecclesiastical council to meet at Winchester under his presidency. It opened on Monday, 7 April, and Archbishop Theobald, all the bishops of England, and many abbots were said to be present. William of Malmesbury tells us that he himself took part in the proceedings and gives a lively account of the meeting. At the beginning, the letters of excuse from those who were unable or unwilling to attend were read, which would indicate that our author exaggerates in saying that all the bishops were present. The legate then conferred in secret with the bishops, the abbots, and the archdeacons separately and in turn.

On Tuesday the legate made a speech to the whole assembly. After pointing out that he stood in the pope's place in England and that it was by the pope's authority that he had convened the council, Henry went on to the delicate matter of explaining why he was now requiring his audience to desert his brother, to whom they had sworn fealty, and to elect Matilda as queen. It was a tricky business, and he succeeded none too well. After touching

[1] *H.N.*, p. 51.
[2] See H. W. C. Davis: 'Some Documents of the Anarchy', in *Essays in History Presented to Reginald Lane Poole* (Oxford, 1927), pp. 181–2.
[3] *H.N.*, p. 51; Florence of Worcester, Vol. II, pp. 130–1.

lightly on the oath that all the bishops and barons had sworn to receive Matilda as heir to England and Normandy if King Henry died without a male successor, he played down his own part in violating that oath and securing the crown for his brother. After King Henry's death, he said, as though all this had taken place when he was far away in a distant land, 'because it seemed tedious to wait for the lady, who made delays in coming to England since her residence was in Normandy, thought was taken for the peace of the country, and my brother was allowed to reign'.

Henry then declared that 'he was vexed to remember and ashamed to tell what manner of man he [Stephen] showed himself as king'. Stephen, he said, had failed to enforce justice against transgressors; he had abolished peace entirely, almost in the very year of his coronation; he had arrested bishops and forced them to surrender their properties; he had sold abbacies and despoiled churches of their treasure, and he had listened to the advice of the wicked and disregarded that of the good.

This was the speech of a bitter and disappointed man. Henry had counted on being his brother's chief advisor in return for his influence in securing Stephen's coronation. The king, however, had not allowed himself to be ruled wholly by the bishop, and at the ecclesiastical council at Winchester he had successfully defied him. That defiance still rankled, as the bishop indicated when he said that the council he had called to judge the king's conduct had brought nothing but hatred.

Henry attributed only the highest motives to himself. 'While I should love my mortal brother, I should esteem far more highly the cause of my immortal Father. Therefore, since God has executed His judgment on my brother in allowing him to fall into the power of the strong without my knowledge', by virtue of his position as legate he had called his audience together 'so that the kingdom may not totter without a ruler'. Since it was the special prerogative of the clergy 'to choose and consecrate a prince', he finished by declaring: 'We choose as lady of England and Normandy the daughter of a king who was a peacemaker, a glorious king, a wealthy king, a good king, without peer in our time, and we promise her faith and support.'

Everyone present either applauded this speech or gave consent to it by silence. If any voices were raised on behalf of the king

to whom they had sworn fealty and allegiance, it must have been
in the secret sessions of the previous day.[1]

The imprisonment and deposition of King Stephen and the
election of Matilda in his stead were surely 'the most important
constitutional event that had taken place since the Conquest', and
not the arrest of Bishop Roger of Salisbury, as Bishop Stubbs
maintains. The political theorists, if one may call them such, of
the twelfth century placed great emphasis upon the sacred
character of the kingship and of the divine authority that the
king exercised.[2] That character and authority were conferred
upon the king by the quasi-sacramental rite of anointing and
crowning, which could be performed by the Church alone.
Once conferred, that sacred character could not be removed,
although Pope Gregory VII had claimed the right to depose
emperors. Yet the council at Winchester offers the extraordinary
spectacle of a group of bishops repudiating the king whom the
Church had anointed, on no other ground than that he had fallen
into the hands of his enemies and thus was unable for the time
being to exercise his authority.

The bishops, furthermore, who took part in this performance
had sworn fealty to Stephen and were thus guilty of perjury, not
to speak of craven disloyalty, in abandoning the lord to whom
they had sworn to be faithful in life and limbs and earthly honour,
unless one assumes that Stephen, in his interview with Archbishop
Theobald at Bristol, had released them all from their oaths of
fealty. The chill wind of treason was blowing over the land, and
the bishops were the first to bow before it, led by the papal legate,
who hoped to 'rise thus nimbly by a true king's fall'.

Although William of Malmesbury says that all the bishops of
England attended the council, that statement is open to question.
Some ecclesiastics did not attend and sent letters excusing their
absence; some bishops may have been amongst the number. In
any case, the council at Winchester, which declared Stephen
deposed and which elected Matilda in his stead, was not a meeting
of the Great Council; it was purely an ecclesiastical affair, summoned by the legate, and if any laymen were present the fact
was not recorded, although the presence of even a minor baron

[1] *H.N.*, pp. 52–4.
[2] Stubbs: *Constitutional History of England*, Vol. I, pp. 352–3; Poole: *From
Domesday Book to Magna Carta*, p. 3.

would hardly go unnoticed by a chronicler whose primary aim was to defend the reputation of Robert of Gloucester, the leader of the rebel party.

Because it was purely an ecclesiastical assembly, Bishop Henry advanced the extraordinary assertion that the clergy had the special prerogative not only of consecrating the king, which no one would deny, but also of electing him in the first place. Such a theory had never been heard before in England. Bishops as members of the Great Council had a voice in choosing the king, if one assumes that the Great Council at this time had the right of electing the king rather than of confirming a choice already made. Henry's assertion that they had a special right to elect the king was sheer fantasy to cover up as best he could the fact that none of the lay magnates of the kingdom was present at this council.

Even Henry could not ignore the leading part that the Londoners had played in securing his brother's accession, and he knew that without their support the empress could neither be crowned at Westminster nor rule over England. He had therefore included them in his summons to the council, and after his proclamation of Matilda as lady of England and Normandy he adjourned the assembly till the arrival of the messengers from the city, whom he expected that day.

The Londoners arrived on Wednesday and announced that they bore a message from the commune of London, which is the first time that we hear of that organisation. All one can say of the commune at this early stage is that, as A. L. Poole defines it, it was 'some sort of sworn association for the defence of their liberties'.[1] Instead of agreeing tamely to the deposition of their king as Bishop Henry seems to have expected them to do, they demanded that he be set free from his captivity. 'All the barons who had earlier been received into their commune were urgent in demanding this from the lord legate, the archbishop, and all the clergy who were present.'

Angered by this unexpected show of that loyalty in which the clergy were so notably lacking, the legate first repeated his arguments of the previous day and then reproached the Londoners, 'who held a special position of superiority in England', for having given aid and comfort to the king's supporters, who, he declared, 'had abandoned their lord in war, by whose advice he had

[1] *H.N.*, p. xviii; Poole: *From Domesday Book to Magna Carta*, p. 143.

dishonoured Holy Church, and who, finally, seemed to favour the Londoners with no other object than that of squeezing money out of them'.

After this speech, a certain Christian, one of Queen Matilda's clerks, gave a document to the legate. Henry read it silently and then 'said at the top of his voice that it was not valid and ought not to be read out in so great an assembly, especially one of persons of rank and religion'. His objection to the letter, apart from its contents, was that one of the witnesses to it had previously used insulting language to the bishops in that very chapter-house. Since the bishop refused to read the letter to the assembly, Christian did so.

> The queen earnestly begs all the assembled clergy, and especially the bishop of Winchester, her lord's brother, to restore to the throne that same lord, whom cruel men, who are likewise his own men, have cast into chains.

The legate refused to honour this request, and the messengers at last agreed to inform the Londoners of the council's decision. The gathering closed by excommunicating many of the king's supporters. The legate himself 'cursed those who cursed her [the empress], blessed those who blessed her, excommunicated those who withstood her, and absolved those who obeyed her'.[1]

When the news of Stephen's defeat and capture reached Normandy, meanwhile, the king's chief supporters, under the leadership of Archbishop Hugh of Rouen, met to discuss the state of the country. Since they were extremely reluctant to have Matilda and her husband as their new rulers, they offered 'the kingdom of England and the duchy of Normandy' to Stephen's brother, Count Theobald. He had no desire, however, to undertake such a difficult and troublesome task as winning over his brother's lands would undoubtedly be, and he therefore offered to recognise Count Geoffrey as Stephen's successor if he would turn over Tours to him, release Stephen from his prison, and restore to him all the lands and honours he had held before he became king. Nothing of course came of these negotiations.[2]

The empress's uncle, King David of Scotland, joined her after Ascension Day, 8 May. In view of Stephen's apparently hopeless

---

[1] *H.N.*, pp. 54-6; Florence of Worcester, Vol. II, p. 130.
[2] Vol. Orderic, V., p. 131.

plight and in the absence of any effective resistance, she seemed to be on the verge of controlling the country. The author of the *Gesta Stephani* says that she 'brought the greater part of the kingdom under her sway', and Henry of Huntingdon says: 'The empress was received as lady by all the people of England, except those of Kent, where the queen and William of Ypres fought against her with all their strength.'

These statements are undoubtedly exaggerations. H. W. C. Davis, after a study of the lists of witnesses to Matilda's charters, concludes that 'the basis on which her power rested was insecure: a minority of the bishops, a minority of the magnates of the west and south-west of England'. Most of the great men of the country were keeping quiet and waiting to see how the struggle would end before they declared themselves for one side or the other. Three of the greatest earls, Waleran, count of Meulan, William of Warenne, and Simon of Northampton, 'and many others' are mentioned by Orderic Vitalis as remaining faithful to the king.[1]

Now that she had been declared lady of England and was soon, she hoped, to be crowned queen, Matilda took advantage of her position to reward her friends and punish her enemies. 'By reckless innovations she lessened or took away the possessions and lands of some, held on a grant from the king, while the fees and honours of the very few who still held to the king she confiscated altogether and granted to others; she arbitrarily annulled any grant fixed by the king's royal decree; she hastily snatched away and conferred on her own followers anything he had given in unshakable perpetuity to churches or to his comrades in arms.'[2]

This reckless alienation of her opponents' lands and the bestowal of them upon her followers led to boundless confusion. The immediate result was that in the territories that were not under her control these transfers of land had no practical effect, but the disappointed recipients of her grants, ineffective though they were, considered that they had claims to the lands thus affected and reasons for trying to obtain them by violence if necessary. In the territories under her control, largely in the west and south-west, such acts were effective, which meant that the lands of many

[1] John of Hexham, p. 309; *G.S.*, p. 80; Henry of Huntingdon, p. 275; H. W. C. Davis: 'Some Documents of the Anarchy', p. 184; Orderic, Vol. V, p. 130.
[2] *G.S.*, p. 79.

of Stephen's supporters were taken from them and given to her friends. The former owners, of course, refused to consider such alienations lawful and strove whenever it was possible to regain their lands. Much of the turmoil of the ensuing years was due not to open warfare between the king's forces and those of the empress but to private contests between two claimants to the same lands who, in the absence in the disputed areas of courts whose jurisdiction was acknowledged by both sides, resorted to force to establish their rights.

This confusion was carried over into the early years of the reign of Henry II, who as Stephen's recognised successor was bound to uphold his actions and yet as his mother's son to honour her grants. Henry's solution in most cases was to recognise the tenant in actual possession as the lawful one, and the possessory assizes that form one of his most important contributions to the development of English law uphold the right of the sitting tenant to continue in possession till his challenger has established his superior right.

The author of the *Gesta Stephani* tells of some of the punishments that Matilda meted out to Stephen's supporters. Alan of Brittany, 'a man of boundless ferocity and craft', who had led the flight from the Battle of Lincoln, laid an ambush for Earl Ranulf of Chester in order to avenge the king. Ranulf and his forces were too strong for him, however, and he was captured, put in chains, and confined in 'a filthy dungeon' till he submitted to Ranulf, did homage to him, and turned over all his castles to him. John of Hexham, however, says that Ranulf summoned Alan to a parley and then treacherously seized him and starved him into surrendering Galclint Castle and the treasure that he had found there when he had seized the castle from William of Aubigny before the Battle of Lincoln. Alan at any rate fell into the hands of his enemies. The empress took away from him the estates in Cornwall that Stephen had given him and bestowed them on her half-brother Reginald, whom she created earl of Cornwall, probably at this time.

Hervey the Breton, the king's son-in-law, to whom he had entrusted the castle at Devizes, was besieged by 'a mob of plain peasants' and at length was forced to surrender the castle to the empress. He is now referred to as Earl Hervey, which would indicate that Stephen had recently made him earl of Wiltshire.

The empress banished him from England.   Hugh 'the Poor' was
forced to surrender Bedford to Miles of Beauchamp, and William
Peverel turned over Nottingham Castle to William Paganel.[1]

This taste of power went to Matilda's head.   'She at once put
on an extremely arrogant demeanour, instead of the modest gait
and bearing proper to a gentlewoman, began to walk and speak
and do all things more stiffly and haughtily than she had been
wont', and gloried in being called queen.   Worse still, she was
haughty and insolent to her three chief advisors, King David,
Bishop Henry, and Earl Robert, 'whom she was then taking
round with her as a permanent retinue'.   She was rude to them
in public and rejected their advice in private, acting in an arbitrary
and capricious manner.[2]

All this while negotiations were going on with the citizens of
London, for until they agreed to receive her she could not hope
to be crowned at Westminster.   One assumes that during this
time she used Oxford as her headquarters.   When the negotiations at last took a favourable turn she went to St. Albans, 'with
great exultation and joy'.   Many of the leading citizens of
London met her there and agreed on the terms of their submission.

She and her retinue set out for London a few days before
Midsummer Day, 24 June.   She was received at Westminster
with processional honours and took up residence there while the
preparations for her coronation were being made.   Anticipating
the royal powers that she thought were soon to be hers, she had a
great seal made with the superscription 'Matilda, Empress of the
Romans and Queen of England', and she transacted a great deal
of business in a queenly style.[3]

One of her first acts was to appoint a bishop to the see of London, which had been vacant since the death of Gilbert 'the
Universal' in 1134.   Stephen had attempted to fill the vacancy
at the meeting of the council at Westminster at Easter 1136, and
he seems to have granted a free election to the canons in com-
pliance with his oath to respect the freedom of the Church.
Part of the chapter chose Anselm, abbot of St. Edmunds, but the
dean and the remaining canons violently opposed the election

---

[1] G.S., p. 77; John of Hexham, pp. 306–9; Cronne: 'Ranulf de Gernons, Earl
of Chester, 1129–53', pp. 117–20; G. de M., p. 68; The Complete Peerage, Vol. XII,
pt. 2, pp. 727–8.
[2] G.S., pp. 78–80.
[3] Florence of Worcester, Vol. II, p. 131; H.N., p. 56; G. de M., pp. 299–303.

and appealed to Rome. When the case came before Pope Innocent II in 1138, he asked the English bishops to let him know their opinions of Anselm. Archbishop Thurstan replied: 'If we consider his life and reputation, it would be much more fitting to remove him from his abbacy than to promote him to be bishop of London.' The pope annulled the election on the ground that it had been made without the consent of the dean, who by law had the first voice in the election; Anselm returned to Bury St. Edmunds, and the pope appointed Bishop Henry of Winchester as administrator of the diocese till a fresh election should be made. To fill this vacancy Matilda appointed Robert, called 'of the Seal' (*de Sigillo*) because he had been King Henry's chancellor. After his master's death he had become a monk at Reading, whence he was now removed to be bishop of London.[1]

In order to secure the support of Geoffrey de Mandeville, constable of the Tower of London, whom Stephen had made earl of Essex, probably in 1140, she issued a charter to him that not only confirmed Stephen's previous creation but added considerably more to it. Since it is one of the few charters of the empress that have survived, it may be of interest to quote the opening words as a sample of her style:

Matilda, the daughter of King Henry, to the archbishops, bishops, abbots, earls, barons, justiciars, sheriffs and ministers, and all her barons and lieges, French and English, of all England and Normandy: greetings.
Let all of you, both those present and those to come, know that I, Matilda, the daughter of King Henry and lady of the English, give and concede to Geoffrey de Mandeville for his service and to his heirs after him by hereditary right that he be earl of Essex and that he have the third penny of the county from the pleas as an earl should have in his county in all things. . . .[2]

She grants him and his heirs custody of the Tower of London, and she assigns rich grants of lands and revenues to him. The most significant passage of the charter, as J. H. Round points out, is that in which she makes him both sheriff of Essex and chief

[1] Ralph of Diceto: *Ymagines Historiarum*, ed. William Stubbs (2 vols., Rolls Series 68, 1876), Vol. I, pp. 247–52; John of Hexham, p. 309; Florence of Worcester, Vol. II, p. 131; *G. de M.*, pp. 67–8.
[2] *G. de M.*, pp. 37–54; R. H. C. Davis: 'Geoffrey de Mandeville Reconsidered,' *English Historical Review*, LXXIX (April 1964), pp. 299–306; *Regesta*, pp.99–101.

justiciar of the county, exempt from the jurisdiction of the royal justices, thus reversing the process by which her father had gradually and with great difficulty asserted the royal supremacy over the local jurisdictions of the sheriffs. Matilda, after appointing him chief justiciar of the county, promises that she will not send any other justiciar into the county with authority over him, but that if the occasion should arise when occasionally she would despatch a justiciar into Essex he would be one of Geoffrey's peers, who would hear the pleas of the Crown with Geoffrey as his colleague.

This passage is of no constitutional importance because it never came into effect, but it is valuable nevertheless because of the insight it gives both into Matilda's character and into the aspirations of the greater barons. It reveals Matilda's profound ignorance of English institutions and of the whole programme of her Norman predecessors, whose constant aim had been to increase and extend the royal jurisdiction. If she had been able and willing to apply the exemptions she thus granted to Geoffrey de Mandeville to the whole country, she would have destroyed the entire system of government, for by granting such a concentration of powers to various earls who would thus be independent of the royal government she would have turned England into a loose confederation of counties, each ruled by its own earl in his combined capacities as sheriff and justiciar, bound to the Crown only by the loose ties of fealty and responsible to it only for the farm of the royal manors within each county. In short, Matilda, if she had become queen and had followed the disastrous policy adumbrated in her charter to Geoffrey de Mandeville, would have turned England into a feudal state after the German and French models. It is evident that although Henry I had regarded Matilda as his heir, he took no pains to teach her any of the principles of government by which, building on the framework established by his father, he had succeeded in giving England the most highly centralised and efficient government in western Europe.

Since Geoffrey apparently dictated his own terms to Matilda, the passage under discussion shows the aspirations of the men of his class. Henry's general policy had been to transfer the power and responsibility for local government from the great landholders to the 'new men' whom he had appointed, who were responsible to him, and whose loyalties lay with him rather than with the particular counties with which they were connected. Geoffrey's ambition and the ambition of others of his class were to reverse this trend and to restore to the local magnates the authority and jurisdiction they had formerly enjoyed. Whilst they might grudgingly tolerate the occasional visits of justiciars sent down from the royal courts, they would like them to be of their own class, not professional judges of the sort that Henry's reforms had tended to produce.[1]

The list of witnesses to this charter, when Matilda was at the height of her power and expecting to be crowned within a few days, shows how limited was her following. Five bishops: Henry of Winchester, Alexander of Lincoln, Robert of Hereford, Nigel of Ely, and Bernard of St. David's; three earls: Robert of Gloucester, Baldwin of Redvers, whom she had made earl of Devon, and William of Mohun, newly created earl of Dorset or Somerset; her faithful followers, Brian fitz Count and Miles of Gloucester; her chancellor, William fitz Gilbert, and eight lesser men attested the charter. To these supporters may be added the names of Archbishop Theobald and Robert, the newly elected bishop of London, who were probably with the empress at this time.[2]

Queen Matilda sent a delegation to the empress to beg that her husband be released from his 'filthy dungeon', where he was being kept in chains. Many of the leading men of England joined their pleas to the queen's, offering 'to turn over many hostages and castles and great riches' to her if she would set the king free, and they promised that if she would release him he would leave the kingdom, become a monk or a pilgrim, and trouble her no more. Bishop Henry joined the queen's envoys in begging that the lands that Stephen had held in England and Normandy before his accession should be given to his eldest son Eustace as his rightful inheritance. Matilda refused these requests 'in harsh and insulting language' and sent the envoys away.

A delegation from the citizens of London appeared before her to beg that the harsh laws that King Henry had imposed on them be abrogated and that the milder laws of King Edward be

[1] *G. de M.*, pp. 81–113; Davis: 'Geoffrey de Mandeville Reconsidered', p. 306; Stenton: *The First Century of English Feudalism*, pp. 223–6.
[2] *G. de M.*, pp. 171, 195, 271–2; Stenton, op. cit., p. 227; *Regesta*, pp. xxix–xxx.

restored. Matilda countered with a demand for 'a huge sum of money'. The citizens replied that 'they had lost their accustomed wealth owing to the strife in the kingdom and the acute famine that threatened them'. They begged her to moderate her demands for a little while till they were better able to meet them, and then 'they would aid her the more eagerly in proportion as their wealth expanded'.

Matilda 'blazed into unbearable fury', reviled the Londoners, and refused to accept their excuses. She accused them of treachery and demanded that they meet her exactions in full. 'On hearing this the citizens went away gloomily to their homes.'[1]

Queen Matilda, meanwhile, with the assistance of William of Ypres and her kinsman Pharamus of Boulogne, had been raising an army in Kent, and with it she advanced on London. They devastated the outskirts of the city on both sides of the Thames, and the queen's envoys had little trouble in inducing the citizens to return to their former allegiance, disgusted and alarmed as they were by the empress's excessive demands and haughty demeanour.

The Empress Matilda 'was just bent on reclining at a well-cooked feast' at Westminster when the citizens set all the bells ringing 'as a signal for battle' and poured out of the gates 'like thronging swarms from beehives'. At the last moment someone warned the empress of the plot against her, and she and her immediate entourage had barely time to mount swift horses and flee in great disorder, leaving their belongings behind them. Hard on their heels came the mob of citizens, who 'entered their abandoned lodgings and found and plundered everywhere all that had been left behind in the speed of their unpremeditated departure'.

The empress and her entourage fled wildly to the north, over the only road, apparently, that was open to them. So great was their panic that each man thought only of himself. 'Taking different turnings, the first that met them as they fled, they set off for their own lands by a multitude of byroads, as though the Londoners were hot on their heels.' Only the king of Scots, Earl Robert of Gloucester, and few others of her most faithful friends remained with her in the disorderly flight.[2]

---

[1] G.S., pp. 80–1; Florence of Worcester, Vol. II, p. 132; H.N., p. 87.
[2] John of Hexham, p. 310; G.S., pp. 81–2; H.N., pp. 55–6; G. de M., p. 147.

Thus, at the very moment 'when it was thought that she might at once gain possession of the whole of England, everything was changed'. By her arrogant behaviour towards those who had most helped her and whose advice she contemptuously rejected and by her intolerable demands upon the Londoners, the empress had thrown away all the advantages that her followers had gained for her with great difficulty over the last two years. The Londoners admitted Queen Matilda to the city, and she immediately seized on this favourable turn of fortune to rally all her husband's supporters. 'Forgetting the weakness of her sex and a woman's softness, she bore herself with the valour of a man; everywhere, by prayer or price, she won over invincible allies; the king's lieges, wherever they were scattered throughout England, she urged persistently to demand their lord back with her.' Thus she succeeded at once in inducing Earl Geoffrey de Mandeville to return to his allegiance.

The empress meanwhile had fled to Oxford and then, not feeling safe even in that stronghold, had gone on to Gloucester. Taking counsel with Miles of Gloucester, who seems to have calmed the panic-stricken woman, she went back to Oxford under his escort to attempt to reassemble her scattered forces. On 25 July she made him earl of Hereford, 'to the pleasure and satisfaction of all there'. Together with her brother Robert, he had been her most faithful and effective helper, and whatever success she had had in her efforts to win the crown she owed to them. Miles himself declared that 'she had not had food for a single day nor a plate to eat it from except through his munificence or providing'.[1]

Although Bishop Henry had accompanied the empress on her flight from London, he had dropped out of her escort on the way to Oxford and had probably taken refuge in Winchester till he could find out how the land lay. Matilda's contemptuous treatment of him had shown him that she was even less likely than his brother had been to act under his advice. William of Malmesbury writes as though Henry's chief grievance lay, not in the ecclesiastical sphere, in which his position as legate and Matilda's explicit promises assured him the chief voice, but in her refusal to allow Stephen's son Eustace to succeed to the estates his father

[1] *H.N.*, p. 56; *G.S.*, pp. 83, 85; Florence of Worcester, Vol. II, pp. 132–3; *G. de M.*, pp. 119, 123–4.

had held in England before his accession. Her ignominious expulsion from London and her failure to launch an immediate offensive from Oxford convinced him now that he had bet on the wrong horse. He conferred with Queen Matilda at Guildford and decided to abandon the empress and work for his brother's restoration. The author of the *Gesta Stephani* places Henry's defection even earlier, for he says that the bishop was reputed to be privy to the plot to expel the empress from London and even to have instigated it.

When Earl Robert of Gloucester heard these rumours he went to Winchester to have an interview with the bishop, but he apparently was unable to pin him down to a definite statement of his loyalties. Robert went back to Oxford and reported to his sister, who was now convinced of the bishop's treachery. She immediately summoned all her followers, who had scattered after the flight from London, and marched on Winchester towards the end of July.[1]

William of Malmesbury says that the people of Winchester remained loyal to the empress and admitted her to the city and that she 'was at once received within the royal castle', no doubt by the castellan, William of Pont de l'Arche, who had gone over to her in the previous spring. She sent messengers to summon the bishop, but Henry was too wily to place himself in her power. He sent back the ambiguous message 'I will get ready' and immediately sent for help from all the king's supporters.

The author of the *Gesta Stephani*, on the other hand, says that the empress had hoped to catch the bishop by surprise, which would hardly have been possible if she had had 'a highly equipped force and a very large retinue'. At any rate, she entered the city by one gate before the citizens knew of her coming, and the bishop, warned in time, mounted a swift horse, fled by another gate, 'and made off to his castles at full speed'. The empress then sent out her summons and 'gathered into a vast army the whole array of those who obeyed her throughout England'. With this army she invested both the bishop's castle in the middle of the town and his palace of Wolvesey, in the south-east corner of the city.

John of Hexham adds to the confusion by saying that when the empress arrived at Winchester she found that the bishop's

[1] *H.N.*, pp. 57–8; *G.S.*, pp. 83–4; Florence of Worcester, Vol. II, p. 133.

forces were already besieging her adherents in the royal castle.[1]

Some of Matilda's followers had accompanied her to Winchester; others arrived soon in response to her summons. The leading men in her army were her uncle David; her three bastard brothers, Robert, earl of Gloucester, Reginald, earl of Cornwall, and Robert fitz Edith, who had married the daughter of Robert of Oilly, castellan of Oxford; three earls of her own creation, Baldwin of Redvers, earl of Devon, Miles of Gloucester, earl of Hereford, and William of Mohun, earl of Dorset or Somerset, and one earl of the older nobility, Roger of Beaumont, earl of Warwick. Brian fitz Count, her most devoted follower, was there, as were Geoffrey Boterel, the brother of Alan of Brittany, and Archbishop Theobald.[2]

Bishop Henry meanwhile had summoned the king's followers and had also hired knights at his own expense. William of Malmesbury, with perhaps some exaggeration, says that almost all the earls of England came in response to the bishop's summons, both because 'they were young and light-minded, men who preferred cavalry-raids to peace' and because they were ashamed of having abandoned the king at the Battle of Lincoln and wanted to wipe out their disgrace on that shameful occasion. Queen Matilda, William of Ypres, and almost a thousand Londoners, 'magnificently equipped with helmets and coats of mail', arrived to help the bishop. Ranulf, earl of Chester, realising that the presence of King David at the empress's side meant that he had no hope of getting Carlisle from her, showed up in the royalist camp, but the queen and her followers, naturally enough, suspected him of still further treachery and drove him away. He then offered his services to the empress, but by this time it was too late for him to give any effective help.

The ensuing siege was a remarkable affair; 'nothing like it' says the author of the *Gesta Stephani* 'was ever heard of in our times'. The empress's forces, using the royal castle as their base, laid siege to the bishop's palace of Wolvesey, which was a castle in itself; the queen's army in turn closely invested the city and laid siege to the besiegers. The bishop's men 'flung out firebrands and completely reduced to ashes the greater part of the town, including two abbeys', the convent of nuns within the city and

[1] *H.N.*, pp. 58–9; *G.S.*, pp. 83–4; *G. de M.*, p. 126; John of Hexham, p. 310.
[2] *G.S.*, pp. 85, 89; John of Hexham, pp. 310–11; *G. de M.*, p. 66.

Hyde Abbey, just outside the walls.   The continuator of Florence of Worcester says that the fire was set on 2 August and that more than forty churches, as well as the greater part of the city, were destroyed.

The royalists commanded all the roads to the east, and Geoffrey de Mandeville, who, it will be remembered, had returned to his allegiance, seems to have been assigned the task of keeping their communications to London open and their supplies moving smoothly.   The empress's forces depended upon their strongholds, Bristol and Gloucester, to the west and north for their supplies.   To cut off these supplies the queen's forces burned Andover, twelve miles to the north, and blockaded the roads on that side of the town.   Cut off from their bases of supply and confined to a city largely in ashes, the empress's forces, to say nothing of the wretched inhabitants of Winchester, were faced by starvation.

According to the author of the *Gesta Stephani*, in an effort to protect their lines of communication to the north, the empress's forces attempted to fortify Wherwell, some eight miles along the road to Andover, at the crossing of the River Test, and establish a garrison of 300 knights at that strategic point.   John of Hexham, however, says that they sent a force of 200 knights to Wherwell under the command of Robert fitz Edith and John Marshal to escort a train of provisions into the city.

The royalist forces, at any rate, under the command of William of Ypres, fell upon the empress's men, captured or killed a great many, and drove the rest, including John Marshal, into the convent church.   When they attempted to turn the church into a castle and defend themselves there, the royalists set fire to the church.   'In one place mutual slaughter was going on, in another prisoners were being dragged off, bound with thongs; here the conflagration was fearfully ravaging the roofs of the church and the houses, there cries and shrieks rang out piercingly from the virgins dedicated to God who had left their cloisters with reluctance under the stress of the fire.'

The empress and her followers had placed great dependence upon the arrival of the supplies from the north, and with the defeat of her forces at Wherwell and the capture of the convoy they were reduced to despair.   They accordingly decided to abandon Winchester and to try to break through the royalist lines. As they were emerging from the gates on Sunday, 14 September, the queen's forces fell on them with such violence that the withdrawal quickly turned into a rout. Robert of Gloucester sent his sister ahead with Brian fitz Count while he guarded the rear of the column. Under the unrelenting pressure of the queen's army the column broke into disorderly flight. Knights fled over the countryside in every direction, shedding their arms and shields and coats of mail in an effort to lighten their horses' burden and abandoning everything they carried. Knights and even barons dismounted and tried to steal away on foot or to hide themselves in the countryside. Men, arms, horses, and valuables of all kinds fell into the hands of the pursuers. King David was captured but succeeded in bribing his captors, and 'in grief and weariness, with a few followers, he fled back to Scotland'. William of Warenne and the Flemish mercenaries captured the richest prize of all, Earl Robert himself, at Stockbridge at the crossing of the Test, eight miles to the west of the city.

Accompanied only by Brian fitz Count and a few others, the empress, 'sorrowful and grieving', reached Ludgershall, twenty miles north-west of Winchester, but she could not feel safe from her pursuers there. Mounting her horse again, she fled to Devizes, seventeen miles to the west. She reached that stronghold more dead than alive, having ridden almost forty miles, but she was so filled with terror that even there she could not stop. Since it was beyond her strength to ride any farther, she was placed in a litter swung between two horses and carried in ignominious fashion a further forty miles to Gloucester. There she was eventually joined by Miles, 'exhausted, alone, and almost naked', who had barely escaped with his life.[1]

Earl Robert was brought before Queen Matilda at Winchester, and she turned him over to William of Ypres to be imprisoned at Rochester. Although King Stephen was being kept in close confinement in chains at Bristol, Queen Matilda had her captive treated with great consideration. She would not allow him to be fettered, and he was kept under a sort of open arrest, free to wander about the town and to see what visitors he liked. He even used the occasion to buy at a high price some horses that had caught his fancy.

[1] *H.N.*, pp. 58–61; John of Hexham, p. 310; Florence of Worcester, Vol. II, pp. 133, 135; *G.S.*, pp. 86–9; Beeler, *Warfare in England, 1066–1189*, pp. 121–8.

Negotiations were opened for the exchange of the prisoners, but Robert showed so little interest and imposed such extravagant conditions that one almost suspects that he was enjoying life too much at Rochester to be interested in returning to the company of his domineering sister and to the problems she had brought with her. His wife, Countess Mabel, was eager to accept the offer of an even exchange in order to regain her husband, but he refused. He, a mere earl, was not worth so much as a king, and he therefore demanded that the scales be balanced by releasing along with him all those who had been captured from his side.

This was by no means pleasing to the men on the king's side, for they had captured a great many valuable prizes and were holding them for ransom. Gilbert of Clare, earl of Hertford, for instance, had taken William of Salisbury, and William of Ypres was holding Humphrey of Bohun. None of these speculators was willing to release his prizes merely to secure the king's freedom. They proposed instead that Robert abandon his sister, whose cause was evidently quite hopeless, and support the king, in whose name but probably not by his authority they promised that 'he would have the lordship over the whole land, so that everything would be dependent upon his will and he would be lower than the king only as regards the crown, dominating all others as he would'.

To this Robert replied, reasonably enough, that as long as he was in their power he could not consider such offers; if he were a free agent he would be able to give them his attention. Since promises had no effect on him, they next threatened to send him overseas to Boulogne and imprison him there for the rest of his life. To this he replied with the even more dreadful threat of having the king sent to Ireland if anything wrong were to befall him.

Although he thus showed a spirited determination to dictate his own terms for the exchange, his friends reminded him that they were in no position to adopt such an intransigent attitude. They had been utterly defeated and dispersed at Winchester, and they were afraid that Stephen's side would follow up their advantage, besiege the rebels' castles one by one, force them to surrender the lands they had seized, and, finally, attack the empress herself.

They therefore urged him not to hold out for a set of impossible conditions but to agree to a simple exchange of himself for the king. Robert at last made such a bargain with Bishop Henry and Archbishop Theobald, and their mention in this connexion by William of Malmesbury probably indicates that these two conducted the negotiations. Robert won the important concession that the empress and her adherents should be allowed to keep all the lands and castles that had fallen into their hands after the king's capture, but he was unable to gain the release of any of his friends who were being held for ransom. The king's friends were especially insistent that Stephen be released first, out of respect for his rank, but Robert would not agree to this till the legate and the archbishop swore that if the king did not release him they would immediately surrender themselves to Robert and allow him to imprison them wherever he chose. He took the further precaution of obtaining letters from the two prelates to the pope, explaining the situation and requesting him to secure both their release and the earl's if the king should break his promise, and these letters Robert put in a safe place, to be delivered to the pope in case of treachery.

Robert was brought from Rochester to Winchester under the escort of the two prelates and a great number of barons. The elaborate machinery, which showed how little each side trusted the other, for the exchange of the two prisoners was then set in motion. On All Saints' Day, 1 November 1141, the king was released from his prison at Bristol, but he was forced to leave Queen Matilda and his son Eustace there as hostages. When he arrived at Winchester, escorted by 'a superb and magnificent procession of barons', on 3 November, he had an interview with Robert in which he attempted to induce him to renounce his allegiance to his sister and return to the fealty he had sworn to the king in 1136, but Robert refused, 'not so much from hatred of the king as from regard to his oath' to his sister. Leaving his eldest son William as a hostage, Robert set out for Bristol. When he arrived there safely, Queen Matilda and Eustace were released, and when they reached Winchester William in turn was set free.[1]

Although the bishop of Winchester, together with Archbishop Theobald, seems to have served as intermediary between the two

[1] Florence of Worcester, Vol. II, p. 135; *H.N.*, pp. 61–2, 66–70; *G.S.*, p. 90.

parties in effecting Stephen's release, now that his brother was free Henry and the other bishops who had taken part in the council at Winchester were in the embarrassing position of having to undo what they had previously done and to proclaim publicly their renewed allegiance to Stephen. Henry, again as papal legate, summoned a council to meet at Westminster on 7 December. If his previous attempt to justify his change of sides was awkward, to say the least, his performance at Westminster was even sorrier, and it must have vexed even his agile mind to come up with a convincing defence of his conduct, which to a less subtle intellect would appear to be treason pure and simple.

According to William of Malmesbury, who says that he was not present at this council as he had been at the one at Winchester, Henry opened the proceedings by trying to make it appear that he was acting in obedience to the pope's command. Innocent II, it will be remembered, was firmly on Stephen's side, and his letter, which the bishop caused to be read aloud to the assembly, was evidently written before the pope had learned of Stephen's release. 'He mildly rebuked the legate for evading the task of his brother's release but forgave him his previous fault and strongly urged him to gird himself to procure his brother's freedom by any means, ecclesiastical or secular.'

At this point the king himself appeared before the assembly. According to William of Malmesbury, he merely complained 'because his men had both captured him and almost killed, by the grievous burden of their insults, one who had never refused them justice', but one may be certain that the king's words were much more direct and to the point. Faced by a pack of men who were at the best cowards who had done nothing to help him when his fortunes were at their lowest ebb and at the worst traitors who had connived at his downfall and had publicly proclaimed his rival lady of England, Stephen would have been of rare self-restraint indeed if he had not let them see what he thought of them.

After the king had spoken, his brother attempted to defend his defection to the empress. He asserted that he had acted 'not of his own will but under compulsion' because, at a time when the king had been defeated and his supporters scattered, Matilda had surrounded Winchester with an army. His audience may have gaped at this interpretation of the events of the previous spring, but the bishop pressed on to the next task, that of explaining why, after he had proclaimed Matilda lady of England and had publicly pledged his support to her, he had deserted her and returned to his former allegiance. Matilda 'had persistently broken all her pledges relating to the freedom of the Church. Moreover, he said, he had been informed on reliable authority that she and her men had plotted not only against his position but also against his life.' Henry concluded his speech by bidding his audience 'aid zealously to the utmost of their power a king anointed with the goodwill of the people and the approval of the Apostolic See'. Just as he had excommunicated many of the king's adherents at Winchester in the preceding April, he now excommunicated 'those disturbers of the peace who supported the countess of Anjou, . . . all except the lady of the Angevins herself', using the lowest of Matilda's titles.

These fumbling attempts at justifying himself did not convince his audience, but at least no one tried to confute them, for many of the bishops were in the same boat with Henry and must have realised that they could have done no better at the job of defending themselves than Henry had done, and all were in awe of him as papal legate. The empress, however, had sent a layman as her delegate to the council, and he spoke up boldly. In her name he forbad the legate to make any decision to her prejudice and reminded him that he had promised her to give no help to his brother beyond sending him twenty knights at the most. The delegate went on to expose the extent of the bishop's commitment to the empress, and if his charges were true Henry stood convicted of having espoused and aided her cause almost from the beginning and of having indulged in the most shameful double-dealing.

Bishop Henry was responsible for the empress's coming to England in the first place, the delegate charged, for he had written frequent letters encouraging her to come. Furthermore, he said, 'the king's capture and imprisonment were mainly due to his connivance.' This charge, at any rate, seems far-fetched unless Henry had aided and abetted Earl Ranulf in his rebellion, and there is no evidence that he did so beyond the fact that Ranulf had shown up at Winchester in September and had attempted to join the bishop's side. While it is barely possible that he did so out of loyalty to the bishop, it is much more likely that Ranulf,

I

the least subtle of men, could hope for nothing from the empress as long as King David was amongst her counsellors and therefore attempted to join the royalists in the hope of profiting from their victory. The bishop did not attempt to answer these charges. The council then pronounced a public and solemn sentence of excommunication upon all despoilers and oppressors of the clergy.[1]

It may have been at this meeting that Bishop Henry as papal legate heard the complaints against William, archbishop-elect of York. Walter of London, archdeacon of the West Riding, who had originally contested the election on the ground that the chapter had been intimidated by William of Aumale, earl of York, acting in the king's name, was now joined by a powerful group representing both the newly-founded Cistercian houses of the north and the Austin canons, who were inspired by their example. He appeared before the council accompanied by William, the first abbot of Rievaulx, Richard, the second abbot of Fountains, Cuthbert, prior of Guiseborough, and Waldef, prior of Kirkham, and they accused the archbishop-elect not only of having been elected uncanonically but also of having bought his election. Bishop Henry had his hands full at this time and did not want to be drawn into the quarrel, even in defence of his nephew. He therefore referred the matter to Rome.[2]

In order to reassert his royal dignity, which had been eclipsed by his capture and imprisonment, King Stephen, accompanied by Queen Matilda and the leading nobles of the realm, went to Canterbury and on Christmas Day was crowned in the cathedral by Archbishop Theobald, whilst Queen Matilda wore her golden crown. Although it is not likely that the anointings of the coronation ceremony, since they were of a quasi-sacramental character, would be repeated, it seems evident that as much of the ceremony as pertained to the investiture with the regalia and the solemn placing of the crown on the king's head by the archbishop in the course of the Mass was repeated, in order to emphasise in the most solemn way possible Stephen's position as king, unimpaired by his imprisonment and now restored to all his power and dignity.[3]

[1] H.N., pp. 62–4; Gervase of Canterbury, Vol. I, p. 122.
[2] John of Hexham, p. 311; Knowles: *The Historian and Character*, p. 82.
[3] Gervase of Canterbury, Vol. I, p. 123; G. de M., pp. 137–8.

We may assume that for the same reason Stephen's Christmas court was held with all possible splendour and magnificence. During this visit to Canterbury he granted to Geoffrey de Mandeville a charter that confirmed what J. H. Round calls 'the lost charter of the queen' that Queen Matilda is presumed to have issued during the previous summer in order to secure Geoffrey's allegiance after the empress had fled from London and that also increased considerably both the honours Stephen had given Geoffrey when he made him earl of Essex, probably in 1139, and the grants made by the empress in the previous June.

Geoffrey's support of the empress had been brief, and he is not recorded as having done much to help her. He was late in coming over to her side, and he did so only when she was apparently on the verge of being crowned queen. If R. H. C. Davis is correct in dating 'the second charter of the empress' at Oxford in late July 1141, Geoffrey accompanied her on her flight or joined her there soon afterwards, but he remained with her for only a short time, for he gave decisive support to the royalist forces at the siege of Winchester. Of all the leading men who supported the empress, Geoffrey did so at the latest possible moment, made the least contribution to her cause, and went back to the king's side at the first opportunity. Stephen therefore had no reason to feel any particular resentment against him, and his charter indicates his readiness to overlook Geoffrey's temporary lapse and his eagerness to bind him firmly to the king's side.

The charter opens by confirming Geoffrey in everything he held at the time of the king's capture at Lincoln. The king, in addition, grants him lands worth £400 a year and gives his son Ernulf lands worth £100 a year, to be held of Geoffrey. Stephen grants him and his heirs 'the custody of the Tower of London with the castle belonging to it', which Geoffrey already had by hereditary right, and makes him sheriff and justiciar, not only of Essex alone, as the empress had done in her first charter to him, but of Hertfordshire, Middlesex, and London as well. The king also grants him the service of sixty enfeoffed knights, whereas the empress had given him only twenty, and permission to build a castle wherever he pleased on his land. Finally, Stephen confirms whatever the queen had given Geoffrey in her lost charter on the occasion of his return to the king's side. There is the possibility, of course, that the extremely generous nature of the

king's grants was forced on him by the terms his queen had previously offered Geoffrey, either to purchase his return or to
reward him for it, at a time when she was desperate for help.

The list of witnesses tells us the names of some who were
present at this Christmas court. It is significant that only one
bishop, the king's brother Henry, witnesses the charter. While
the absence of the names of other bishops from this charter does
not prove that they absented themselves from Stephen's court,
it may perhaps indicate that they did not stand high in his regard.
The bishops of England, including Archbishop Theobald, certainly had not played a distinguished part in the events of the
year now drawing to a close. They seem to have followed the
legate's lead like sheep as he changed from one side to the other,
and such conduct would hardly win for them a large measure
of the king's esteem. Henry, the officious busybody, probably
could not have been prevented from setting his seal to any official
document that would testify to his importance, but his fellow
bishops stayed well in the background. J. H. Round offers the
explanation that they may have been at enmity with Geoffrey,
but it may have been simply that they were not high in the
king's favour.

On the other hand, eight earls, those of Warenne, Pembroke,
Hertford, York, Northampton, Sussex, as William of Aubigny
is now styled, Richmond, and Derby, witnessed the charter, and
they were among Stephen's most faithful adherents. Among the
eight remaining witnesses are William of Ypres, the captain of
Stephen's mercenaries; William Martel, his steward; Baldwin
fitz Gilbert, the brother of the earl of Pembroke; Pharamus, the
queen's kinsman, and Richard of Luci, who was to distinguish
himself in future years as Henry II's justiciar.[1]

Crowned again as king and surrounded by his court, with his
enemies put to ignominious flight, Stephen was now in the
strongest position he had attained since his rival's landing in
England.

---

[1] G. de M., pp. 136–56; Davis: 'Geoffrey de Mandeville Reconsidered', pp.
299–307; Regesta, pp. 102–3.

VII

1142–1143

KING Stephen now had two principal aims, according to John of Hexham: to avenge his former injuries, that is, to punish the supporters of the empress, and to restore order and peace to his kingdom. He therefore went north 'to settle some affairs' and to raise an army in Yorkshire, where he had a loyal following. Together with Queen Matilda, he went to York, and there he put a stop to a projected tournament between William of Aumale, earl of York, and Alan of Brittany, earl of Richmond. This was no time, in Stephen's opinion, for such knightly sports as tournaments, and they had the added disadvantage that although they started out as games, played in dead earnest, they often aroused such intense feelings that they turned into the small-scale wars of which they were simulacra. Stephen needed all the men he could get, and he seems to have raised a sizable army in Yorkshire.

On the way south with his forces, however, he fell ill at Northampton at Easter, and his illness was so grave that he was forced to send his army back to their homes and it was rumoured throughout the country that he was dead.[1]

The empress meanwhile had recovered her health and spirits, badly shaken by her flight from Winchester, and had established her headquarters at Oxford at the previous Michaelmas. Taking advantage of the king's absence in the north and of the truce that prevailed during the season of Lent, she and her counsellors went to Devizes, which seems to have been as far as Earl Robert of Gloucester was willing to go from his stronghold of Bristol, to confer regarding their next steps. It was now obvious that they could have no hope of overcoming the king with the forces

---

[1] John of Hexham, p. 312; *H.N.*, p. 71; R. H. C. Davis: 'King Stephen and the Earl of Chester Revised', pp. 654–60; H. W. C. Davis: 'The Anarchy of Stephen's Reign', *English Historical Review*, XVIII (October 1903), p. 631.

at their disposal, and they agreed that their best hope lay in summoning to their help Count Geoffrey of Anjou, who was fighting doggedly to gain the whole of Normandy. They accordingly despatched some of their number to point out to him that it was 'his duty to maintain the inheritance of his wife and children in England'.

When the envoys returned, a second meeting of the empress and her councillors was held at Devizes on 14 June 1142 to hear their report. Geoffrey had been quite lacking in any enthusiasm for his suggested invasion of England. He was a single-minded man whose one ambition was to win the whole of Normandy for his son, and from that aim he refused to be deflected. He was a realist who considered his wife's ambitions and schemes little better than hare-brained, although he must have rejoiced that they were sufficiently attractive to that imperious and disagreeable woman to keep her occupied across the Channel. He had no desire to join her.

He accordingly replied to her invitation that although he did not entirely disapprove of the proposition her messengers had laid before him, he knew nothing about any of her supporters except the earl of Gloucester, whom he had long admired. If Earl Robert, then, would come over and discuss his plans with him, Geoffrey would give him an attentive hearing, but it would be a waste of time for the empress to send over any more of those unknown English adventurers with whom she had surrounded herself.

In spite of the unpromising nature of this reply, the assembly agreed that Robert should go to see Geoffrey. Robert, naturally enough, was reluctant to start out on a mission whose outcome could only be unfavourable, and he raised a host of difficulties. It would be a perilous journey, he said, 'through a mass of enemies on both sides of the sea'. Furthermore, he pointed out, the very men who were urging him to leave his sister and cross the sea had abandoned her when he had been captured; how could he now go away and leave her under the protection of men who had thus shown their lack of faith in her cause?

When they all insisted that he go on this mission on which they pinned such high hopes, Robert demanded that all the leading men give him hostages whom he could take with him to Normandy to ensure their fidelity to his sister while he was out of the country.   The nobles gave the hostages he required, and Robert, with the hostages and 'knights ready for action', sailed from Wareham, which he had entrusted to his eldest son William, shortly after Midsummer Day.

Geoffrey met him at Caen, but when Robert urged him to set out for England, the count objected that he could not leave just at that moment, when a number of Norman castles were revolting against him, and suggested that Robert help him put his affairs in Normandy in order so that he might be free to leave. Robert accordingly joined forces with him, and they spent the remainder of the summer in capturing ten castles, lying roughly in the triangle Bayeux–Falaise–Domfront, which would indicate that at this time Geoffrey had only a precarious hold over the western part of Normandy.[1]

Stephen did not recover his health till after Whitsunday, 7 June. He then reassembled his army and began operations against the empress.   His strategy apparently was first to seize Wareham, from whence Earl Robert had sailed, in order to prevent his landing there unexpectedly if he should return to help his sister, and then to approach Oxford, Matilda's stronghold, from the west, reducing the castles she had fortified in that area to protect her communications with Bristol and Gloucester and thus cutting her off from her chief sources of supply.

When he appeared suddenly before Wareham as the first step in his campaign, he found only a small garrison there. Earl Robert, it will be remembered, had entrusted the castle to his eldest son William, whom the author of the *Gesta Stephani* characterises as 'effeminate and more devoted to amorous intrigue than to war', and William had apparently failed to take adequate measures to protect it.   Stephen plundered and burned the town and had no difficulty in seizing the castle.

He went next to Cirencester, some seventy miles to the north, where Matilda's knights held the castle.   When he arrived there, however, he found that the garrison had fled at the news of his approach.   He burned the castle and destroyed the rampart and stockade that protected it.   Then he turned towards Oxford, thirty miles to the east.   Half-way there he captured the twin fortifications at Bampton and Radcot, only a few miles apart. One can form a good idea of what was considered a castle at this

[1] *G.S.*, p. 91; Gervase of Canterbury, Vol. I, p. 124; *H.N.*, pp. 71–3.

time when he reads that the castle at Bampton was built 'right on the church-tower'.[1]

Having cut the empress's lines of supply to the west, Stephen hastened to attack her headquarters at Oxford, 'a city securely protected, inaccessible because of the very deep water that washes it all round, most carefully encircled by the palisade of an outwork on one side, and on the other finely and very strongly fortified by an impregnable castle and a tower of great height'.

When he reached the city, on 26 September, he and his army swam rather than waded across the Thames at 'an old, extremely deep ford', and attacked the empress's troops with such vehemence that they drove them back into the city. Stephen's forces followed hot on their heels, set the town afire, and forced Matilda's knights back into the castle with their mistress.

When his army had finished sacking and burning the city and had either killed, or put in chains to be held for ransom, as many of Matilda's supporters as they could capture, the king settled down to besiege the empress and the remnant of her forces in the tower. He had at last learned that as long as the empress was at large he could have no peace, and he declared that 'the hope of no advantage, the fear of no loss should make him go away unless the castle had been surrendered and the empress brought into his power'.

Matilda's supporters massed their forces at Wallingford, Brian fitz Count's stronghold fifteen miles down the Thames, but they did not dare attack the army at Oxford, and Stephen refused to be drawn away from his objective, which was to capture the tower and the empress within it. He began the dreary business of starving his opponent into submission, and since the garrison were well supplied with food the siege promised to be a long-drawn-out affair.

When the news of his sister's plight reached Earl Robert in Normandy, he again urged Count Geoffrey to come to England with him, but again Geoffrey brought up fresh excuses. He refused to be diverted from the business immediately at hand, the subjugation of Normandy, but, 'as a great favour', he allowed Robert to take to England with him the young Henry, then nine years old, 'so that in seeing him the nobles might be inspired to fight for the cause of the lawful heir'. The

[1] *G.S.*, pp. 91-2, 139-40; *H.N.*, p. 73.

unprepossessing character of the empress was the chief drawback to her cause, and Geoffrey, who was acutely aware of the more unpleasant side of his wife's temperament, shrewdly suggested that their son might be a more inspiring figure about whom the rebels could rally.

Robert set sail for England with his nephew and a force of between 300 and 400 knights in fifty-two ships. He landed at Wareham and as a point of honour laid siege to the castle before moving inland. Stephen had placed a courageous garrison there under the command of Herbert of Luci, but even they 'were shaken and terrified by the earl's siege-engines'. They asked for a truce so that they might summon help from the king and agreed to surrender if he did not come by a stipulated date. Robert gladly agreed, for he hoped by this means to draw Stephen away from Oxford, but the king refused to rise to the bait.

Robert seized Wareham after a siege of three weeks and went on to take the Isle of Portland and the castle at Lulworth, a few miles north-west of Corfe Castle. Then he summoned all who were faithful to his sister to assemble at Cirencester early in December to march to her relief at Oxford.[1]

As the siege at Oxford entered its third month the empress and her knights within the tower were reduced to the extremity of hunger. Their supplies were exhausted; they had no hope of help, and the king had an army of over a thousand knights closely guarding the castle and battering it with stone-throwers. One night shortly before Christmas, when the ground was covered with snow and the Thames frozen over, the empress either stole out of the castle by a little postern gate or, according to the more dramatic narrative of the Peterborough Chronicle, had herself lowered from the tower by ropes. With only three or four companions, all clad in white so that they could not be seen against the snow, she stole through the pickets, 'who everywhere were breaking the silence of the night with the blaring of trumpets and loud shouts', and crossed the frozen river.

The little party went six miles on foot, 'through snow and ice, through ditches and valleys', to Abingdon, where they found horses and thus rode to Wallingford and a warm welcome from Brian fitz Count. The news of her daring escape was brought to Earl Robert, and he and his young nephew joined her. 'And

[1] G.S., p. 92; H.N., pp. 73-6; Gervase of Canterbury, Vol. I, p. 124.

when the empress saw her brother and her first-born son she was cheered beyond measure and held her earlier griefs and labours as nothing.'

Henry was sent to the safety of Bristol, to be taught his letters and manners by Master Matthew. He had as his companion in his studies his cousin Roger, a younger son of Earl Robert. Although Gervase of Canterbury, writing some forty years later, says that the young Henry was at Bristol for four years, A. L. Poole has shown that he was with his father at Angers early in 1144.[1]

Once the empress had made her escape, the garrison at Oxford surrendered to Stephen. He installed a garrison of his own men and apparently devoted considerable time to subduing the surrounding countryside, over which the empress had established control, and expelling her adherents. He had previously attempted and failed to capture Wallingford, where his adversary had taken refuge, and he was unwilling to repeat the attempt. After re-establishing his authority in the neighbourhood of Oxford, he took his army to Wareham, but he found the castle so strongly defended that he did not embark upon another siege that would have consumed time and supplies without bringing him any great gain. He devastated all the country around Wareham and then marched to Wilton. The author of the *Gesta Stephani*, influenced perhaps by local pride, calls Wilton 'the master-key of the whole kingdom'; at any rate, it seemed of great importance to the king. His purpose in going there was 'to strengthen the castle with the object of preventing the earl's raids through the counties', and it looks as though he intended to establish an outpost to protect Winchester and perhaps to serve as a base for an advance against Bristol; in any case, it would serve to halt an extension of Earl Robert's influence to the south-east.

Once Wilton was strongly fortified, Stephen summoned his barons from every part of England, and those who were not already with him 'came flocking in to him with all the reinforcements they could raise'. Bishop Henry appeared with a strong body of troops. All these preparations might indicate that

---

[1] *H.N.*, p. 77; *The Peterborough Chronicle, 1070–1154*, ed. Cecily Clark (Oxford, 1958), p. 59; *G.S.*, pp. 94–5; Gervase of Canterbury, Vol. I, pp. 124–5; Austin Lane Poole: 'Henry Plantagenet's Early Visits to England', *English Historical Review*, XLVII (July 1932), p. 450.

Stephen was contemplating an attack on Bristol or at any rate an extensive foray into Earl Robert's territory. So at any rate Robert interpreted the assembling of this army, and he sent urgent appeals to all his followers to join him. When he advanced on Wilton he must have had a sizable army; the author of the *Gesta Stephani* mentions Miles of Gloucester, William, the castellan of Salisbury, and Robert son of Hildebrand, of whom we shall hear more later, as being present.

Stephen, his brother Henry, and their army came out of the town to meet Robert and his forces. Just as he had at Lincoln, the king left the town and fought in the open rather than risk the danger of being besieged and thus bottled up, perhaps for months. The king and his brother were put to ignominious flight, and only the stout resistance put up by William Martel, the king's steward and castellan of Sherborne, saved him from being captured a second time. William Martel and many other knights were captured; others fled as best they could, and some took refuge in the town. Robert and his men pursued them into Wilton, set the town afire, and killed or captured as many as they could. The last remnants of the king's forces took refuge in the convent church. Robert's men smashed the doors, plundered the convent, and dragged out those who had taken refuge there.

The victorious earl and his army took their booty and prisoners to Bristol. William Martel was the earl's most important captive, and Robert put him in close confinement till at last he purchased his freedom by surrendering Sherborne.[1]

We are not told of Stephen's movements immediately after his defeat at Wilton, beyond that he made good his escape. His brother returned to Winchester, and the account of the *Gesta Stephani* indicates that a curious situation existed there. Although the Angevin forces had been defeated and put to flight at the Rout of Winchester in September 1141, it would seem that William of Pont de l'Arche, the custodian of Winchester Castle, continued to hold it for the empress even after her defeat. The *Gesta Stephani* characterises him as 'a man utterly loyal to King Henry and his descendants' and says that he now picked a quarrel with Bishop Henry. One may surmise that although William

[1] G.S., pp. 92–3, 96–8; William of Newburgh: *Historia Rerum Anglicarum*, ed. Richard Howlett, in *Chronicles of the Reigns of Stephen, Henry II, and Richard I* (Rolls Series 82, 4 vols., 1884–9), Vol. I, p. 42; *Regesta*, p. xviii.

contrived to hold the castle, he did not feel secure enough to challenge the bishop till after his flight from Wilton. When the empress's party appeared again to be in the ascendant and the bishop had narrowly escaped capture, William may have felt that the time was opportune for him to challenge Henry's hold upon the city.

Whatever the circumstances of the quarrel may have been, William at any rate appealed to the empress for help. Matilda and her party were delighted to receive this message, for they saw in him the instrument with which to overcome the fickle bishop and thus extend the territory under their control. They accordingly sent 'a fine body of knights' under the command of Robert son of Hildebrand, who had fought at Wilton and whom the author of the *Gesta Stephani* describes as 'a man of low birth indeed but also of tried military qualities, and, what disgraces and sullies the prime and fame of soldiers, he was likewise a lustful man, drunken and unchaste'.

It is indicative of the weakness of the bishop's position in Winchester itself that Robert and his body of knights apparently met with no opposition but were able to join William in the castle, where Robert received 'a most cordial reception'. Having gained William's confidence, Robert, instead of concerting with his host that attack on the bishop for which his help had been requested, set to work to seduce William's wife. When he had succeeded in that objective, he then, with the help of his paramour, seized his host, bound him with chains, and imprisoned him in a dungeon. In possession of William's wife, his castle, and his wealth, Robert then made an agreement with Bishop Henry and transferred his allegiance to the king.

Our author describes with the greatest satisfaction Robert's unhappy end.

God most justly avenging his injuries, a worm was born at the time when the traitorous corrupter lay in the unchaste bosom of the adulteress and crept through his vitals, and slowly eating away his entrails it gradually consumed the scoundrel, and at length, in affliction of many complaints and the torment of many dreadful sufferings, it brought him to his end by a punishment he richly deserved.[1]

[1] G.S., pp. 100–1.

After he had transferred his allegiance back to his brother, Bishop Henry attempted to induce Brian fitz Count to follow his example. There was apparently an extended correspondence between the two. Part of one of Henry's letters to Brian and the whole of Brian's reply have been preserved, and they tell us a great deal about the characters of both writers.

The bishop begins his letter by warning Brian to remember Lot's wife, who was turned into a pillar of salt for having looked back. 'While you are always looking back at the things that are behind you, you pay no attention to the transgression that is before your eyes and that you can more easily correct.' Henry reminds him that in a previous letter he had asked Brian to grant a firm peace to all who were on their way to the bishop's fair of St. Giles, held in September, and that Brian in his reply had not refused the bishop's request. Now, however, the bishop's possessions have been seized and his lands and men and the roads leading to Winchester have been disturbed by Brian's men. The bishop concludes that Brian and his men are not to be trusted and that unless they mend their ways they are to be numbered amongst the infidels of England. Since St. Giles's Fair was certainly not held during the siege of 1141 and since Bishop Henry styles himself legate, a title that he lost in September 1143,the correspondence probably belongs to the autumn of 1142.

Brian's reply shows a lively intelligence, quick to seize on all the points at which the turncoat bishop had laid himself open, a lively wit to taunt him with his inconsistency, and a burning sense of the injustice of his charges. Although Henry had styled himself 'by the Grace of God bishop of Winchester and legate of the Apostolic See', Brian addresses him as 'Henry, King Henry's nephew', to remind him of who had made him what he is. The bishop had cited in a previous letter the case of Adam, who sinned through disobedience; now he tells Brian to remember Lot and his wife. 'I have never seen or known them', Brian writes with broad irony, 'or been in their city, but I have heard tell that it was an angel that ordered them not to look back. No one ever ordered me not to look back; on the contrary, I do well to look back to Holy Church's orders so that by remembering what I have been ordered to do I may avoid the contrary.

'Now you yourself, a prelate of Holy Church, ordered me to

support the daughter of King Henry your uncle and help her to gain what is rightfully hers and had been taken away from her by force and to hold on to what she now has.   And I not only look back to your orders; I take the worthy deeds of our illustrious ancestors as an example even for me.   And as I look back to the examples of Count Stephen your father and of many others of the noblest and richest knights, who obeyed the pope's order, left everything they had, and conquered Jerusalem, and as I look back to your order that I should help King Henry's daughter with all my might, I have no fear of doing wrong where the precept of Holy Church sustains me.'

In his indignation, Brian rises to the highest point of eloquence. 'King Henry gave me land.   But it has been so taken away from me and my men because of your order that I obeyed, that in this time of great need I do not reap one acre of corn from the land he gave me, and therefore it is no wonder that I take from others what I need to keep me and my men alive.   And to do what you ordered me to do, I should not need to take anything from another if what is mine had been left to me.   I tell you that neither I nor my men do this for money or fief or land that has been promised or given to us, but solely in obedience to your order and out of the respect that I and my men have for what is lawful.   And as witnesses to this order that I say you gave me', Brian cites a list of those who supported the empress in her brief hour of glory, a list more extensive than is supplied by any of her surviving charters.   It begins with 'Theobald, whom they call archbishop of Canterbury', to mark Brian's contempt for the man who should have been the leader of the English clergy, and continues with the names of twelve bishops.   David, king of Scots, heads the list of laymen, and it is interesting to find amongst them 'Osbert Eight-Pence and all the citizens of London and William of Pont de l'Arche and all the citizens of Winchester'.

Brian closes with a formal challenge to the bishop, offering to prove himself in the right either by trial by battle or by one of the ordeals, against anyone whom the bishop may name as his champion.   'Therefore let all the faithful of Holy Church know that I, Brian fitz Count, whom good King Henry brought up and to whom he gave arms and honour, am ready to prove what I assert in this letter against Henry, King Henry's nephew, bishop of Winchester and legate of the Apostolic See, either by battle or by ordeal, by one clerk or one layman.'[1]

Brian also wrote a book or pamphlet (*libellus*) in defence of the empress, which inspired Gilbert Foliot, abbot of Gloucester and a staunch partisan of Matilda, to send him a letter of congratulation on the clarity with which Brian presented the case, all the more gratifying because Brian had not 'been brought up to letters'.[2]

After they had defeated the king at Wilton, Earl Robert and his party devoted their energies to consolidating their hold upon the territory under their control. The author of the *Gesta Stephani* says, with great exaggeration, that they 'put almost half of England, from sea to sea, under their own laws and ordinances', and he grudgingly concedes that the earl 'restored peace and quietness everywhere'. Robert, however, exacted forced labour from the inhabitants in order to build castles with which to defend his territory, and he maintained his army by demanding knight-service or scutage from all the landholders.[3]

This picture of 'a shadow of peace but not yet peace complete' is belied, however, by the general account of the unhappy state of the country in the pages immediately following. This description refers not to the particular results of any one campaign by either of the opposing forces but rather to the general state of misery to which the country had been reduced by four years of civil war and the disorder attendant upon it. Almost all the fighting had taken place west of a line running from Oxford to Winchester, and the description given in the *Gesta Stephani* may be taken as applying particularly to Wiltshire and Gloucestershire and the neighbouring regions.

Some of the inhabitants had been driven into exile; some 'lived in fear and suffering' in the shelter of a church; some were driven by famine to eating dogs and horses and 'raw and filthy herbs or roots', and some 'wasted away and died in droves'. To add to the miseries of war and famine, a horde of mercenary soldiers swarmed over the land, pillaging and robbing.[4]

[1] H. W. C. Davis: 'Henry of Blois and Brian FitzCount', *English Historical Review*, XXV (April 1910), pp. 297–303.

[2] *The Letters and Charters of Gilbert Foliot, Abbot of Gloucester (1139–48), Bishop of Hereford (1148–63) and London (1163–87)*, ed. Z. N. Brooke, Adrian Morey, and C. N. L. Brooke (Cambridge, 1967), pp. 60–6.

[3] G.S., p. 99.

[4] G.S., p. 101.

VIII

1143–1145

WITH Stephen's defeat at Wilton the war reached a stalemate. The king could not wrest any further territory from Earl Robert, whose positions in Bristol and Gloucester seemed impregnable, and Robert and his party, instead of trying to enlarge their sphere of influence, were forced to devote their energies to consolidating their hold upon what they had. In addition to the physical damage that the war had wrought on the country, the moral effect of Robert's rebellion was extremely damaging to Stephen's authority. It had been openly challenged by a group who sought to depose the king and place another on the throne, and they had almost succeeded. Even when they failed, the king was unable to punish them, and they remained safely in their strongholds within the kingdom as a perpetual threat to the peace and stability of the realm, as a centre to which all the disaffected might rally, and as an example of the impunity with which men might flout the king's authority.

Their example was not lost upon some of the barons, and the next phase of Stephen's struggle was concerned with putting down the rebellions of individual barons whose aim was not to make Matilda queen of England but to defy and shake off Stephen's authority. The civil war entered into a period of abeyance and was followed by a series of revolts that were fully as dangerous to the king's authority and as destructive to the country as the war itself had been.

Of all the barons who were ostensibly faithful to him, Stephen most distrusted Geoffrey de Mandeville, earl of Essex, who had briefly sided with the empress during Stephen's captivity but had returned to his previous allegiance before the siege of Winchester. It is difficult to believe that Stephen bore a grudge against him on that account, for, as R. H. C. Davis points out, Geoffrey's conduct in 1141 was 'no worse than that of a very large number of bishops and barons, including the king's own brother, Henry of Blois'.

William of Newburgh explains Stephen's distrust of Geoffrey by saying that Geoffrey had taken Constance of France, the bride of Stephen's son Eustace, away from her mother-in-law and kept her in custody, while sending Queen Matilda away 'with ignominy'. Mr. Davis conjectures that Geoffrey perpetrated this outrage during the king's captivity in 1141. Afterwards the king, 'concealing his just rage for the time being, demanded her back, and Geoffrey reluctantly surrendered his illustrious captive.' Stephen bided his time and waited for an opportunity to avenge the insult.[1]

The author of the *Gesta Stephani*, however, who was much nearer to these events than was William of Newburgh, does not mention the kidnapping of Constance. He depicts the earl as surpassing all the chief men of the kingdom 'in the extent of his wealth and the splendour of his position' and says that 'everywhere in the kingdom he took the king's place and in all transactions was listened to more eagerly than the king and received more obedience when he gave orders'. It was also commonly reported, he says, that Geoffrey 'had determined to bestow the kingdom on the countess of Anjou'. Geoffrey had, it is true, briefly supported the empress, but his support had been neither enthusiastic nor effective. If he had indeed intended to further the empress's cause, he chose an inopportune time to do so, after having let pass many better chances.

The earl, however, enjoyed great wealth and influence, which in the eyes of Stephen's loyal supporters he had done little or nothing to deserve, for his support of the king had been lukewarm at best. All the writers of the period emphasise the jealousy with which Stephen's friends regarded the earl of Essex, and their jealousy, combined with the distrust that the king felt for a man who had been grudging in his support, may explain the decisive action that Stephen at last took against him.

The king's friends had long been urging him to seize the earl, but Stephen, although apparently convinced of the truth of their accusations, hesitated to act, 'lest the royal majesty should be disgraced by the foul reproach of betrayal'. Matters came to a

[1] R. H. C. Davis: 'Geoffrey de Mandeville Reconsidered', pp. 301–2, 306; William of Newburgh, Vol. I, pp. 44–5.

head at a meeting at St. Albans, apparently in the autumn of
1143. A quarrel broke out between Geoffrey and the king's
barons. The king attempted to 'calm both parties and settle the
disagreement between them'. Geoffrey's opponents, however,
openly accused him of treasonable intentions against the king.
Geoffrey made no attempt to clear himself of the charge and tried
to pass it off as a joke. This gave the king and his friends the
opportunity they had been waiting for, and they seized the
earl and his followers.[1]

As in the case of the arrest of the bishops in 1139, Stephen's
overriding consideration was his own safety and that of his realm,
and he felt that the seizure of a traitor was more important than
the observance of niceties of behaviour. Henry of Huntingdon
remarks that the king acted 'more in accordance with the punishment of the earl's villainy than in accordance with established
usage, more from necessity than from honourableness, for if
he had not done this, the earl's treachery would have deprived
him of his realm'. William of Newburgh, perhaps echoing his
words, says that the king seized Geoffrey 'not honourably and
according to established usage but according to his deserts and
out of fear, looking more to what was expedient than to what was
fitting'.

Stephen brought his captive to London and threatened to hang
him unless he surrendered his castles. The source of Geoffrey's
strength was the Tower of London, which placed the city in his
power, and in order to save his neck he surrendered the Tower
and his two castles in Essex, Saffron Walden and Pleshy, near
Chelmsford.[2]

Stephen's depriving Geoffrey of his castles differed from the
similar action he took against the three bishops in 1139 because
in their cases the custody of the castles had been a personal favour
conferred on them by Stephen's predecessor and hence revocable
at the king's will; the question of hereditary right could not have
been raised. Geoffrey, however, held the Tower by hereditary
right, and that right had been recognised and confirmed by
Stephen in his second charter to the earl. 'I have given and confirmed to him the custody of the Tower of London with the

[1] G.S., pp. 106–7; G. de M., p. 202.
[2] Henry of Huntingdon, p. 275; William of Newburgh, Vol. I, p. 44; G.S.,
p. 108.

castle dependent on it, to have and to hold by him and his heirs
of me and my heirs, with all the things and liberties and customs
pertaining to the aforesaid Tower', Stephen had declared, and at
the close of the charter he repeated that the custody of the Tower
and all his other grants to Geoffrey were given 'in fief and inheritance of me and my heirs to him and his heirs for his
service'.[1]

Even though the grant had been made in the most solemn and
binding fashion, underlying it was the assumption that the
recipient would remain faithful to the king; treason would of
course invalidate the grant, and it was of treason that Geoffrey
was accused. Again Stephen asserted the basic principle that
tenures and custodies bestowed by the Crown did not give the
recipients absolute and perpetual possession but were revocable
at the king's will when the foundations upon which all tenure
rested, fealty and loyalty to the king, were found to be wanting.

It is characteristic of Stephen that having deprived Geoffrey of
his castles he did not go all the way and imprison the earl for
life, as his uncle King Henry would have done. He released
Geoffrey, who then embarked on a career of plundering and
devastation without parallel even in that age.

The earl fled to the fen country and gathered about him a
formidable army made up of his own knights, all the disaffected
and landless men of the district, mercenary soldiers who sold
their services to whoever would pay them, and 'robbers who had
collected enthusiastically from every quarter'. With this lawless
mob he fell upon the king's town of Cambridge. They pillaged
the town, broke into the churches, in which the inhabitants had
stored their treasures, carried off everything they could lay their
hands on, and then set fire to the town.[2]

Geoffrey then led his forces to Ramsey, twenty miles north-west
of Cambridge, where a rich abbey stood on what was then an
island amidst the fens, approachable only by a narrow causeway.
The monastery was peculiarly vulnerable at this time because
of the dissension within its walls. The abbot, Walter, had been
prevailed upon to resign his office in favour of one of his monks,
the same Daniel who in 1140 had shown the king's army the
ford that enable them to invade the Isle of Ely. Daniel, to

---

[1] *G. de M.*, pp. 141–3; *Regesta*, p. 103.
[2] *G.S.*, pp. 108–9.

whom the unworldly Walter had already committed the management of the abbey's affairs, had bribed the king, the queen, and their close advisors, according to the Ramsey chronicler, so that when Walter presented himself before the king at Stamford and resigned his staff of office into Stephen's hands, the king immediately conferred the office on Daniel and went to Ramsey and installed him in his new post.

The tenants of the abbey, 'the barons, knights, and freemen', meanwhile were appalled to learn what Walter had done and overwhelmed him with reproaches. Walter, who seems to have been of an astonishing simplicity, realised too late that he had been tricked by Daniel, now firmly installed as abbot, and immediately set off for Rome to lay his story before the pope.

Eighteen days after Daniel thus became abbot, Earl Geoffrey and his army, early in the morning while the monks were still sleeping after having recited matins, broke into the abbey and drove the monks off in the mere clothes in which they had been sleeping. Geoffrey and his men pillaged the monastery, stripped the altars and the reliquaries of the saints, and carried off the vestments and sacred vessels to be sold. Geoffrey then turned the bare shell of the monastery into a castle and quartered his troops there, and the manors belonging to the abbey he distributed as rewards amongst his followers. Ejected from the monastery along with the other monks, Daniel followed Walter to Rome to lay his side of the case before the pope.

Geoffrey had chosen his ground well. Although Stephen came at once with an army when he learned of the earl's rebellion, Geoffrey was far too crafty to meet him in pitched battle. He and his men vanished into the trackless fens when danger threatened, and Stephen was never able to come to grips with them. He built castles in various strategic places and installed garrisons in them in order to contain Geoffrey, and then he 'turned in another direction to deal with other affairs of the realm'.

Hemmed in by the king's castles, Geoffrey and his men plundered the fenlands and turned the district into a desert. It is noteworthy, however, that he received no help from the empress's adherents in the west; his chief allies were his brother-in-law, William of Saye, and Hugh Bigod, who now rebelled for the third time against the king. They plundered the inhabitants, held them to ransom, and subjected them to fiendish tortures 'till they paid the money demanded of them to the last farthing'.[1]

The chronicler at Peterborough, only ten miles from their headquarters at Ramsey, described their doings in the famous last pages of the Anglo-Saxon Chronicle:

Then they took those that they thought had any goods, both by day and by night, men and women alike, and put them in prison and tortured them for their gold and silver with unspeakable torture, for never were martyrs so tortured as they were. They hanged them up by the feet and smoked them with foul smoke. They hanged them up by the thumbs or by the head and hung fires on their feet. They tied knotted cords about their heads and twisted them till they went to the brain. They put them in prisons in which were adders and snakes and toads and slew them thus. Some they put in a *crucethus*—that is, in a chest that was short and narrow and shallow—and put sharp stones therein and pressed the man therein so they broke all his limbs. In many of the castles were 'loath-and-grims'; these were fetters of which two or three men had enough to bear one, so made that they were fastened to a beam and put a sharp iron about a man's throat and his neck so that he could neither sit nor lie nor sleep in any position without bearing all that iron. Many thousands they killed with hunger. I neither can nor may tell all the wounds and all the tortures that they inflicted on wretched men in this land; and that lasted the nineteen winters while Stephen was king, and ever it was worse and worse. They laid imposts on the towns again and called it 'tenserie' [protection-money]. When the wretched men had no more to give, then they robbed and burned all the towns, so that you might journey all a day's journey and never would you find a man dwelling in a town or the land tilled. Then corn was dear, and meat and cheese and butter, for there was none in the land. Wretched men died of hunger. Some went begging alms that were once rich men. Some fled out of the land. Never yet was there more wretchedness in the land, and never heathen men did worse than they did; for against all custom they spared neither church nor churchyard, but took all the good that was therein and then burned the church and all together. Nor did they spare bishop's land nor abbot's nor priest's, but robbed monks and

---

[1] *Chronicon Abbatiae Rameseiensis*, ed. W. Duncan Macray (Rolls Series 83, 1886), pp. 7, 325–9; William Dugdale: *Monasticon Anglicanum*, rev. by John Caley *et al.* (London, 1817–30, 6 vols. in 8), Vol. IV, p. 142; G.S., pp. 109–10.

clerks and every man save the overmighty. If two or three men
came riding to a town, all the township fled before them, thinking
that they were robbers. The bishops and learned men cursed them
ever, but nothing came of it, for they were all accursed and for-
sworn and lost. However men tilled, the earth bore no corn, for
the land was all defiled with such deeds. And they said openly that
Christ slept and all His saints.[1]

This account, written after Stephen's reign was over, certainly
exaggerates in saying that such conditions prevailed throughout
the whole of the reign, and it cannot be applied to England as a
whole. It must nevertheless be taken as an accurate description
of what the writer saw in his immediate surroundings as a result
of the depredations of Geoffrey and his men.

Abbot Walter meanwhile had conducted his appeal with a
despatch that makes one wonder if he were really as simple as
his resignation of his office would make him appear to be. All
in the space of three months, he went to Rome, won the pope's
favour, returned to England, and had his abbey restored to him
by judges delegate, who must have heard his case with extraordinary speed, particularly since the king tried to block the
action. When Walter went to Ramsey to claim his abbey,
however, he found it occupied by Geoffrey's soldiers, who had
turned it into a barracks, pitched their tents round it, and made
the outer gate into a castle. He braved their arrows and swords
and set fire to their tents and the castle, but the soldiers drove him
away with threats. He went next to Geoffrey, their master.
The earl promised often to restore the abbey to him but did
nothing to fulfil his promises, 'finding it easier to delude him
with vain promises than to give back what he had taken'.

The king's forces meanwhile had built a castle at Burwell, nine
miles north-east of Cambridge, which threatened both to cut
Geoffrey's lines of communication and to force him deeper into
the fenlands. If he was to preserve the freedom of movement
that was his chief asset, he had to remove this threat. He therefore laid siege to the castle in August 1144. Whilst he was riding
round the castle and directing operations, a bowman from within
the fortification loosed an arrow that struck the earl in the head.
Geoffrey at first made light of the wound, but he became so ill

[1] *The Peterborough Chronicle*, pp. 55–6.

that he was forced to retire to Mildenhall in Suffolk, eleven miles to the north-east.

The monks of Walden Priory, which Geoffrey had founded in 1136, claimed that as he lay on his deathbed their founder had repented of his sins and attempted as best he could to satisfy both God and man. No priest could give him absolution, however, for a legatine council convoked by Bishop Henry in the spring of 1143 had decreed that anyone who laid violent hands on a cleric could be absolved only by the pope, to whom the suppliant had to go in person. Hearing that Geoffrey was on the point of death, Abbot Walter hurried to Mildenhall, but when he reached there the earl had neither 'voice nor sense'. He had, however, shortly before this dictated a letter directing his eldest son Ernulf to restore the abbey and all its lands to the abbot.

Walter found Ernulf engaged in building a castle at Walton, just outside Peterborough, and Ernulf, albeit 'after many delays, not without difficulty, and unwilling, for he loved that place and its surrounding neighbourhood dearly', ordered the garrison to withdraw and to turn the abbey over to Walter. The abbot regained little more than the bare walls and devastated lands of his monastery. When he at last returned to Ramsey, there was not even so much as a pot left in which to boil a cabbage-stalk. In all the demesne lands he found only one and a half plough-teams; there was no food of any kind; all the land lay unculti-vated. Through the queen's intercession he regained the king's favour; he collected together his scattered monks and restored the monastic life, and he reclaimed his manors. By the end of Stephen's reign he was able to build the great stone tower of the abbey, which, as Professor Knowles points out, indicates how rapidly the monastery could recover from the devastation inflicted upon it.

As Earl Geoffrey lay dying, some Knights Templar came to his bed and clothed him in the cloak of their order, with its red cross, but he died excommunicate, without any of the sacra-ments of the Church. The Templars took his body to London, and since he could not be buried in consecrated ground they wrapped him in a leaden coffin and hung him in the branches of a wild apple tree in their orchard, according to the Walden chronicle, or threw him in a pit outside their cemetery, as the Ramsey chronicler tells it. Twenty years later his second son,

Geoffrey, succeeded in obtaining absolution and Christian burial for his father.[1]

Geoffrey's death marked a great triumph for Stephen, for his fiercest opponent had been removed from the scene, his policy of containment rather than direct assault upon the rebels had proven successful, and his action in depriving even the greatest of his earls of his castles had been vindicated. He had successfully asserted the rights of the Crown over his barons, and 'a kind of darkness and dread filled all the king's enemies'. Geoffrey's son Ernulf was captured and sent into exile. He apparently made no attempt to join the empress's forces; in any case, the fact that he too was excommunicate would hardly make him welcome to the rebels.[2]

The empress meanwhile had lost one of her most faithful supporters, and he too died excommunicate. Miles of Gloucester, whom she had made earl of Hereford, in his pressing need for money to support the large army he maintained, laid heavy exactions on Robert, bishop of Hereford, and all the churches in the area that he controlled. The bishop protested against these levies and at last refused to meet Miles's ever-growing demands. Miles thereupon ordered all the bishop's lands to be ravaged. Robert summoned his clergy together and in their presence pronounced the sentence of excommunication upon Miles and all his helpers and laid the diocese under interdict till Miles should restore all that he had plundered from it.

On Christmas Eve 1143, whilst he was hunting deer, Miles met a death similar to that of William Rufus. A knight in his party shot wildly at a stag and struck Miles instead. The arrow pierced his chest, and he died without any of the sacraments of the Church. He was not only a skilful soldier in the empress's cause; he, almost alone of her followers, seems to have felt a personal affection for her. He, rather than her brother Robert, sheltered her at Gloucester and supported her household; the author of the *Gesta Stephani* says that 'he always behaved to her like a father in deed and counsel'.[3]

Earl Geoffrey's rebellion had set an evil example for the king's

[1] *Chronicon Abbatiae Rameseiensis*, pp. 330–6; Henry of Huntingdon, pp. 276–7; Dugdale: *Monasticon*, Vol. IV, p. 142; Knowles: *The Monastic Order in England*, p. 272; *G. de M.*, pp. 220–6.
[2] *G.S.*, p. 110; Henry of Huntingdon, pp. 277–8.
[3] *G.S.*, pp. 63–4, 104–6.

enemies. Ranulf, earl of Chester, who acted always out of self-interest rather than on the empress's behalf, seized the opportunity to ravage the north. He attacked all the king's barons in that part of the country whenever he saw a chance of taking their castles for himself, and William of Aumale, earl of York, seems to have borne the brunt of his attacks.[1]

In the midst of this confusion, the empress's friends stirred themselves to fresh activity in order to break the stalemate that followed Stephen's defeat at Wilton. William of Dover, with the support of Robert of Gloucester, built a castle at Cricklade and filled it with mercenary knights and bands of archers. From this fortification he could threaten the king's forces both at Oxford to the east and at Malmesbury to the west and ravage the upper valley of the Thames.

Robert of Gloucester followed this up by building three castles close to Malmesbury and succeeded in bottling up the king's forces in Malmesbury Castle. Stephen hurried up with a large army to relieve the garrison. After stocking the castle with large quantities of supplies, he laid waste the land surrounding the earl of Gloucester's three castles and then laid siege to Tetbury, five miles north-west of Malmesbury, which was apparently one of Robert's three castles. He succeeded in breaching the outer walls and then, after what was left of the garrison had taken refuge in the keep, brought up siege engines to batter the keep. Robert, meanwhile, and his ally Roger, who had succeeded his father as earl of Hereford, 'assembled a cruel and savage army of foot-soldiers' from Bristol and the surrounding towns, enlisted as many Welsh mercenaries as they could, and summoned all the knights who owed allegiance to them.

The two earls and their forces pitched their camp close to Tetbury and waited for the remainder of their army to gather. As the vast array of troops came pouring in from the west, the hearts of the king and his barons sank. They realised that they were greatly outnumbered and that their men were 'far from home and exhausted by the fatigue of the journey'. No warrior would willingly face a pitched battle in such circumstances. Stephen followed 'the good advice of his barons' and quickly withdrew to the north. Taking advantage of the fact that the earl of Hereford and his men were at Tetbury, he marched to

[1] G.S., p. 111; John of Hexham, p. 315.

Winchcomb, twenty-five miles to the north, where Earl Roger had built a castle.

Although it was sited on a high mound and surrounded by a strong palisade, the castle was manned by only a small garrison. The author of the *Gesta Stephani* says that part of the garrison had fled when they learned of Stephen's sudden and unexpected arrival, and it is likely that Earl Roger had withdrawn most of them in order to help him at Tetbury. Stephen ordered 'that the most vigorous men should arm themselves and make ready with all speed for the storming of the castle, that some should advance shooting clouds of arrows, others should crawl up the mound, and everyone else should rush rapidly round the fortifications and throw in anything that came to hand'. They captured Winchcomb in short order, and then from that stronghold they penetrated deep into Gloucestershire and built 'a very large number of castles' in a part of the country where the earls of Hereford had had undisputed sway.

Although his ally, Geoffrey de Mandeville, was no longer on the scene, Hugh Bigod took advantage of Stephen's absence in the west to lay siege to some of his castles in East Anglia and 'plunder with all his might'. Hugh, like Geoffrey, was not interested in helping the empress; he was simply seizing the occasion to strike out on his own. Having regained a large part of Gloucestershire, Stephen arrived unexpectedly in East Anglia in the early part of 1145 and caught Hugh by surprise. Stephen scattered the rebel's forces, ravaged his lands, and built three castles 'just where Hugh was most in the habit of raiding'.[1]

Stephen, as we have seen, was firm in holding that the royal castles were not to be regarded as the personal property of the men to whose care they were committed and that these custodies were revocable at the king's will. When he had asserted his rights and deprived Geoffrey de Mandeville of the castles that Geoffrey had tried to hold as his own, he gave the castle of Saffron Walden and the neighbouring district to one Turgis of Avranches, a Norman of humble origin whom he had taken into his favour and enriched with gifts and honours. Turgis, heedless of the fate that had befallen his predecessor, took it into his head to rebel against the king, and when Stephen, in the course of his stay in East Anglia, wished to occupy Saffron Walden, which he

[1] G.S., pp. 115–16; Henry of Huntingdon, p. 278.

had given Turgis, as the author of the *Gesta Stephani* points out,
'to guard rather than to possess', Turgis refused to admit him.

One day Turgis 'left that castle to devote himself to hunting,
and when some of the hounds were straining with keen-scented
nostrils and others pursuing the quarry at headlong speed, and
Turgis himself was joyfully following, sounding his horn,
behold! the king suddenly and unexpectedly arrived with a very
strong body of knights'. Turgis was seized in the midst of his
sport, and Stephen threatened, as he had threatened Geoffrey de
Mandeville, to 'hang him on high right before the castle entrance'
if he did not surrender. 'At last he took thought for his life and
met the king's demand as he wished.'

Whilst the king was thus occupied in East Anglia, William of
Dover, from his stronghold at Cricklade, kept up a continual
harassment of the king's forces both at Oxford and at Malmesbury. At last he succeeded in capturing Walter of Pinkney,
the castellan of Malmesbury, and turned him over to the empress.
After his spectacular success, 'repenting of the woes and sufferings
that he had pitilessly brought on the people', William went on a
pilgrimage to the Holy Land, and 'at last he was killed and died
a blessed death'.

Matilda tried her best both by fair words and by threats of
torture and death to induce Walter of Pinkney to order the
garrison at Malmesbury to surrender the castle to her, but Walter
held out against her. She then had him tightly fettered and cast
into 'a filthy dungeon'. To take William of Dover's place she
installed at Cricklade her nephew Philip, a younger son of Robert
of Gloucester. The author of the *Gesta Stephani* characterises
him as 'a man of strife, supreme in savagery, daring in what should
not be dared, in fact a perfect monster of every kind of
wickedness'.

Philip, in addition to the usual plundering, burning, and
devastating of all the countryside within reach, kept up an unrelenting pressure against the royal garrison at Oxford. When
his efforts began to promise some success, he summoned his
father to help him. Earl Robert collected all the forces at his
command and advanced to Faringdon, about half-way between
Cricklade and Oxford, where he built a castle 'strongly fortified
by a rampart and a stockade' and manned by 'the flower of his
whole army'. From this post he was able to exert such pressur

on Oxford that the king's men were unable to leave their castles.

William of Chamai, to whom Stephen had entrusted Oxford, realised that he was on the point of losing the city. He sent messages to the king, and Stephen hurried to help him. He arrived at Oxford in the summer of 1145 with an army and meanwhile summoned reinforcements. His friends the Londoners sent 'a terrible and numerous army'. When his forces were assembled he led them to Faringdon and set to work reducing Earl Robert's castle. First he had his men build a rampart and stockade behind which they could take shelter if necessary, and then he had siege engines set up all round the castle. A dense ring of archers surrounded the fortification.

When Stephen began his attack on Robert's men, 'on the one hand stones or other missiles launched from the engines were falling and battering them everywhere; on the other a most fearful hail of arrows, flying around before their eyes, was causing them extreme affliction; sometimes javelins flung from a distance or masses of any sort hurled in by hand were tormenting them; sometimes sturdy warriors, gallantly climbing the steep and lofty rampart, met them in most bitter conflict with nothing but the palisade to keep the two sides apart'.

This was not the usual type of siege in which the besieging army relied on the slow course of starvation to bring the enemy to terms, for Henry of Huntingdon tells us that a great deal of blood was shed. Stephen's forces pressed the attack with such ferocity that 'those who were chief in command, without the knowledge of the others, sent secretly to the king and made an agreement conceding his demand for the surrender of the castle'.

The storming and capture of Faringdon was the greatest triumph of Stephen's career, and both the author of the *Gesta Stephani* and Henry of Huntingdon describe it as the turning point in the war. The immediate and most tangible result, from his soldiers' point of view, was the seizure of a large number of knights whose ransoms enriched their captors and of a great store of arms and booty within the castle. Robert of Gloucester had been checked in his advance to the east and driven back to his base at Bristol. That Stephen had at last gained the upper hand over his enemies was most convincingly shown by the actions of Ranulf, earl of Chester, who the author of the *Gesta Stephani* says 'by force of arms had seized on almost a third of the country' and who now came to the king and made a humble submission.

This may have been at the meeting at Stamford mentioned by the Peterborough chronicler, when 'they swore oaths and plighted troth that neither should harm the other'. Even Philip, the earl of Gloucester's son, went over to Stephen's side and fought against his late allies, including his father, with the same ferocity that he had lately exercised on their behalf.[1]

[1] *G.S.*, pp. 116–21; Henry of Huntingdon, p. 278; *The Peterborough Chronicle*, p. 5.

IX

1145–1147

THE submission of the earl of Chester brought a great increase to Stephen's military strength. Sir Frank Stenton has pointed out that 'at the height of his power the earl was by far the greatest lord in England'.[1] In his eagerness to show his loyalty to what he obviously considered the winning side, Ranulf captured Bedford and turned it over to the king.

Having broken the rebels' communications between the Thames valley and their strongholds at Bristol and Gloucester by the capture of Faringdon, Stephen set to work to reduce their outpost at Wallingford, where Brian fitz Count had been holding out against him with little apparent help from the empress. Ranulf, 'with a retinue of three hundred stout-hearted cavalry', accompanied the king to Wallingford, where Stephen built a castle of such strength that he was able to check Brian's raids on the surrounding countryside and effectually cut him off from his allies to the west.

These triumphs so impressed Matilda that she endeavoured to make peace with her rival. She sent her half-brother Reginald, earl of Cornwall, to treat with the king. Her nephew Philip, in his excess of zeal, captured Reginald 'with a mighty array of his knights' as he was on his way to meet the king, but since Stephen had granted Reginald a safe-conduct and a truce had been declared, Philip was forced to let his uncle go free. Soon after this exploit, Philip fell into a long illness, and when he at last recovered he went on a pilgrimage to the Holy Land.

The author of the *Gesta Stephani* says that King Stephen and the Empress Matilda 'met together to establish peace'. Since neither one would make the slightest concession to the other, their meeting had no result, and in view of the inflexibility of Matilda's pretensions it is difficult to see why she should have

[1] Stenton: *The First Century of English Feudalism*, p. 104.

asked for the meeting in the first place. She still claimed to be the rightful heir to England, and Stephen, all the more confident because of his recent successes, quite naturally refused to admit her claim.

In spite of the valuable assistance that Earl Ranulf had given him at Bedford and Wallingford, Stephen and his advisors by no means trusted him whole-heartedly. He had not surrendered any of the castles, including Lincoln, that he had seized by force; he did not turn over to the Exchequer any of the proceeds from the king's manors that he had appropriated, and 'he had in no wise given security, by the offer of hostages or guarantors, against that fickleness and instability of mind which was a characteristic engrained in him by nature'. The author of the *Gesta Stephani* says that the king and his counsellors accepted Ranulf's help for the time being but put no confidence in him, holding their hands till he should either make a full submission, with the restitution of all that he had taken, or else by his refusal to do so afford the king an opportunity to challenge his loyalty and put him under arrest.[1]

The opportunity came when Ranulf arrived at the king's court at Northampton with only a few followers and complained that the Welsh were ravaging and plundering his lands and besieging and burning the towns. He proposed that the king come to his aid by mounting an expedition into Wales for his benefit. Ranulf made it all appear extremely easy. The Welsh, he said, would flee in terror at the mere sound of the king's name; the king's presence would be worth more to him than many thousands of fighters, and he would pay most of the expenses of the expedition, which need not be a long one, for the king could win a glorious victory, almost in passing, as it were.

One does not know whether to marvel more at Ranulf's simple-mindedness in making such a proposal or at Stephen's gullibility in agreeing to it. The author of the *Gesta Stephani* says that Stephen was already 'gladly and gaily' promising to go to Ranulf's aid when all his chief counsellors raised their objections. They might have pointed out that Ranulf, who had devastated the north of England, was only getting a taste of his own medicine from the very allies who had rushed to help him fight the king at Lincoln. His barons reminded the king that it

[1] G.S., pp. 122–4, 126–7.

was foolhardy to lead an expedition into Wales when his presence
was urgently needed to quell discord and disorder in England;
that the difficulties of a campaign in the mountains of Wales,
with its attendant problems of supplying his army, were formidable, and that it was rash in the extreme for him to entrust himself
to a man, recently his enemy, who had seized a large part of his
kingdom and had neither returned any of the lands that he had
appropriated nor given hostages for his fidelity.

They proposed a simple test of Ranulf's loyalty: let him restore
the king's lands that he had taken unjustly and by force and let
him take an oath of fealty and give hostages to make sure that
he would keep it. If he agreed to do this, they said, the king
might then consider his pleas for help; if he refused, let him be seized
and thrown into prison as the traitor he had shown himself to be.

Stephen agreed to this sensible advice, and the barons laid their
proposal before Ranulf. Taken by surprise, the earl replied that
he had not come to court for this purpose, that he had not been
given any notice in advance, and that in any case he would have
to consult with his advisors. Some of the barons openly accused
him of treason, and the court broke into an uproar. Ranulf at
first denied the charge, and when they pressed him to comply
with the king's conditions he attempted to change the subject.

By his refusal to give any solid evidence of his fidelity he had
in effect admitted his treachery. The barons 'suddenly laid
hands on him, delivered him to the king's guards, chained him,
and put him in prison'. Then it became evident why he had
appeared at court with so few followers; he had left most of
them at their posts in the castles throughout his lands, ready to
take action if anything amiss should happen to him. The more
hot-headed of these, when they learned of his capture, flew to
arms, assembled their 'cut-throats', and harassed the king's supporters in the way they had been doing before the earl's
submission.

The more cautious ones, however, decided that it was foolish
for them to fight without their leader, and they and a number
of Ranulf's friends went to the king and bargained for his release.
They promised on his behalf to surrender the castles that Stephen
claimed as his and to provide hostages and securities for the earl's
good behaviour in the future. After taking counsel with his
barons, Stephen agreed to these conditions. Ranulf and his men

surrendered the king's castles, chief amongst which was Lincoln, which Ranulf had held since late in 1140 and which Stephen had tried in vain to take away from him in 1144. They also provided hostages and men willing to stand as securities. Chief amongst these latter was Gilbert fitz Richard, whom Stephen had made earl of Hertford, probably in 1138, and who was the nephew both of Earl Ranulf through his mother, Ranulf's sister, and of Gilbert, earl of Pembroke, his father's brother.

Stephen should have known, from his experience with Geoffrey de Mandeville, what would be the probable result of releasing Ranulf, but on the other hand he and his counsellors had proposed the terms of the bargain; once Ranulf met the terms they had no choice but to set him free, even though they specified that he was 'to enjoy the honours of his own earldom only'. Regarding neither his own oaths nor the safety of those who had stood security for him, Ranulf broke into wild revolt as soon as he was free. He attacked such of the king's castles as were within reach, built new castles from which to plunder and burn, and wherever he passed 'he turned everything into a desert and bare fields', exercising 'the tyranny of a Herod and the savagery of a Nero'.[1]

Stephen attached particular importance to having regained Lincoln, for that city stood in his mind as a symbol both of Earl Ranulf's rebellion and defiance and of his own capture and humiliation. Its strategic importance was of course immense, both as a gateway to the north and as the eastern base of that area of the Midlands that Ranulf had converted into an almost independent principality.[2] The king stationed the flower of his troops there, and at Christmas 1146 he wore his crown in regal splendour at Lincoln, defying an ancient superstition that forbad the king to wear his crown in Lincoln.[3]

[1] G.S., pp. 131-2; Henry of Huntingdon, pp. 277, 279.

[2] Cronne: 'Ranulf de Gernons, Earl of Chester, 1129-1153', pp. 127-8.

[3] Henry of Huntingdon, p. 279. I am not able to account for this superstition, but that it existed is testified to by the writers of the time. In addition to the passage cited in Henry of Huntingdon, William of Newburgh twice refers to it as 'an old superstition' in connexion with Stephen's crown-wearing of 1146 (Vol. I, p. 57) and with Henry II's crown-wearing at Lincoln at Christmas 1157, when he so far deferred to the superstition as to wear his crown, not in the city itself, but in a suburb of the city (Vol. I, pp. 117-18). Roger of Howden repeats the tale, naming the suburb as Wickford (Vol. I, p. 216). Stephen's misfortunes at Lincoln in 1141 could hardly have given rise to an 'ancient superstition' within the short period of six years unless there had been some previous basis for it.

After Stephen left the city, Ranulf attempted to recapture it early in 1147. The citizens hated him with a bitterness that shows how oppressive his rule must have been, and they united with the king's troops to repulse him. The leader of Ranulf's army, 'a most strong and unconquerable man', was killed before the northern gate of the city, and Ranulf was forced to flee with his army.[1]

He turned next to Coventry, the southern base of his principality, which he had also been forced to abandon. When he laid siege to the castle there, Stephen led 'a fine and numerous body of knights' to the relief of the garrison, and in the heavy fighting that ensued the king was wounded. Ranulf was put to flight and almost killed, and after the surrender of the castle the king had it demolished. Stephen then embarked on a vigorous campaign against Ranulf and harried him from one castle to another.[2]

At the very beginning of Ranulf's revolt the king seized Gilbert, earl of Hertford, who had stood security for his uncle, and cast him into prison. Stephen offered him the choice of surrendering all his castles or going into exile and banishment. Gilbert surrendered all his castles and then hastened to join his uncle Ranulf. His other uncle, Gilbert fitz Gilbert, whom Stephen had made earl of Pembroke, demanded that the king turn these castles over to him, since they belonged to him by hereditary right. This claim could be justified only by the supposition that as his nephew had no children[3] he was the earl of Hertford's heir, and it overlooks the fact that Hertford had forfeited the castles to the king. As he always did when claims of hereditary right conflicted with the welfare of the realm, Stephen refused to regard those claims as conferring an absolute right that overrode all other considerations. The king had given the earl the castles, and it was within his right to take them back.

The earl of Pembroke, after his request had been denied, stealthily withdrew from the court with the intention of joining the earl of Chester. Stephen and his army set out in pursuit and caught him up at one of his castles. The king would have captured him if he had not disguised himself and fled with a few companions. The castle surrendered, and Stephen quickly seized

---

[1] Henry of Huntingdon, p. 279; G.S., p. 132.   [2] G.S., pp. 132–3.
[3] It is assumed that he was unmarried. See *The Complete Peerage*, Vol. VI, p. 499.

two other castles belonging to the earl. He then led his army
to Pembroke's fourth castle at Pevensey, on the Sussex coast
twelve miles west of Hastings, a much harder nut to crack. The
author of the Gesta Stephani describes it as 'a castle rising on a very
lofty mound, fortified on every side by a most beautiful wall,
fenced impregnably by the washing waves of the sea, almost
inaccessible owing to the difficulty of the ground'. Deciding
that he could not take it with the ease with which he had seized
the other three, Stephen left 'a loyal and resolute body of troops'
to besiege it till the garrison should submit.[1]

Stephen had acted with great strength and resolution, and as a
result of his energetic campaigns, first against the supporters of
empress, culminating in their defeat at Faringdon, and then
against the rebel earl of Chester and his allies, his enemies were
forced into defensive positions in the two areas left to them, the
party of the empress in the country about Bristol and the Welsh
Marches and the rebel earls into Chester and the western Midlands. It is significant that the two groups did not attempt to
join forces, and the events of the early months of 1147 show
how demoralised and discouraged they had become.

The young Henry had returned to his father after his brief stay
in England. Count Geoffrey meanwhile had made great head-
way in his conquest of Normandy, to which he had given a
pretext of legality by claiming to act on his son's behalf. He captured Rouen on 20 January 1144, although William, earl
Warenne, faithful to King Stephen, refused to surrender the castle
to him. After a long siege, Geoffrey took the castle and thence-
forward assumed the title of duke of Normandy. With the surrender of Arques in 1145, he became master of the whole duchy.[2]

Early in 1147 the young Henry landed in England 'with a fine
company of knights' on an expedition so strange as to be incredible if it were not for the authority of the writer of the Gesta
Stephani, the only chronicler who mentions this singular adven-
ture. The lad was not yet fourteen years old, and he could
hardly have undertaken the expedition without the knowledge of
his father, who, however, apparently did nothing to help him.
The counts of Anjou matured early, and Geoffrey may have
decided simply to let the boy have his own way and learn by
experience; at this low state of his mother's fortunes in England

[1] G.S., pp. 134–5.   [2] Robert of Torigni, pp. 147–50.

Henry could hardly do anything to hurt a cause that seemed irretrievably lost, and the long succession of revolts against the king's authority may have led Geoffrey to think that the rebels would welcome the young pretender as a figure-head about which to rally. On the other hand, there is no indication that Henry or his father had consulted the lad's mother or any of the leaders of her party in England, for once he had landed they did not lift a finger to help him. Henry and his company came 'without forethought or judgment'.[1]

They probably landed at Wareham, since that would be the only port open to them other than Bristol, and wild rumours immediately spread that 'he was at the head of many thousand troops, soon to be very many thousand, and had brought with him a countless quantity of treasure'. Henry marched his company to Cricklade, where the king's garrison quickly put them to flight, and then to an unidentified place called *Burtuna*, where they were driven into a panic.

The clearest indication of the strength of Stephen's hold upon the country is the fact that the young Henry, attempting to challenge the king at a place where either his mother and Earl Robert to the west or the earl of Chester and his associated rebels to the north could easily have sent him help, received no assistance from either group. They idly watched as the foolhardy boy was repulsed at every place he attempted to attack. His companions began to desert him, and then it was learned that instead of the 'countless quantity of treasure', Henry had nothing with which to pay them. Like his great-grandfather the Conqueror, Henry had enlisted his followers with promises of the rich lands he would give them when he should have conquered England.

Henry turned first to his mother, 'but she herself was in need of money and powerless to relieve his great need'. He then appealed to his uncle Robert, which would indicate that Matilda was not living with her brother or at his expense. It may be that Roger, earl of Hereford, inherited from his father, Miles of Gloucester, the burden of supporting the empress. Earl Robert in turn, 'brooding like a miser over his money-bags', refused to help him.

As a last resort the lad, lacking neither ingenuity nor effrontery, sent messengers to beg King Stephen 'in friendly and imploring terms to regard with pity the poverty that weighed upon him and

[1] G.S., p. 136.

harken compassionately to one who was bound to him by close ties of kinship and well-disposed to him as far as it in him lay'. Stephen apparently was touched by the very effrontery of the whole affair, both of the lad's having undertaken the conquest of England in such an off-hand way and of his turning to the man whose crown he was trying to usurp and asking him to pay the expenses of such an expedition. Stephen gladly sent the lad the money he asked for, and Henry returned to Normandy, where he arrived before the end of May 1147.[1]

In the autumn of this year the empress's cause received a blow so severe that it put an end to all her hopes of depriving Stephen of his crown. Her brother Robert died suddenly at Bristol on 31 October 1147, and her party was thus deprived of the one man with the ability and determination to direct operations against the king. He was succeeded by his eldest son William, whom the author of the *Gesta Stephani* characterises as 'a man already advanced in years but effeminate and more devoted to amorous intrigue than to war'.[2]

Although William succeeded in driving Henry of Tracy away from Castle Cary, which Henry was besieging at the time, he made no attempt to follow up this exploit, and he showed no inclination to step into his father's shoes as the leader of his aunt's party. Roger, earl of Hereford, likewise showed little enthusiasm for Matilda, and David, king of Scots, also was not interested in helping her. She was not the sort of person to inspire either loyalty or affection, and her domineering behaviour during the few months of her ascendancy in 1141 had shown her supporters what sort of treatment would be in store for them if she should ever be crowned. After that brief period she was only a figure-head about which the discontented could gather, but they were interested only in their own advancement, not hers. After her brother's death she sank into such insignificance that the author of the *Gesta Stephani* does not even notice her departure from England; it is only a passing reference by Robert of Torigni that enables us to place it sometime in 1148.[3]

[1] G.S., pp. 135–7; A. L. Poole: 'Henry Plantagenet's Early Visits to England', pp. 451–2.

[2] *Annals of Margam* in *Annales Monastici*, ed. H. R. Luard (Rolls Series 36, 5 vols., 1864–9), Vol. I, p. 14; G.S., pp. 139–40.

[3] Robert of Torigni, p. 160. Gervase of Canterbury, writing long afterwards, places her departure before Lent 1147 (Vol. I., p. 133).

X

1147–1148

WITH the death of Earl Robert of Gloucester and the Empress Matilda's departure from England, Stephen at last reached the end of the almost constant warfare that had claimed most of his attention and energies since 1139, and at the same time the decisive defeat of Earl Ranulf of Chester put a check to the revolts of various barons, few of whom were active supporters of the empress, that had aggravated his troubles. He had shown himself to be resourceful, courageous, and daring, and no mere weakling could have brought himself from Stephen's abject position after his defeat at Lincoln in 1141 to the height of power that he had reached by 1147. Defeated and deposed, he had nevertheless fought on with such determination that he had overcome all his enemies, put down the rebellious earls, and asserted his authority in the whole of England, except for the few strongholds about Bristol, Gloucester, and Chester that sheltered the remnants of the rebels. His authority was far from absolute, for the machinery of government had of course been much disrupted by the warfare of these years, but at least the country was at peace, although it was a precarious peace at best, and there was no open challenge to his position in England.

It was at this point that Stephen got himself into trouble with the Church. It may be that finding himself master in his own house at last gave him a new confidence that led him into his difficulties; on the other hand, the situation of the Church in England and the attitude of various popes had changed so greatly in the last few years that trouble was almost inevitable between a king who insisted on exercising the same supervision over the Church in his realm that his predecessors had always done and a body of churchmen who subscribed with growing conviction to the new ideals of the freedom of the Church from lay interference. The situation had changed, also, in that the anomalous position of the archbishop of Canterbury, subject for a time to a humiliating subservience to one of his own suffragans as papal legate, had been improved by the termination of Bishop Henry's legatine authority, whilst at the same time the archbishop, who seemed at first to be almost lost in his new position, found himself, as it were, rose to the responsibilities of his great office, and began to exercise his authority in a way he could not have done, or at any rate was too timid to do, when he first became archbishop.

Stephen's conflict with the three bishops in 1139 had not been a conflict with the authority of the Church itself, for he had dealt with them as rebellious keepers of castles, not as bishops, and although churchmen criticised him for his harsh treatment of them, their conduct, on the other hand, has been so little in keeping with the sacred character of their office that their best friends would have found it difficult to defend them.

The conduct of the bishops in 1141, when his brother, the archbishop of Canterbury, and most of the bishops had declared him deposed, certainly could not have deepened Stephen's respect or admiration for them. Far from helping him, they had united to deprive him of his crown. Stephen, then, had little reason to feel either gratitude to his bishops or respect for them. Pope Innocent II had helped him when he became king, but a new pope now showed himself hostile to Stephen, and Stephen countered that hostility by insisting on the customs and rights that previous kings of England had exercised in respect of the English Church.

William I and his successors had demanded a voice in the election of bishops, since they were among their chief counsellors, enjoyed large fiefs as tenants-in-chief, and exercised great authority in the land. The kings had disapproved of appeals to Rome, maintaining that the English hierarchy, with the assistance of the king and his counsellors, were capable of deciding all questions that came before them, and they forbad English clerics to leave the realm without their permission, which in practice meant that bishops had to obtain the king's leave in order to attend general councils of the Church or to go to consult the pope.[1] In their efforts to maintain the control over the Church in England that they considered an essential part of their rights and dignities, they had all fallen foul of the Church, and it was over

[1] Z. N. Brooke: *The English Church and the Papacy*, pp. 136–8.

these same principles that Stephen found himself in trouble.

The occasion for his first open conflict with the Church over a matter of principle, as distinguished from his troubles with various unruly bishops over purely secular matters, was the complicated case of William, archbishop of York. It will be recalled that Stephen's nephew had been elected archbishop of York, in spite of vigorous protests from the Cistercians and the reforming party in the north, and that the king, shortly before the Battle of Lincoln early in 1141, had given William possession of the temporalities of his see. Later in that troubled year, when the archbishop-elect and his opponents appeared before the papal legate, Bishop Henry of Winchester had sent them to the pope. It is not clear why he did this, for he was never lacking in confidence in his own abilities and in his authority as legate. One may suggest two reasons for his action: in the first place, since William was his nephew, he would be laying himself open to charges of nepotism if he decided in his favour, and in the second place the Cistercians opposing William not only enjoyed a great deal of respect in the north; they had also reported the matter to the redoubtable Bernard, abbot of Clairvaux, and enlisted his help in the matter. Henry was so occupied with the violent political changes of this year that he perhaps welcomed the opportunity to wash his hands of the affair by referring the contestants to Rome and thus avoid a decision that would either involve him in a bitter quarrel with some of the most powerful churchmen of the north or else force him to humiliate his nephew and quarrel with his brother.

After an adjournment in 1142, Pope Innocent II on 7 March 1143 referred the matter back to Henry with instructions that if the dean of York, William of Ste-Barbe, who had not been amongst those present at Rome, would swear that William of Aumale, earl of York, had not delivered an order from the king to the chapter to elect William and if, furthermore, William himself would swear that he had not purchased his election, he might be consecrated. This was a clever move on the pope's part to avoid the necessity for making a decision, and it illustrates how appeals to Rome, which were increasing greatly in number at this time, could introduce almost endless delay and confusion into the affairs of the Church. Now that canon law was being codified and studied with great care, it was natural that appeals should be made to the supreme law-giver of the Church for guidance in disputed or uncertain points of law. All too often, however, points of fact, which could best be settled in the place where they arose, rather than points of law, formed the substance of these appeals, as they did in this case. No doubtful point of law was involved; the question was simply whether or not the king had forced his choice on the chapter of York, thus violating their right of free election, and whether or not William had obtained his election by simony.

When Henry heard the case at Winchester in September 1143, none of William's enemies appeared in order to oppose him, and William of Ste-Barbe, whom Henry had meanwhile consecrated bishop of Durham and whose testimony was vital to the case, sent word that he was unable to come because of troubles in his diocese. Bernard of Clairvaux wrote later that William of Ste-Barbe had not only refused to take the prescribed oath but was ready to swear to the contrary. The archbishop-elect, however, produced a second document from Rome that Professor Knowles believes 'was either forged or (as would seem more likely) issued informally and dishonestly, and not by Innocent himself', authorising the judge to act on the testimony of witnesses other than the dean if the latter was not present at the hearing. Ralph Nowell, bishop of Orkney, a suffragan of York, and Severin and Benedict, abbots respectively of St. Mary's, York, and Whitby, supported the archbishop-elect in his oath; no one opposed him; the people of York wanted him, and the king and his brother favoured him. The legate therefore consecrated him on 26 September and 'many people rejoiced at his promotion'.[1]

The death of Innocent II on 24 September changed the ecclesiastical situation in England, for with his death Henry's appointment as legate came to an end. Both Henry and Archbishop Theobald set out for Rome before Christmas, the first to try to have his legation renewed and the second both to prevent a renewal of a situation in which he was subordinated to his suffragan and to attempt to secure the office for himself. Unfortunately for Henry, the new pope, Celestine II, favoured the Angevins and was seeking some means by which to harm

[1] John of Hexham, pp. 311, 313, 315; G. Hüffer: *Der heilige Bernard von Clairvaux*. Vol. I, *Vorstudien* (Münster, 1886), p. 234; Knowles: 'The Case of St. William of York', p. 86.

Stephen and his friends.   Learning of the pope's frame of mind, Henry spent the winter with his friends at Cluny. Celestine died on 8 March 1144 and was succeeded by Lucius II, whose views were the opposite of his predecessor's.   Henry then went on to Rome and was received with great favour, but he did not succeed in inducing the pope to name him legate.   Neither, however, did Archbishop Theobald secure the office for himself, and William of Newburgh suggests maliciously that each one's bribes cancelled out the other's.[1]

The fact that neither of them won the appointment, however, meant that the victory was Theobald's in the end, for as archbishop of Canterbury he could claim the bishop of Winchester's obedience.   Henry, fertile in expedients, conceived a plan that would lift him above the merely temporary station of legate, with his powers dying with each pope, and place him beyond the reach of the archbishop of Canterbury.   He proposed that the pope raise Winchester to the dignity of an archbishopric, a plan that, as Dr. Saltman points out, was 'by no means absurd', since the province of Canterbury, with seventeen suffragan dioceses, was unusually large for Western Europe.   The author of the *Annals of Winchester* says that Henry proposed that Winchester should be made an archbishopric, that Hyde Abbey be made a bishopric, and that Chichester should be taken from Canterbury and added to the new province.   Ralph of Diceto says that seven dioceses were to be assigned to Winchester.[2]

Exactly what happened to this proposal, beyond that it eventually came to naught, is not known.   Ralph of Diceto says that 'Pope Lucius sent a pallium to Henry, bishop of Winchester, to whom he proposed to assign seven bishops'.   Dr. Saltman conjectures that the news of Pope Lucius's death reached England before the legate, Cardinal Imar, bishop of Tusculum, could confer the pallium, and one must accept this in the absence of a better explanation, although the legate, who probably arrived in England just about the time the pope died, on 15 February 1145, would have had ample time in which to attend to this piece of business before the news of the pope's death would have reached

[1] Henry of Huntingdon, p. 277; John of Hexham, pp. 315–16; William of Newburgh, Vol. I, pp. 43–4.

[2] Avrom Saltman: *Theobald, Archbishop of Canterbury* (London, 1956), p. 21; *Annals of Winchester*, in *Annales Monastici*, ed. H. R. Luard (Rolls Series 36, 5 vols., 1864–9), Vol. II, p. 53; Ralph of Diceto, Vol. I, p. 255.

him and terminated his powers. In any case, Lucius's successor, Eugenius III, would have cancelled such an arrangement immediately.

Henry seems also to have explained to the pope his decision in the matter of the archbishop of York and to have requested or to have conveyed William's request that the pallium be given to him, which would set the seal of the pope's approval on William's consecration and confer on him the jurisdiction, as distinct from the sacramental powers conferred by his consecration, of arch-bishop of York, for Lucius sent Cardinal Imar to England with the pallium for William. Unfortunately for William, the cardinal, as he passed through France on his way to England, met Bernard of Clairvaux, who had been denouncing William's election to succeeding popes in letter after letter of venomous vituperation, and Bernard made him promise not to give the pallium to William unless the original instructions of Innocent II were obeyed to the letter and William of Ste-Barbe took the required oath, no matter what the present pope may have decided.[1]

When Imar arrived in England with, one assumes, two palliums, one for Henry and one for William, the latter, John of Hexham says, 'delayed to go to meet him through negligence, occupied, as was his custom, with other less important matters'. This hardly seems credible, and Professor Knowles suggests that William knew that William of Ste-Barbe would not take the oath. If this was the case, William was wise in evading the issue and thus avoiding a formal refusal by the bishop of Durham, which would of course be placed on record against him. The opposition to William amongst the Cistercians of the north was now led by Henry Murdac, whom Bernard had made abbot of Fountains and who of course followed his master's directions in the matter. They all appealed to the new pope, and Eugenius ordered Cardinal Imar to return to Rome with the pallium that had been intended for William.[2]

Belying John of Hexham's imputation of sluggishness and indifference, William himself now went to Rome to ask for the

[1] Bernard of Clairvaux: Epistola CCCLX, in J. P. Migne: *Patrologia Latina*, Vol. CLXXXII, columns 561–2.
[2] John of Hexham, pp. 317–18; Knowles, 'The Case of St. William of York', p. 88.

pallium, since without it he could exercise no jurisdiction in the archdiocese of York. The new pope, Eugenius III, who had been elected on the very day on which his predecessor had died, had been a Cistercian monk and a disciple and friend of Bernard of Clairvaux. Bernard's influence with him was boundless, so that even Bernard wrote to him: 'People say that it is now I who am pope'.[1] Bernard's letters to succeeding popes on the subject of William of York do not make pleasant reading; there is something unbalanced in the extravagance of language with which he denounces the unfortunate William and his supporter, Bishop Henry, whom Bernard, with something less than Christian charity, calls 'that old whore of Winchester'.[2]

Although a majority of the cardinals favoured William, Bernard's influence carried the day. Eugenius took his stand on Pope Innocent's original letter to Henry, setting up the commission of enquiry, and suspended William from the episcopal office till such time as William of Ste-Barbe should take the required oath. Since the bishop of Durham had evaded taking the oath at various times in the past, this suspension effectively put an end to William's hopes of being recognised as archbishop of York, and he took refuge with his kinsman Roger, king of Sicily.[3]

When the news of this latest defeat reached William's friends in Yorkshire, the enraged knights, regarding Henry Murdac 'as the author of his downfall', visited their wrath on Fountains Abbey. They invaded the monastery, carried away its few possessions, and set fire to the buildings, although they failed to find Henry, who was prostrate in prayer at the foot of the altar.[4]

These outrages were duly reported to the pope and furnished Bernard and his party with fresh reasons for calling for the strictest measures against William. Early in 1147 Pope Eugenius deposed him from the archbishopric of York on the ground that 'Stephen, king of England, before his canonical election, nominated him'. There can be no doubt that his deposition was due

---

[1] Bernard of Clairvaux: Epistola CCXXXIX, in Migne, Vol. CLXXXII, column 431.
[2] *Seductor ille vetus Wintoniensis*, in a letter to Lucius II, quoted by G. Hüffer, op. cit., Vol. I, p. 236. See Knowles: *The Monastic Order in England*, p. 290.
[3] John of Hexham, p. 318; A. L. Poole: 'The Appointment and Deprivation of St. William, Archbishop of York', pp. 279–80.
[4] *Memorials of the Abbey of St. Mary of Fountains*, Vol. I, ed. John Richard Walbran, Publications of the Surtees Society, Vol. XLII (Durham, 1863), pp. 101–2.

to the continued and unrelenting campaign that Bernard carried on against him, for throughout this dreary affair a majority of the cardinals had supported William, and he had the enthusiastic backing of the people of Yorkshire. It was, furthermore, an established practice in the Church in England for the king to nominate bishops to the more important sees, and Archbishop Theobald himself owed his position to just such a nomination.

Bishop Henry loyally gave refuge to his deposed kinsman, received him and his household as his guests, and supported them out of his great liberality. William in all humility stayed with the monks of St. Swithun's as much as his uncle would permit, eating with them and sleeping in their dormitory. John of Hexham says that in all the long-drawn-out affair of his humiliation and deposition, William never murmured or complained, never spoke evil of his persecutors, and turned his mind and hearing away from his detractors. He turned his thoughts to study and to prayer and became a wholly new man.[1]

To fill the vacancy thus created, the pope ordered William of Ste-Barbe and the chapter of York to elect 'a learned, discreet, and religious man' as archbishop within forty days of the receipt of his letter. The bishop of Durham was afraid to come to York because of the enmity of William of Aumale, earl of York, whom he had excommunicated in the course of a quarrel over the bishop's manor of Howden, and the election was consequently held at Richmond on 24 July. Again dissension sprang up. Robert of Gant, the king's chancellor and dean of York, and Hugh of Le Puiset, treasurer of York and the king's nephew, two men whom William had appointed to their ecclesiastical offices during the brief period when he had any say in affairs, and their party chose Master Hilary. This was a clever move, for Hilary had first distinguished himself in the service of the bishop of Winchester and had then served the papal court as a lawyer and gained a great reputation for himself. Those who nominated him might thus assume that their choice would be pleasing to the powerful bishop of Winchester and thus to the king, and to the pope as well.

The opposition, consisting of William of Ste-Barbe and Æthelwulf, bishop of Carlisle, both suffragans of York; William

[1] Gervase of Canterbury, Vol. I, p. 134; *Annals of Winchester*, p. 54; John of Hexham, p. 320.

of Eu, cantor of York, and the archdeacons, voted for a man who would be even more pleasing to the pope, though certainly much less so the king: Henry Murdac, abbot of Fountains.

Since the two parties could not agree, the matter was referred to the pope, and he of course came down on the side of his fellow Cistercian, at the same time consoling Hilary by naming him bishop of Chichester. Archbishop Theobald consecrated Hilary at Canterbury on 3 August 1147, and the pope himself consecrated Henry Murdac at Trèves on 7 December.[1]

In the earlier stages of the affair of the archbishop of York, the king had been involved in such difficulties that he had had no time to spare for intervening in the matter. By the time Henry Murdac returned to York, however, the king had overcome his enemies, peace had been restored, and Stephen was ready to assert that control over the affairs of the Church that his predecessors had exercised. He had two causes for complaint: that William had been deposed and that Henry Murdac had been elected and consecrated without either his knowledge or his consent. He regarded Henry's consecration in these circumstances both as a grave act of discourtesy on the pope's part and as an infringement of his own rights. He had good precedent for doing so; only two years before this, Eugenius had consecrated Peter as archbishop of Bourges without consulting the king of France, and Louix VII had been so infuriated that he had sworn that Peter should never enter Bourges as long as he, the king, lived.

Henry Murdac had all the high Gregorian ideals of the Cistercians and other reformers concerning the complete independence of the Church from the state, as the reforming party saw it, although to others it appeared that they asserted not only the independence of the Church but also its superiority to the secular power and the duty of temporal rulers to defer to their wishes even in secular matters. William of Newburgh says that Henry Murdac asserted his independence, upon his return to England, by refusing to swear fealty to the king.[2]

Stephen at any rate refused to recognise him as archbishop of York, confiscated all the temporalities of the see, and diverted the income from them to his own treasury. He was not alone in repudiating Henry, who seems to have been as unpopular in

---

[1] John of Hexham, pp. 320–1; Gervase of Canterbury, Vol. I, p. 132.
[2] Ralph of Diceto, Vol. I, p. 256; William of Newburgh, Vol. I, p. 56.

Yorkshire as William, whom he had supplanted, was popular. The citizens of York refused to allow him to enter the city, and if any of the clergy went to visit him they were beaten upon their return, deprived of their goods, and cast out of the city. Henry also angered Archbishop Theobald by refusing to defer to him and by reviving the claim that his see was of equal dignity to that of Canterbury. Henry took refuge in Ripon and launched a series of excommunications upon Hugh of Le Puiset, treasurer of York and apparently the leader of the opposition to him, all the citizens of York who sided against him, and William of Aumale and all his supporters. He also laid York under an interdict.

The stout-hearted Hugh would not allow the sentence to be observed. He ordered that all services be continued in York as usual, and in turn he declared Henry and all his followers to be excommunicated. The archbishop's two suffragans, however, William of Ste-Barbe and Æthelwulf, who had both voted for him, received him with all due reverence.[1]

In his measures to regain the control over the Church that his predecessors had enjoyed and that he now felt strong enough to claim as his right, Stephen next attempted to prevent Archbishop Theobald from obeying the pope's summons to a general council. He had made no attempt to interfere with Theobald's attending the Second Lateran Council in 1139, both because his hands were full with other matters of more importance to him and because he did not feel sufficiently secure in his position to precipitate a quarrel with the pope.

Early in 1148, however, when Eugenius III summoned the English bishops and particularly the archbishop of Canterbury to a council to meet at Rheims on 21 March, Stephen refused to give them permission to attend. Gervase of Canterbury says that Stephen did this at the prompting of his brother Henry, who saw an opportunity to damage Theobald's standing with either the king or the pope. If he disobeyed the king and attended the council, he would bring the king's wrath down upon his head and risk being proscribed; on the other hand, if he disobeyed the pope and failed to attend, Eugenius might suspend him or even depose him, which would open up vast new possibilities for the ambitious bishop of Winchester. Whilst this may

[1] John of Salisbury: *Historia Pontificalis*, p. 5; John of Hexham, p. 322.

be partially true, Dr. Saltman has pointed out that Stephen's main purpose was to assert his control over the English Church by restricting its contacts with the papacy.[1]

After forbidding the archbishop to leave England, Stephen named three bishops, Robert of Hereford, William of Norwich, and Hilary of Chichester, to represent the English hierarchy at Rheims and to present the apologies of the remainder for their absence. John of Salisbury says that 'the intention of the king and queen and their council as well as of certain bishops was merely to deceive and injure the archbishop of Canterbury', which would indicate that the king was displeased with the increasing control over the Church that Theobald was exercising, now that he had found himself and was beginning to realise the extent of his powers.

To make sure that his commands were obeyed, Stephen went to Canterbury and had the archbishop closely watched. He also had the ports guarded so that Theobald could not leave the country. The archbishop, however, had already, with the king's permission, sent some of his clerks to Rheims, ostensibly to convey his apologies to the pope, and he had hired a fishing smack and had it hidden in a remote cove 'far from the haunts of men'. Accompanied by one of his clerks, Thomas Becket, Theobald eluded the king's guards, reached the coast, and set sail in the smack, a vessel so small that it would carry no more than a dozen men and so unseaworthy that John of Salisbury says that 'he crossed the Channel rather as a survivor from a shipwreck than in a ship', and the pope declared, when the archbishop presented himself before him, that he had swum rather than sailed across the Channel.[2]

The pope received Theobald with the greatest favour and kindness because of his courage in defying the king and his loyalty in obeying the pope's summons. The business enacted at the council, according to John of Salisbury's report, was so trivial that it hardly seemed worth all the stir it occasioned in England, and one suspects that Eugenius's motive in convening it was more to assert his authority than to settle any momentous

[1] Gervase of Canterbury, Vol. I, p. 134; Saltman: *Theobald, Archbishop of Canterbury*, p. 25.

[2] John of Salisbury: *Historia Pontificalis*, pp. 7–8; Gervase of Canterbury, Vol. I, p. 132; *Materials for the History of Thomas Becket*, ed. J. C. Robertson (7 vols., Rolls Series 67, 1875–85), Vols. III, p. 356, and VI, p. 58.

place the kingdom under interdict and warn Stephen that the pope would excommunicate him at Michaelmas.[1]

While these negotiations were proceeding, Theobald took a further step to alienate himself from the king. Robert of Béthune, bishop of Hereford, died during the Council of Rheims, which Stephen had permitted him to attend. John of Salisbury says that 'by the advice and at the desire of the archbishop of Canterbury', Gilbert Foliot, abbot of Gloucester, was elected to succeed him. Hereford was of course in the Angevin sphere of influence, and John says that Gilbert was acceptable to the young Henry, 'who then controlled the election to this see'. The details of the election are not clear, and Professor Knowles has suggested that the pope directly appointed Gilbert without the formality of an election; at any rate it is evident not only that Stephen was not consulted but also that an adherent of the empress and her son was being made an English bishop.

John of Salisbury says that the young Henry 'was unwilling to confirm the election or grant the regalia until the bishop-elect had sworn on the gospels to do fealty to him within a month of consecration, and not to do fealty to King Stephen, whom the whole English Church followed by papal decree', and that later on, when Gilbert did do fealty to the king, Henry reproached him with having broken an oath that he had sworn to in public and on the gospels. Messrs Morey and Brooke, however, think it probable that Gilbert did not swear such an oath.[2]

All this makes it look as though Theobald was going out of his way to defy the king. When, at Theobald's request, the pope ordered three English bishops, Robert of London, Jocelin of Salisbury, and Hilary of Chichester, to go to Flanders and assist Theobald in the consecration of the bishop chosen under such unfortunate auspices, they refused to do so. It was contrary to the customs of the kingdom for an English bishop to be consecrated outside the realm, they declared, and they made their loyalty to Stephen quite clear by pointing out that Gilbert had

---

[1] Gervase of Canterbury, Vol. I, p. 135; John of Salisbury: *Historia Pontificalis*, pp. 44-5.

[2] John of Salisbury: *Historia Pontificalis*, pp. 47-9; Adrian Morey and C. N. L. Brooke: *Gilbert Foliot and His Letters* (Cambridge, 1965), pp. 96-7; David Knowles: *The Episcopal Colleagues of Archbishop Thomas Becket* (Cambridge, 1951), pp. 43-4.

not received the royal assent or done fealty to the king. The bishops' action indicates that Stephen certainly had control over the Church in England at this time, since the bishops' loyalty to him overrode their obedience to both the pope and the archbishop of Canterbury. Theobald nevertheless persisted in his intention, in spite of this warning, and on 5 September 1148 he consecrated Gilbert at St. Omer, with Nicholas, bishop of Cambrai, and Miles, bishop of Térouanne, assisting.

Stephen, quite naturally, showed no signs of being willing to forgive the archbishop and restore his possessions as the pope had ordered, and the English bishops, far from admonishing him as Eugenius had directed, sided with him. Since the bishops clearly had no intention of obeying the pope and laying the kingdom under interdict, Theobald himself proclaimed the sentence, to take effect on 12 September. The interdict was an almost complete failure. No one paid the slightest attention to it except in the diocese of Canterbury, and even in the city itself the monks of St. Augustine's continued to celebrate Mass.

The situation had now reached a stalemate. The archbishop had used all his powers short of excommunicating Stephen, and the king had not budged. Gervase of Canterbury implies that the queen and William of Ypres, Stephen's closest friend, were working on Theobald's behalf, and John of Salisbury says that the archbishop, in what followed, acted 'on the advice of able men', including Hugh Bigod of Norfolk. At any rate, he returned to England without having received any of the promises of restoration and reformation from the king that he had been demanding. He did not dare, however, to land in Kent, which was under Stephen's immediate control; he went instead to Suffolk, where Hugh Bigod was supreme.

Hugh met him with the greatest reverence and honour and conducted him to Framlingham. Theobald took up residence in the castle and from there he 'carried out all the duties of his office'. Emissaries were no doubt going between him and the king all this time in an effort to bring the anomalous situation to an end. At last Bishops Robert of London, Hilary of Chichester, and William of Norwich and a number of prominent laymen came to Framlingham and succeeded in making peace between the king and the archbishop. Theobald lifted the interdict, and Stephen for his part offered compensation for the seizure of

David assembled 'an immense multitude' of Scots, and Ranulf and his adherents joined forces with them. Their first objective was the city of York; if they could succeed in capturing it, they could control the north of England. The citizens, however, had sent word to Stephen of the threatening preparations that David and his allies had been making, and the king quickly assembled a large body of knights and hurried to York. From thence he went to meet the Scots, and his army kept growing from day to day 'as robust warriors poured in from every part of England'. David of course had not forgotten the drubbing he had received at the Battle of the Standard, and when he and his army perceived that they were greatly outnumbered they quietly disbanded, and each man individually crept back to his home.

Henry and his companion Roger were in mortal terror of being captured by Stephen's men, and they fled along little-used byroads till at last, 'worn out with fear and fatigue', they reached Hereford. Stephen meanwhile had sent word of Henry's escape to his son Eustace, whom he had left in charge of affairs in the south and who was then near London. Eustace, who also had been made a knight in this same year, hastened to Gloucester with a body of knights in order to intercept Henry on his way to Bristol. Learning that Henry was spending the night in Dursley Castle, near Stroud, Eustace arrived there before daybreak and laid ambushes for him in three places. Henry, however, had been warned of Eustace's approach, and he fled from the castle in the middle of the night and reached Bristol safely. Eustace set out in pursuit, but he dared not attack Bristol with his small force. He inflicted as much damage as he could on the country-side and then took up his headquarters at Oxford. From there he mounted raids against the rebels in Gloucestershire, harried the garrisons at Marlborough and Devizes, and penetrated as far south as Salisbury.[1]

Whilst his son was thus occupied in the south, the king was forced to remain in the north through the month of August, for he feared that if he left York King David, who had retired, discouraged but undefeated, to Carlisle, would reassemble his army and attack the city. At this point we learn something of Stephen's financial dealings. One of the major mysteries of his reign is how he contrived to raise the money to pay his

[1] G.S., pp. 143–4; Henry of Huntingdon, p. 282.

mercenaries. He seems to have maintained a large standing army,
to judge by the speed and efficiency with which he met his
opponents, and he certainly could not have done this if he had
relied on the cumbersome machinery of the feudal army with its
limited terms of service. To maintain a standing army of
mercenaries, however, requires large sums of money, and
although parts of England were removed from the effective
control of the king and hence contributed nothing to his treasury,
Stephen seems never to have been at a loss for money. The
revenues from his private estates, as well as from the royal
demesne, would no doubt have been large, but certainly not
large enough to pay the expenses of his many military campaigns.[1]

John of Hexham tells us something of how Stephen contrived
to raise money at this time. His loyal supporters, the citizens of
York, complained to him that a group of rebels had built a castle
at Wheldrake, seven miles south-east of the city, and were block-
ing the road into York from that quarter. He agreed to demolish
the castle, but he suggested to the citizens that they should pay the
costs of the operation. Thus he succeeded in raising a large sum
of money from them. Next, at the suggestion of his friends at
York, he went to Beverley, where Henry Murdac had taken
refuge after the townspeople of York had refused to receive him,
and laid a heavy fine on the people of Beverley for having
sheltered the archbishop without his permission. Finally, when
he returned to York, he demanded money from his nobles
according to their rank and holdings. This was probably an
arbitrary exaction of the sort that would euphemistically be
called a 'gift' later in the century. There is no suggestion that it
bore any relation to the recognised feudal dues or that it was
levied in lieu of military service. Stephen probably advanced
the argument that he was protecting them from the ravages of the
Scots and that they should be willing to pay for that protection.[2]

Stephen's measures both to repel the Scots and to replenish his
treasury were highly successful, for the author of the *Gesta
Stephani* says that he went back to London 'enriched by many
gifts and with immense glory'. Now that he had put the young

---

[1] For a discussion of the finances of Stephen's reign, see J. O. Prestwich: 'War
and Finance in the Anglo-Norman State', *Transactions of the Royal Historical
Society*, 5th Series, Vol. IV (1954), pp. 19-45.

[2] John of Hexham, pp. 323-4.

Henry to ignominious flight and had forced King David and Earl Ranulf to retire from the field, he took counsel with his advisers as to how he could best follow up his successes. Reluctantly, for he was well aware of the misery that such a course would inflict on the helpless and innocent inhabitants of the regions concerned, he determined 'to attack his enemies everywhere, plunder and destroy everything they had, set fire to the crops and whatever else could sustain human life, and let nothing remain anywhere, so that, held in check by these measures and reduced to the very extremity of want, they might at last be forced to yield and surrender.' By turning the country they occupied into a desert, Stephen hoped literally to starve the rebels into submission. It was a brutal policy, for the first to suffer from it would be the peasants, while the castles would be well stocked with provisions to meet a siege.

Gathering his army and accompanied by Eustace and his troops, Stephen went to Wiltshire and started to put his policy into effect at Salisbury. They laid waste the country, burning houses and churches and the crops stacked in the fields, and then moved north to Marlborough and Devizes. If Stephen had been able to finish what he had started, he might well have succeeded, although at a fearful cost, in forcing his opponents to surrender. As always happened, however, when he put intense pressure on his enemies in one section, their friends in another part of the country seized the opportunity to create such a disturbance that he was forced to divide his forces and thus weaken his attack. Earl Ranulf of Chester, forgetting the speed with which the king manœuvred his army, took advantage of Stephen's preoccupations elsewhere and made a foray into Lincolnshire. He ravaged a large part of the county and mounted an assault on Lincoln, still the object of his strongest ambition. The citizens hated him as much as the men of Yorkshire hated the Scots, and they withstood his assaults on their city manfully whilst sending messengers to the king to beg for help.

Stephen hastened to Lincolnshire, for just as Ranulf had made the capture of Lincoln his chief objective in life, the king was equally determined that he should not have it, and not even the prosecution of his well-planned campaign against the young Henry and his allies could outweigh in his mind the necessity for defending Lincoln against Ranulf. He was not able, however, to inflict a decisive defeat on the earl, for the fighting seems to have been sporadic, and Ranulf preferred raids and ambushes to pitched battles. At last the king built a castle 'in the most suitable spot' (we are not told where) and thus was able to hold Ranulf in check.

At about the same time, Eustace was forced to move part of his army to East Anglia in order to cope with Hugh Bigod. The young Henry took advantage of his opponents' absence to mount an attack on the king's adherents in the south-west. Assisted by his cousin, William, earl of Gloucester, and Roger, earl of Hereford, he captured Bridport and inflicted great damage on the lands of Henry of Tracy, Stephen's chief supporter in that region. Henry of Tracy, however, wisely manned his numerous castles and refused to be drawn into a battle, so that the rebels, who apparently were not prepared to undertake siege operations, could only devastate the countryside and then retire. Their retreat was hastened by the news that Eustace, who had learned from his father the importance of moving his army quickly, had appeared before Devizes and was planning either to set out in pursuit of Henry or to capture the castle, Henry's base of operations. By the time Henry and his allies reached Devizes, Eustace had already taken and burned the town and driven the garrison into the castle. After a furious battle, Henry succeeded in driving Eustace off, and another stalemate occurred.[1]

Although Henry had been assisted during this year by the greatest and most powerful of his supporters, the king of Scots and the earls of Gloucester and Hereford, and although the earl of Chester and Hugh Bigod had made their characteristic contribution of creating powerful diversions in the rear, the young pretender with all this help had accomplished nothing beyond forcing Stephen to reduce the lands of Henry's supporters to a desert. The only prospect before him if he remained in England was an indefinite continuation of sieges and occasional raids that would result only in further devastation and misery. Seeing no hope for him in such a continuation, his advisors eased him out of the country as tactfully as possible by suggesting that he go back to Normandy and enlist the aid of both the Normans and his father, Count Geoffrey. Since Geoffrey had never given his son the slightest encouragement in his previous expeditions to England and the Normans had shown a similar indifference to his

[1] G.S., pp. 144-8.

grandiose designs, Henry's English friends and relations probably hoped that the troublesome lad would leave them to that state of armed truce with the king from which he had so disastrously disturbed them.   The earls of Gloucester and Hereford were supreme in their respective parts of the country and had been little troubled by the king, whilst the earl of Chester and Hugh Bigod were interested only in advancing their own interest, not Henry's.   The young man therefore returned to Normandy in 1150, probably in January.[1]

With the departure of the young Henry, an uneasy peace was restored.   Stephen and his son did not press the advantage they had gained over their opponents, probably because everyone was so sick of war that Stephen could not count on the support of his barons if he were to attempt to disturb the tacit truce that prevailed between the two sides.[2]

Stephen now embarked on a complicated scheme to ensure the succession to his son Eustace and thus bar Henry from the throne. He knew that if he merely designated Eustace as his successor and had his barons swear fealty to him as such, his own death would only open the question of the succession all over again and possibly afford an opportunity to the young Henry to secure the crown, as he himself had done, by a legitimate election and consecration. If, however, he could have Eustace crowned immediately, he could confront his opponents with an accomplished fact.   In order to gain his end, he decided to bypass the archbishop of Canterbury, who, he felt sure, in his heart favoured the Angevin cause, and appeal directly to the pope. If the pope approved the plan and himself crowned Eustace, Stephen reasoned, the young Henry would not have a leg to stand on.

This was an audacious scheme, for Stephen well knew that the pope was no friend of his and could hardly be expected to further his designs.   The king, however, had an ace up his sleeve in the person of the archbishop of York.   It will be remembered that he had refused to recognise Henry Murdac as archbishop or to give him possession of his estates and had supported the citizens of York when they drove him out of the city.   If Stephen now laid

---

[1] G.S., p. 148; Robert of Torigni, p. 161; Gervase of Canterbury, Vol. I, p. 142; Z. N. Brooke and C. N. L. Brooke: 'Henry II, Duke of Normandy and Aquitaine', *English Historical Review*, LXI (January 1946), p. 84.

[2] For the probable attitude of the magnates at this time, see Davis, p. 111.

aside his enmity against the archbishop, restored his estates, and received him into his favour, he hoped that the pope would be so impressed by this gesture to his cherished friend Henry Murdac that he would return the favour and grant Stephen's request. One is tempted to see in this scheme the hand of the bishop of Winchester, particularly since if it were successful it would entail the humiliation of the archbishop of Canterbury, whose privilege it was to crown the king, by having the pope take the matter out of his hands. Bishop Henry had had such poor success on his recent visit to Rome that he could not be used as a messenger to the pope, but Henry Murdac, as a fellow Cistercian and a friend of Pope Eugenius, might be considered an ideal ambassador.

Eustace accordingly went to Yorkshire late in 1150 and had an interview with Archbishop Henry, in the course of which he explained the bargain to him and gained his consent. Eustace thereupon laid aside all enmity against the archbishop. As a part of the bargain, no doubt, Henry Murdac released Hugh of Le Puiset, treasurer of York and the king's nephew, from the excommunication he had laid upon him for his part in barring the archbishop from his cathedral.

With the bargain concluded, Stephen received Murdac into his favour, gave him possession of the estates of his see, and ordered the clergy and people of York to receive him as their archbishop. Henry took possession of his see on 25 January 1151 and shortly thereafter set out for Rome. He spent Easter with Eugenius, but he was unable to obtain the pope's approval of the scheme. It will be remembered that Innocent II had recognised Stephen as king of England shortly after Stephen's coronation, and that recognition had tied the hands of Innocent's successors, no matter how much they may have favoured the Angevin cause. When the matter was raised again, Celestine II had written to the archbishop of Canterbury and forbidden 'that any innovation should be made in the realm of England concerning the crown'. Eugenius now used that prohibition, which had originally been made in order to confirm Stephen's position, to quash Stephen's plans for his son, for the coronation of the king's successor while the king was still alive would certainly be considered an innovation in England, though not in France.[1]

Stephen probably and quite rightly attributed his failure to the

[1] John of Hexham, pp. 325-6; John of Salisbury: *Historia Pontificalis*, pp. 85-8.

low esteem in which Eugenius held him, and it may have occurred
to him that he had made a mistake in recognising Henry Murdac
before he sent him to the pope instead of holding his recognition
as a bargaining point to be conceded if the pope granted his
request. Once Henry had been recognised Stephen had no
way of applying pressure on the pope. He therefore turned
to clerics nearer at hand on whom he could apply pressure.
Early in 1152 he summoned a meeting of his council in London,
at which were present the archbishop of Canterbury and the
bishops and great men of England, and demanded that the archbishop and his colleagues anoint and crown Eustace as king.
Henry of Huntingdon says that the pope had written to Archbishop Theobald and forbidden him to crown the king's son
because 'Stephen appeared to have seized the realm contrary to
his oath'. Gervase of Canterbury repeats this, adding that the
letter had been obtained 'through the very clever foresight and
instigation of a certain clerk, Thomas of London' (later known as
Thomas Becket). This would imply that after Henry Murdac's
visit the pope, foreseeing Stephen's next move, had forestalled
him by forbidding the archbishop of Canterbury to do what the
pope himself had refused to do.

Theobald and his colleagues refused to comply with the king's
orders, even though Stephen's anger was so vehement that they
feared for their very lives. Stephen confiscated their property
and had them all locked up in an effort to force their surrender.
Theobald contrived to escape, fled to Dover, and crossed over
to Flanders. When Stephen's anger cooled, however, he realised
that he had put himself in an untenable position. Theobald was
allowed to return, and Stephen made restitution to him and the
other bishops for the properties he had confiscated.[1]

It seems evident that Stephen's relations with the pope had
been on an unfriendly basis ever since the incidents of 1148,
when he had clashed with the archbishop of Canterbury over his
attending the council at Rheims. In that same year Stephen and
his brother had been sorely disappointed in their efforts to make
one of their nephews bishop of Lincoln. Bishop Alexander had
died in February 1148, and Stephen and Henry immediately proposed three candidates for the vacant post: Henry of Sulli, abbot

[1] Henry of Huntingdon, pp. 283-4; Gervase of Canterbury, Vol. I, pp. 150-1;
Saltman: *Theobald, Archbishop of Canterbury*, pp. 37-8.

of Fécamp, a son of their eldest brother William, the same Henry
who, it will be remembered, had been proposed as archbishop of
York in 1140 and rejected by Innocent II; Hugh, abbot of St.
Benet's Hulme, an illegitimate son of their brother Theobald,
count of Blois, and finally Gervase, abbot of Westminster, an
illegitimate son of King Stephen. This was a poor time for both
King Stephen and Bishop Henry to ask for any favours from the
pope, for the one was in disgrace for his persecution of the archbishop of Canterbury and the other was suspended from his
office. The pope, not unnaturally, rejected all three names 'with
great indignation and severity', and the chapter at Lincoln, freed
from royal interference, chose one of their own number, Robert
of Chesney, archdeacon of Leicester and Gilbert Foliot's uncle.
It has already been mentioned that the pope had made Gilbert
bishop of Hereford without any reference to the king. Furthermore, in addition to refusing Bishop Henry's request that he
be made legate, Eugenius gave the position to Archbishop
Theobald in 1150, thus putting an effective end to Henry's
pretensions.[1]

Failing in his efforts to influence episcopal elections, Stephen
did the next best thing, from his point of view, and in two
instances exacted large sums of money as the price of his assent to
elections. He had, to be sure, promised to safeguard the freedom
of the Church in his coronation charter, but nothing had been
said about not exacting a price for that freedom. It may well be
that Stephen was at this time in such pressing need of money
that he undertook this course of action in order to replenish his
treasury rather than primarily to oppress the Church. Whatever his motive may have been, his actions laid both him and the
clerics concerned open to the charge of simony, as John of
Salisbury points out.

In 1151 Stephen forced the monks of St. Augustine's at Canterbury to pay him £500 for the privilege of electing their prior,
Silvester, as abbot. In the preceding year, Robert 'of the Seal',
whom the Empress Matilda in the short period of her ascendancy
had appointed bishop of London, had died, from having eaten
poisoned grapes, according to John of Hexham. When the
pope, in January 1152, ordered the chapter of St. Paul's to elect a
bishop and put an end to the vacancy of a year and a half, they

[1] *The Letters and Charters of Gilbert Foliot*, pp. 109-10; Saltman, op. cit., pp. 30-1.

wanted to elect one of their number, Richard of Belmeis, whom
his uncle of the same name, bishop of London from 1108 to
1127, had appointed archdeacon of Middlesex whilst he was still
a child.   Stephen did not approve of their choice, although we
are not told on what grounds or who his own nominee was, but
at last he exacted the sum of £500 as the price of his consent.
After his election was thus assured, the burden of paying the
money fell on the bishop's shoulders, and Bishop Stubbs says
that 'the debt thus incurred hampered him all his life'.[1]

During this time there was little military activity, primarily
because both sides were exhausted and had had their fill of
fighting.   Stephen, however, mounted a campaign against
Worcester in 1150, according to Henry of Huntingdon.   It will
be remembered that the king had given the city to Waleran,
count of Meulan, and made him earl of Worcester.   Waleran,
however, had gone over to the Angevin side in order to protect
his estates in Normandy, where the greater part of his holdings
lay, when Count Geoffrey consolidated his conquest of the
duchy.   Stephen now captured the city and burned it, but he
was unable to seize the castle.   After plundering the surrounding
countryside, he withdrew his forces.

He returned to the attack in the following year, and this time
he built two 'castles' or fortified positions facing the castle.   He
then left some of his nobles, chief amongst whom was Robert,
earl of Leicester, in charge of operations and went back to his
own affairs, because, Henry of Huntingdon explains, 'it was the
king's habit to begin many things strenuously but to follow
through slothfully'.   Earl Robert was one of Stephen's most
faithful supporters, but on the other hand Waleran was the earl's
twin brother.   Once the king had left, Robert allowed the garrison to destroy the king's counter-fortifications, and thus the
siege came to nothing.[2]

The author of the *Gesta Stephani* tells a different story, and it is
impossible to determine whether his account is a continuation of
Henry of Huntingdon's or a different version of the same events.
According to this account, after the young Henry had left the

---

[1] John of Salisbury: *Historia Pontificalis*, pp. 90–1; John of Hexham, p. 324;
William Stubbs, Introduction to Ralph of Diceto, Vol. I, p. xxv; *The Letters
and Charters of Gilbert Foliot*, p. 137.
[2] Henry of Huntingdon, pp. 282–3.

country Stephen 'bore himself manfully and victoriously throughout England', building castles to contain his enemies and destroying their castles, fighting battles and raiding far and wide, making
pacts of peace and friendship, and, 'holding the upper hand everywhere, he did everything in the kingdom as he pleased', which
would indicate that with Henry's withdrawal the resistance to
Stephen had pretty well collapsed.

Secure, as he thought, in possession of the kingdom, Stephen
turned his attention to Wallingford, which had been a thorn in
his flesh ever since the first outbreak of the revolt and which he
had never succeeded in subduing. Brian fitz Count was dead
by now,[1] and Roger, earl of Hereford, seems to have been the
leader of the rebel garrison. With the help of his ever-loyal
supporters, the citizens of London, and of 'barons who flocked
in to help him from every part of England', Stephen built two
elaborate fortifications and gained possession of the bridge across
the Thames, thus investing the castle tightly. Earl Roger and
some of the garrison sallied forth, and Stephen's army, after
killing some of them and capturing others, forced them to
retreat.

Seeing that they had no hope of breaking the siege, Roger sent
word to the king that he wanted to make 'a pact of inviolable
peace and friendship with him and to fight steadfastly and whole-
heartedly with him against his enemies', on condition, however,
that the king would help him capture Worcester Castle, which
Count Waleran's knights had taken from William of Beauchamp,
Earl Roger's friend, and where they were keeping William
prisoner. R. H. C. Davis advances the conjecture that the two
rivals, both of whom claimed Worcester, had arrived at a com-
promise whereby Waleran held the city and William the castle,
but that when Stephen had burned the city in 1150 Waleran's
men had seized the castle and held William prisoner.

With the approval of most of his advisers, Stephen accepted
Roger's proposal. Having the upper hand in England and with
his rival in Normandy making no move to help his supporters in
their dire straits, Stephen might naturally look for defections in
their ranks, and Earl Roger had apparently been so thoroughly
defeated that his surrender at this point might well be expected.

[1] He died at some unknown date between 1147 and September 1151. See
Davis, p. 117.

Leaving a strong besieging party at Wallingford, Stephen led a large army to Worcester and with Earl Roger's help closely besieged the castle.

Roger meanwhile sent messengers to the young Henry in Normandy, and Henry's uncle, Reginald, earl of Cornwall, may have led the delegation, for Robert of Torigni records that he came to Normandy during the Lent of 1152 to urge his nephew to return to England. They told him of their desperate condition and besought him, 'if he had any regard for his supporters or any care for recovering the kingdom, to return to England as soon as possible and help them in their extreme distress'.

Stephen heard of this treachery, but he did not want to make an open break with Roger till he had more definite evidence. He therefore withdrew from Worcester, but he left part of his army behind to help the earl. Roger, as soon as the king was gone, made a bargain with the besieged, gained control of the castle, and resumed his revolt.[1]

Although his adherents in England may have felt that he had abandoned both them and his aspirations to the throne, Henry was kept so busy in Normandy that he could not come to their aid. After he returned in 1150, his father turned over the duchy to him as his inheritance through his mother, although Geoffrey might well have pointed out that Henry owed it rather to his father's valour than to his mother's vigilance. King Louis VII meanwhile had returned from the Second Crusade in August 1149, and Stephen's son Eustace seems to have gone to him soon after Henry's arrival in Normandy and stirred him up against Geoffrey and his son. Eustace, it will be remembered, had married Louis's sister Constance, and it was probably he who pointed out to Louis the dangerous encroachments of the Angevins, for the French king was a placid and most unwarlike man who would otherwise have seen nothing alarming in the Angevin conquest of Normandy.

Louis and Eustace then besieged the castle at Arques-la-Bataille a few miles south-west of Dieppe. Arques had been one of the last Norman strongholds to fall to Count Geoffrey; it had held out till 1145, a year after the rest of Normandy had fallen, and the two may well have considered it the best place at which to begin operations. The young Henry arrived on the scene with

[1] G.S., pp. 150–2; Davis, pp. 113–14; Robert of Torigni, p. 164.

N

an army of Normans, Angevins, and Bretons, but the leaders of his army, 'who were more mature than he, both in wisdom and in age', would not permit him to make war against the king of France without more direct provocation. They were aware of the fact that Louis was the feudal overlord of Normandy, although neither Geoffrey nor his son had yet done homage for it, and they did not want to jeopardise Henry's position as prospective duke of Normandy by a direct attack on his overlord. One must assume, although the chronicler does not say so, that Henry withdrew and left Louis and Eustace in possession of the castle. Count Geoffrey now entered the fray by seizing a castle belonging to the king's brother, Robert, count of Perche. Louis and Robert retaliated by staging a raid across the southern frontier of Normandy and burned Séez.

In August 1151 the French king assembled his army along the Seine between Meulan and Mantes for a full-scale invasion of Normandy, and Geoffrey and Henry lined up their forces to protect the threatened border. Just when war was imminent, Louis fell ill of a fever, and through the intervention of 'wise and religious men' a truce was arranged till the king should recover. When the truce expired, Louis apparently realised the impossibility of wresting Normandy from the Angevins. Peace was declared, and Geoffrey and his son went to Paris, where Louis accepted Henry's homage for Normandy and recognised him as duke.

With Normandy thus assured to him, Duke Henry issued a summons to his Norman nobles to meet him at Lisieux on 14 September to discuss his return to England. Before the council could assemble, Count Geoffrey died on 7 September, bequeathing Anjou to his eldest son. Henry, now count of Anjou as well as duke of Normandy, apparently spent the remainder of the year in taking possession of Anjou.[1]

During Lent 1152, as has already been mentioned, Earl Reginald of Cornwall came to Normandy to urge his nephew to return to England, and Henry assembled his council at Lisieux shortly after Easter, 6 April, to lay his plans. King Louis and his queen, Eleanor, who was duchess of Aquitaine in her own right, meanwhile had secured a declaration from a council of French bishops on 18 March that their marriage was null and void because they

---

[1] Robert Torigni, pp. 149–50, 160–3.

were related within the forbidden degrees of kinship, although
Pope Eugenius, when they had visited him on their way back
from the Holy Land in 1149, had confirmed their marriage and
forbidden that their consanguinity should be mentioned or that
their marriage should be dissolved under any pretext whatever.[1]

As soon as she had gained her freedom, Eleanor offered herself
to Henry, who was eleven years her junior, and he accepted her
and her great duchy of Aquitaine with alacrity. They were
married about 18 May, to the great chagrin of King Louis, who
had intended that Aquitaine should go to the two daughters
whom Eleanor had borne him. After his hasty marriage Henry
continued with his plans to return to England. Near midsummer he assembled his army at Barfleur and was ready to sail when
he learned that Louis had formed a redoubtable coalition against
him, made up of Eustace; Louis's brother Robert, count of Perche;
Henry, who on Theobald's death earlier in the year had succeeded his father as count of Blois, and Geoffrey, Duke Henry's
brother. Their avowed object was to wrest Normandy, Anjou,
and Aquitaine away from him and divide these territories amongst
themselves.

The first four of the allies began operations by capturing Neufmarché, on the Norman frontier east of Rouen, whilst the fifth,
Geoffrey, stirred up trouble in Anjou. In August Louis and his
army crossed the Seine at Meulan and headed for Pacy, midway
between Évreux and Mantes. Henry contrived to cut him off,
and Louis withdrew to Mantes. Louis prosecuted the war, if it
could be called such, so half-heartedly that Henry felt safe in
entrusting the defence of Normandy to the Normans themselves,
and towards the end of August he went to Anjou to subdue his
brother Geoffrey. Louis confined himself to a few raids across
the border and at last agreed upon a truce. Henry then turned
once more to his projected invasion of England.[2]

---

[1] Robert of Torigni, p. 164; John of Salisbury: *Historia Pontificalis*, p. 62.
[2] Robert of Torigni, pp. 165–6, 169–71.

XII

1153-1154

DUKE Henry landed in England either on the feast of the
Epiphany, 6 January 1153, or within the week following
the feast. He brought with him 140 knights and 3,000
foot-soldiers in 36 ships, and it is interesting to note that whereas
Henry of Huntingdon and William of Newburgh considered
this only a small force, the author of the *Gesta Stephani* says that
he landed with 'an immense army'. He probably landed either
at Wareham, the only port open to him on the south coast, or,
which is unlikely in view of the season, at Bristol, the permanent
headquarters of the Angevin faction.[1]

After his English supporters had joined him, Henry marched
without delay to Malmesbury, Stephen's chief fortress in that
area. The townspeople manned the walls, but Henry's foot-
soldiers, protected by a hail of arrows, succeeded in scaling the
walls. They sacked the town, and when the defenders took
refuge in the monastery they broke into the sacred precincts,
slaughtered priests, monks, and townspeople indiscriminately,
and plundered the very altar itself. The conduct of these
mercenary soldiers that Henry had brought with him was so
barbarous that his English friends, realising the revulsion that
such atrocious conduct would arouse in the country, advised him
to dismiss them, for his ultimate success would depend upon his
being able to win over the English to his side. After operations
were completed at Malmesbury Henry sent them back to the
Continent, but they were shipwrecked in the Channel, and 500 of
them drowned.[2]

Although he had taken the town with little trouble Henry had

[1] Gervase of Canterbury, Vol. I, p. 151; Robert of Torigni, p. 171; Henry of
Huntingdon, p. 285; William of Newburgh, Vol. I, p. 88; G.S., pp. xxvi, 152;
Davis, p. 118.
[2] G.S., pp. 152-3.

not been able to seize the castle.   The garrison, closely besieged, sent word of their plight to the king.   Accompanied by his son Eustace, who had returned to England on Henry's heels, Stephen assembled 'a countless army of his supporters' and went to the relief of Malmesbury Castle.   The royal forces encamped on the north bank of the Avon, since they came by way of Cirencester,[1] and Henry drew up his army to face them across the river.   A pitched battle, the one thing that the strategists of the time tried their best to avoid because it was so wasteful of life and limb, seemed imminent.

Stephen declined the battle and withdrew.   Henry of Huntingdon says that the river was so swollen by rain and snow that neither army could cross it and that on the day the battle should have been fought such a torrent of icy rain and freezing wind blew into the faces of Stephen's army that it was impossible for them to fight.   Once he declined to do battle, Stephen was forced to withdraw because of the bitter winter and because the country-side, already suffering from a severe famine, had been so plundered by Henry's mercenaries that he could not provision his army.   The real reason was probably the one given by the author of the *Gesta Stephani*: Stephen was aware 'that some of his leading barons were slack and very casual in their service and had already secretly sent envoys and made a treaty of peace with the duke'.[2]

The only open defection of any importance at this time, however, was that of Robert, earl of Leicester, who went over to the duke's side and turned over to him thirty or more castles, in addition to supplying him with provisions for some time.[3] It was not out-and-out treachery that Stephen feared at this time but rather an attitude of disinterested neutrality on the part of his barons.   They recognised him as their king, to be sure, but they were no more willing to risk their lives in defence of his crown than they were to help Henry gain the crown.   They had had some fifteen years of intermittent civil war by now, with no profit except to those robbers amongst them who had taken advantage of the disorder to prey on their weaker neighbours, and they were weary of it.

[1] Gervase of Canterbury, Vol. I, p. 152.
[2] Henry of Huntingdon, p. 286; G.S., p. 154.
[3] Gervase of Canterbury, Vol. I, pp. 152–3.

Stephen was probably forced to withdraw by the advice of his barons, who dissuaded him from risking everything, as he had done at Lincoln, on the outcome of a pitched battle under adverse conditions. He exacted only one condition of his opponent: that Malmesbury Castle be demolished so that Henry could not use it as a stronghold from which to dominate the area about it. The man whom Stephen sent to slight the castle, a certain Jordan, expelled the loyal garrison, however, and turned it over intact to Henry while Stephen was withdrawing to London.[1]

Henry lost one of his most powerful supporters during this spring. His great-uncle David, king of Scots, died on 24 May and was succeeded by his grandson, Malcolm IV, who was only eleven years old. Henry could expect no help from him.

His next important acquisition was also gained by treachery. Gundreda, countess of Warwick, while her husband was in attendance on the king, turned out the loyal garrison and surrendered Warwick Castle to Henry's men. Earl Roger died of grief and shame when he learned of his wife's treachery. Since Henry had no part in this affair, being engaged in another part of England when it took place, one may perhaps ascribe it to the influence of Robert, earl of Leicester. Gundreda was Robert's half-sister; her mother, Isabel, had married first the earl of Leicester, to whom she had borne the twins who later became the count of Meulan and the earl of Leicester, and then William of Warenne, earl of Surrey and Gundreda's father.[2]

Henry's next important military operation, at any rate, was undertaken on the earl of Leicester's advice. Collecting 'an immense army' from all his adherents, which would indicate that after taking Malmesbury he had not endeavoured to keep a large force under arms, he went to Tutbury in Staffordshire, the head of the earl of Derby's honour. Robert of Ferrers, one of the commanders at the Battle of the Standard, had, it will be remembered, been made earl of Derby by King Stephen in gratitude for the part he had played. He had died shortly thereafter. His son, also named Robert, now put up a stout resistance to Henry's attack, but after a long siege he at last capitulated, and he and all his followers went over to Henry's side. The young

[1] G.S., p. 154; Henry of Huntingdon, p. 287.
[2] Robert of Torigni, p. 172; G.S., p. 155.

duke next appeared before Bedford and sacked and burned the town, but apparently he did not capture the castle, in which the king's supporters had taken refuge.

Henry had now been in England for over six months, and he appears to have been acting without any logical plan of operations. At last he went to the relief of the garrison at Wallingford. Collecting all his followers, he first launched an attack, which was briskly repulsed, and then laid siege to the castle that Stephen had built at Crowmarsh, from which the royal forces were besieging Wallingford. Stephen immediately sent a force of 300 knights to Oxford, from which base they harassed Henry's army, to contain the rebels whilst he was raising his forces. He then came to Wallingford, accompanied by Eustace 'and many earls and barons beyond number', at the head of 'an inexpressibly large army of knights and foot-soldiers from every part of England'.

The two armies again faced each other, this time on opposite banks of the Thames, and Henry of Huntingdon notes that although Henry's was the smaller it was lined up against the king in splendid fashion. Gervase of Canterbury adds the detail, of great significance to the medieval mind, that while Stephen, with his earls and barons, was forming his lines, he was thrown from his horse three times in succession. Again, as at Malmesbury, a pitched battle was imminent, and again the leading men refused to fight. Gervase of Canterbury puts a speech into the mouth of William of Aubigny, earl of Sussex and the husband of King Henry's widow, that no doubt expressed the feelings of all of them. He pointed out that kinsman was pitted against kinsman and even brother against brother, and he proposed that to avoid 'the abominable madness of civil war' a truce be arranged. The author of the *Gesta Stephani* says that the leading men on both sides shrank from a conflict that would mean the desolation of the whole kingdom and arranged for a truce. Henry of Huntingdon, taking a more cynical view of the matter, says that the nobles of both sides, who loved nothing more than discord, did not want either contender to win a decisive victory that would place him in effective control of the realm and hence of the nobles. All accounts make it clear that both Stephen and Henry were eager for a battle, that the leading men on both sides forced them to agree to a truce, and that the two contenders complained bitterly of the treachery of their followers.[1]

The king and the duke had a private interview, although it could not have been very private if, as Henry of Huntingdon states, it was conducted from opposite banks of the Thames. The negotiations, however, were taken out of their hands. Robert of Torigni gives the most complete account of the terms agreed upon. A fortnight's truce was declared; both sieges were lifted, and Stephen agreed to raze the castle he had built at Crowmarsh. The eighty knights who remained in that castle were to be released; Henry's forces had already captured an additional twenty in one of the outworks, and these presumably would have to arrange for their own ransoms. Robert adds as an afterthought that Henry had captured sixty bowmen, and these men he had had beheaded. The terms were decidedly favourable to the young duke, and Wallingford remained in his followers' hands.[2]

The truce, however, settled nothing; it merely averted a battle and left the issue over which it was to have been fought still undecided. The truce was arranged in order to afford an opportunity for the more responsible men on each side to conduct negotiations that would lead to a lasting peace. Eustace knew well that any such negotiations could serve only to prejudice his right to the throne, and he was furious with his father for having so tamely laid down his arms and avoided fighting the battle through to its proper conclusion, as Eustace saw it. He could be sure of the throne only if Henry were decisively defeated and driven from England. In his rage and disgust he left his father's court and went into Cambridgeshire, ravaging the countryside on every hand.

He brought his marauding army to Bury St. Edmunds, the site of one of the greatest monasteries in England, about 10 August. The monks received him with great honour and gave him a splendid dinner, but when they refused to give him the money he demanded with which to pay his soldiers he devastated their lands and destroyed their crops.

Stephen, meanwhile, had also gone into Suffolk. Hugh Bigod, a persistent rebel against the king's authority, had taken

[1] G.S., pp. 155, 157; Henry of Huntingdon, p. 287; Gervase of Canterbury, Vol. I, pp. 153–4.

[2] Henry of Huntingdon, p. 288; Robert of Torigni, pp. 173–4.

advantage of the situation to seize the castle at Ipswich. While his father was engaged in laying siege to the castle, Eustace joined him. On 17 August 1153, a week after he had ravaged St. Edmund's lands, Eustace suddenly died. The author of the *Gesta Stephani* says that he died of grief and disappointment when he realised that his father's consenting to treat with Henry would inevitably mean his own disinheritance as his father's successor. Gervase of Canterbury ascribes his death to the vengeance of St. Edmund. When Eustace was sitting at table, says Gervase, he was struck by a miserable madness as he took the first bite of food and underwent the dire pains of death because of the insults he had offered the martyr. On the same day that Eustace died, Henry's first legitimate son, William, was born.[1]

Eustace was buried beside his mother, who had died on 3 May 1152,[2] in the abbey at Faversham that she and her husband had founded. Stephen's reign was remarkable for the great number of religious houses founded; in those twenty years the number increased by a half, rising from about 193 at the beginning of the reign to about 307 at the end. Stephen deserves none of the credit for this extraordinary increase in religious fervour, unless one holds that he deliberately created the unsettled conditions of his reign in order to drive men to seek refuge in monasteries. Almost all the increase was amongst the new orders, particularly the Cistercians and Augustinians.[3] Considering his treatment at the hands of Bernard of Clairvaux and Pope Eugenius, Stephen had little reason to feel any fondness for the Cistercians, and his foundation, as one might expect, was of the Cluniac order, a conservative, wealthy, and highly respected branch of the black monks, or Benedictines as we call them now, of which his brother the bishop had been a member.

While Stephen was engaged in East Anglia, Henry laid siege to Stamford. Although the garrison sent messengers to the king to beg for help, Stephen apparently could not spare any troops. The garrison at last surrendered to Henry. He planned to go next to the relief of Ipswich, but when he learned that Stephen had gained possession of the castle he turned in the opposite

<hr />

[1] Gervase of Canterbury, Vol. I, p. 155; William of Newburgh, Vol. I, p. 89; Robert of Torigni, p. 176; *Regesta*, p. 127.
[2] Gervase of Canterbury, Vol. I, p. 151.
[3] Knowles: *The Monastic Order in England*, pp. 297–8.

direction and went to Nottingham, probably at the instigation of
Earl Ranulf of Chester. Ranulf was with Henry at the siege of
Stamford on 31 August, and the earl, 'whose hand was against
every man, and every man's hand was against him', now
attempted, as was his custom, to use Henry to further his own
ends.[1]

Soon after his landing, Henry, in order to hold Ranulf to his
side, had granted him, amongst many other lands and honours,
'the whole fee of William Peverel, wherever it may be'.
Peverel's fee was centred on Nottingham, and the custody of
Nottingham Castle had been in his family since it was built in
1068. He had played a leading part at the Battle of the Standard
and was taken prisoner with Stephen at the Battle of Lincoln.
The Empress Matilda had then granted Nottingham to one of
her followers, William Paynel, but Peverel had recovered it in
the following year and had held it ever since. He was a baron
of considerable importance, and his daughter was married to
Robert of Ferrers, earl of Derby.[2]

Since the earl of Chester was the most important man on his
side, as well as by far the most grasping and self-seeking, Henry
led his army to Nottingham to secure it for his fickle adherent.
William Peverel and his men, however, were resolute fighters,
and when Henry succeeded in taking the town the garrison of
the castle set fire to it. The duke, 'moved to pity and grieving
over the burning of the town', as Henry of Huntingdon,
perhaps with his tongue in his cheek, puts it, took his army
elsewhere.[3]

This was the last military engagement recorded during the
year. Henry did not have a great deal to show for his campaigns. He had gained Malmesbury, Warwick, Tutbury, and
Stamford; Bedford and Nottingham had been sacked and
burned; he had won over to his side the earls of Leicester and
Derby, and he had relieved the pressure on Wallingford. Stephen,
however, was far from defeated. He still held London, the
greatest source of men and treasure, and all the other cities and

[1] C. W. Foster: *The Registrum Antiquissimum of the Cathedral Church of Lincoln*
(Publications of the Lincoln Record Society, Vol. XXVII, Lincoln, 1931), Vol. I,
p. 97; G.S., p. 156.

[2] *Regesta*, p. 66; Orderic, Vol. II, p. 184; Henry of Huntingdon, p. 264; John
of Hexham, Vol. II, pp. 308–9, 312.

[3] Henry of Huntingdon, p. 288; William of Newburgh, Vol. I, pp. 89–90.

towns of importance except Bristol; he still commanded the allegiance, such as it was, of most of the English barons, as was shown by the large number who obeyed his summons and joined his army at Wallingford, and he was still able to subdue such powerful rebels as Hugh Bigod.

There was no question whatever of Stephen's losing his crown; it was the problem of the succession to the crown that was now causing all the difficulty. The timely death of Eustace, as William of Newburgh points out,[1] removed the chief obstacle to a peaceful settlement, for as long as he was living he would have defended his right to the throne, and, given his determination and Duke Henry's, the civil war and the consequent disorders would have been wellnigh unending. Stephen's younger son, William, on the other hand, had never had any expectation of being king, and his brother's death left him handsomely provided for. In addition to giving William all the lands and honours that he himself had held before he became king, Stephen had also arranged for his marriage to Isabel, the daughter and heiress of William of Warenne, earl of Surrey, who had died in 1148. With such an inheritance, William would easily be the second richest man in England, next only to the king.[2]

With such an ample provision having been made for William, those who were working for a lasting peace felt that they might fairly pass him over and try to persuade Stephen to designate Henry as his successor and Henry to accept such a settlement. The chief negotiator was Archbishop Theobald, who was at last coming to his full stature as the leader of the Church in England and the most respected man in the realm. His principal helper in these negotiations was his old rival, Bishop Henry of Winchester, who was beginning to realise the unseemliness of his past conduct, regret his partisanship, and acquire the statesmanship and wisdom that were henceforth to mark his conduct and to make him one of the most respected figures in the English episcopate.

Theobald stayed at the king's side, frequently urging him to arrive at a peaceful settlement, and sent delegates, of whom Bishop Henry may well have been the chief, to the young duke to

---

[1] William of Newburgh, Vol. I, p. 90.
[2] Round: *Studies in Peerage and Family History*, pp. 167–71.

try to bring him to the same frame of mind.[1] Their task could not have been an easy one, for, as it has been pointed out, Henry's successes in England had been only moderate at best, Stephen was undefeated and still in control of the larger part of the kingdom, and, to judge from the importance that was given in the final treaty to all the provisions made for William, the king's son was driving a hard bargain before he would renounce the prospect of succeeding his father.   The negotiators, however, had a dreadful threat to hold over the heads of both sides: the prospect of renewed and never-ending civil war, with Henry and William, if he succeeded in having himself crowned, carrying on the struggle that had been devastating the kingdom for so long.   The archbishop of Canterbury had a powerful voice in the negotiations, for he alone could crown the king, and he probably used this argument for all it was worth in forcing the two parties to come to terms.

At last Stephen and Henry met at Winchester on 6 November 1153 and agreed to a final settlement.   Robert of Torigni says:

First, the king, in the assembly of bishops and earls and other great men, recognised the hereditary right that Duke Henry had in the kingdom of England.   And the duke graciously conceded that the king should hold the realm all his life, if he wanted to, on the condition, however, that in the present circumstances the king himself and the bishops and the other great men should declare on oath that after the king's death the duke, if he should survive him, should have the kingdom peacefully and without opposition.   It was also sworn that the possessions that had been snatched away by usurpers should be restored to the ancient and lawful possessors to whom they had belonged in the time of the excellent King Henry and that the castles that had been built since the death of that king should be destroyed; their number had swollen to a total of 1115.[2]

This seems to have been only a verbal agreement, although made particularly binding by the oaths of the witnesses to the reconciliation, preliminary to the embodiment of the terms in a formal charter.   Stephen and Henry went to London together before Christmas, and it seems likely that the interval was spent in hammering out the exact terms.[3]   The document embodying

[1] Henry of Huntingdon, p. 289.   [2] Robert of Torigni, p. 177.
[3] Henry of Huntingdon, p. 289; Gervase of Canterbury, Vol. I, p. 156.

them was probably promulgated at Stephen's Christmas court, when many of his earls and barons would be present as witnesses.

Stephen, king of England, to the archbishops, bishops, abbots, earls, justiciars, sheriffs, barons, and all his faithful men of England: greetings. Be it known that I, Stephen, king of England, have appointed Henry, duke of Normandy, my successor to the kingdom of England after me and my heir by hereditary right, and thus I have given and confirmed the kingdom of England to him and his heirs. The duke, in turn, because of this honour and gift and confirmation that I have made to him, has done homage to me and has given me a guarantee by oath that he will be faithful to me and will guard my life and honour with all his might according to the agreements already made between us, which are contained in this charter. I likewise have given the duke a guarantee by oath that I will guard his life and honour with all my might, and I will uphold and guard him as my son and heir in everything I can against all men over whom I have power. William my son likewise has done liege homage and given a guarantee to the duke of Normandy, and the duke has conceded to him that he shall hold of him all the holdings that I held before I obtained the kingdom of England, whether in England, whether in Normandy, whether in other places, and whatever he received with the daughter of the earl of Warenne both in England and in Normandy, and whatever pertains to those honours.

Then follows a host of detailed provisions concerning the additional lands and honours that William is to hold.

Because of the honour I have done their lord, the duke's earls and barons who were never my men have done homage to me and given me guarantees, saving the agreements made between me and the duke; the rest, who had done homage to me before, have done fealty to me as their lord. And if the duke departs from the aforesaid, they shall entirely cease from his service till he corrects his errors; my son also, according to Holy Church's advice, shall thereupon hold fast if the duke departs from the aforesaid. My earls and barons have likewise done liege homage to the duke, saving their fealty to me as long as I live and hold the kingdom, and by the same token if I depart from the aforesaid they shall entirely cease from my service till I correct my errors. At my order the citizens of the cities and the men of the castles that I have under my dominion have done homage and given guarantees to the duke, saving their fealty to me as long as I live and hold the kingdom; those, however, who have custody of the castle of Wallingford have done homage to me and have given me hostages for their fealty to me. Concerning my castles and fortifications, I, by Holy Church's counsel, have given the duke such guarantees that the duke, upon my death, will incur no damage or hindrance to the kingdom because of it.

Next follow the provisions concerning the chief of the king's castles. Those at Windsor, London, Oxford, and Lincoln were entrusted to castellans acceptable to both sides, who gave hostages and swore to turn them over to the duke upon Stephen's death. Winchester and Southampton were already in the custody of Bishop Henry, and he made his pledge to the archbishop in the presence of the other bishops that he would do the same.

The archbishops, bishops, and abbots of the realm of England, at my order, have done fealty to the duke by oath. Those, moreover, who in the future become bishops or abbots in the realm of England shall do the same. If any of our men withdraw from this agreement, the archbishops and bishops on both sides have undertaken to restrain him by ecclesiastical law till he corrects his errors and again observes this treaty. The duke's mother and wife and brothers and all whom he associates with this treaty shall be protected by these provisions. In the affairs of the kingdom I will act with the duke's advice. I, however, in the whole realm of England, as much in the duke's part as in my own, will exercise royal jurisdiction.

The charter was witnessed by Archbishop Theobald, Bishop Henry and twelve other bishops, Robert, prior of Bermondsey, Otto, a Knight Templar, twelve earls, and eight other laymen.[1]

One is immediately struck by the great difference between the preliminary terms agreed upon at Winchester as reported by Robert of Torigni and the final terms as set forth in this charter. The two provisions of supreme importance, that Stephen should remain king for his lifetime and that Henry should succeed him by hereditary right, are common to both and are strengthened in the second by Stephen's declaration that he will uphold Henry as his 'son and heir' and by the reciprocal acts of homage and oaths of fealty. Stephen's son William is not so much as mentioned in the first, whereas a third of the text of the charter is

[1] *Regesta*, pp. 97–9.

devoted to an enumeration of the lands and honours that Stephen has granted him and that Henry swears to confirm, thus indicating that William, and Stephen on his behalf, drove the hardest possible bargain to recompense him for renouncing his claim to the throne.

Equally significant is the omission from the charter of the provision that lands and honours should be restored to 'the ancient and lawful possessors' who had held them during King Henry's reign. Although the idea would of course appeal to the 'disinherited' who are frequently referred to in the chronicles of the time, such a provision would be almost impossible to frame in precise legal language whose terms would satisfy all the parties concerned. In the first place, the ruthless King Henry himself had confiscated the holdings of rebellious barons, and to attempt to examine those confiscations would be a difficult matter and would involve passing a judgment on the late king's acts that neither Stephen nor the young duke would like to undertake and that, if carried through, would involve the deprivation of some of the most important families of the kingdom, on whom Henry had bestowed the confiscated estates.

In the second place, the confiscation of a rebel's estates and his banishment were the ultimate weapons with which the Anglo-Norman kings could punish rebellion and treason. Now that Henry was assured of becoming king, he naturally would not want to weaken his own future powers by forcing Stephen to remit the punishment he as king had exacted of rebels, lest Henry might later find this precedent used against him, and Stephen could not reasonably be asked to undo the acts in which he had exercised his royal powers to punish treason. In other words, if Henry were to declare that Stephen could not lawfully punish treason, he would by the same token declare that when he became king he would not do the same thing. Matters looked quite different to the assured heir to the throne from what they did to a mere pretender who was trying to depose the king by force.

Finally, a general and indiscriminate restoration of property to those who had held it in King Henry's time, apart from being an act of almost insuperable difficulty and complexity that might well keep every court in England busy for years, was a sword that would cut both ways. Not all the 'usurpers' who had snatched away the possessions of others were Stephen's men, by any means;

Henry's followers had in many cases enriched themselves in precisely the same fashion.

As the two parties discussed the matter before the charter was drawn up they must have realised all this and agreed not to attempt to cover the matter in such a formal fashion but rather to examine the more outstanding complaints at their leisure and attempt to arrive at an equitable settlement by common consent.

The provision concerning the unlicensed castles was likewise dropped, since it also was a two-edged sword, but that a general agreement concerning them was in force is evident from subsequent events.

Now that the treaty of peace had been agreed upon and the terms embodied in a formal document, Stephen summoned the chief men of the kingdom to meet at Oxford on 13 January 1154, and at his command they did homage to the young Henry and swore fealty to him as their lord, saving, of course, the honour and fealty that they owed the king during his lifetime. Stephen and Henry met again at Dunstable, and Henry complained that although the greater part of the castles that had been built since King Henry's death had been demolished in accordance with the agreement made at Winchester, Stephen had nevertheless allowed some of his men to keep their castles, even though they were in that category. Henry of Huntingdon says that Henry suffered a repulse on this point and, not wanting to 'extinguish the light of concord', deferred the matter to a later day.[1]

One may assume that in this matter Stephen appealed to the royal authority that it was to Henry's interest to uphold. If Stephen advanced the argument that as king he had the authority to build castles where he chose or to designate fortifications already existing as royal castles and to appoint his own men as castellans in either case, Henry could not well gainsay the proposition without advocating a limitation on the royal power that he would not be prepared to admit when he became king. Henry was probably beginning to find that his position as heir apparent led him to view the king's actions in a more sympathetic light than he had formerly done.

Stephen and Henry were later received with great honour at Canterbury, and during Lent they went to Dover together to

[1] Henry of Huntingdon, pp. 289-90.

meet Count Thierry of Flanders.   Gervase of Canterbury, who
may well have been reporting a local tradition, says that when
Stephen and Henry returned to Canterbury the young duke
learned that the king's Flemish mercenaries, with the connivance
of Stephen's son William, were plotting to kill him and that
he then returned hastily to Normandy.   Henry's position in
England, where he had no real authority and where he would
appear to be waiting only for Stephen's death, could not have
been a pleasant one, and his lands across the Channel demanded
his attention.   He accordingly crossed over to Normandy about
Easter, 4 April 1154.[1]

The closing years of Stephen's reign saw a number of deaths,
in addition to that of his son Eustace, that had a profound effect
on the current of events both political and ecclesiastical. Stephen's
queen, Matilda of Boulogne, died on 3 May 1152, as has already
been mentioned.   She was a courageous, energetic, and resourceful woman, and her absence from the scene may perhaps have
contributed to Stephen's acceptance of the final settlement with
Henry.   William of Ste-Barbe, bishop of Durham, died on 24
November 1152; the results of his death will be commented
upon later.   The death of David, king of Scots, on 24 May 1153,
has also been mentioned previously.   On 8 July 1153 Pope
Eugenius III died, to be followed on 20 August by Bernard of
Clairvaux, and with them passed the ascendancy of the Cistercians in the affairs of the Church in England.   Henry Murdac,
whom they had made archbishop of York, died on 14 October.
Finally, that inveterate rebel, Ranulf, earl of Chester, who had
probably caused more disturbances and inflicted more damage
on the country than any other one man, died on 16 December.
Gervase of Canterbury says that he was poisoned by William
Peverel of Nottingham and sums up his career with the remark,
'He did little for the duke unless it fitted in with his own designs,
and for the king, nothing.'   The author of the *Gesta Stephani*,
however, says that although William Peverel gave poisoned wine
to Ranulf and his followers when they were guests in his house
and that although three of the followers died, Ranulf, after long
agonies, escaped death on this occasion only because he had not
drunk much of the wine.[2]

[1] Gervase of Canterbury, Vol. I, p. 158; Robert of Torigni, p. 179.
[2] Gervase of Canterbury, Vol. I, p. 155; G.S., p. 156.

o

After the death of William of Ste-Barbe, the prior of Durham, the two archdeacons, and all the clergy of the diocese on 22 January 1153 elected Hugh of Le Puiset, treasurer of York Cathedral and archdeacon of Winchester, to succeed him as bishop of Durham.   From a worldly point of view, at least, their choice was a wise one.   Hugh was well connected, being the nephew of King Stephen and Bishop Henry; he must already have been a wealthy man, and he was no doubt well known in Durham. He was no ascetic after the Cistercian model, of which the clergy of the North must by now have had their fill under the rigid rule of Archbishop Henry Murdac.   Most important of all, no doubt, was the fact that he was a seasoned warrior who would be able to occupy this frontier outpost and repel the Scots, if need should arise, for he had already covered himself with distinction in defending Bishop Henry's lands whilst his uncle was on one of his trips to Rome.   Hugh had captured a castle during the bishop's absence and gave promise of being as capable a fighter as his uncle.

When the clergy of Durham brought the news of the election to Archbishop Henry Murdac, he refused to confirm their choice and excommunicated the prior, the archdeacons, and Nicholas, prior of Brinkburn, who had been one of the delegates informing him of the election, because they had conducted it without his permission.   He rejected Hugh because of his youth, his worldliness, and his ignorance; he had neither holiness of life nor the authority of learning to recommend him.   Hugh, to be sure, was only twenty-five at the time and was of a decidedly wordly character, but one may be sure that Murdac's chief objection to him, apart from his not belonging to the Cistercian brotherhood, was his relationship to Bishop Henry and his close friendship with him, whom Murdac hated with all his narrow soul.

The people of York were loyal in their support of the king, and they saw in Murdac's rejection of the king's nephew 'a slight on the royal majesty'.   They had always hated the archbishop that had been forced on them, and they now drove him out of the city for the second time.   Eustace, Stephen's son, who had arranged Murdac's reconciliation with the king, visited him at his retreat at Beverley and tried to induce him to change his mind, but Murdac was inflexible.   The prior and archdeacons appealed to Archbishop Theobald as papal legate.   They convinced him that the election had been a free and canonical one and that there was nothing blameworthy in their actions. Theobald then succeeded in persuading Murdac to retract his sentences of excommunication, but he still refused to confirm the election. Hugh himself went to York in August 1153 and appealed to his fellow members of the chapter, but they gave him neither advice nor help. Armed with letters from Archbishop Theobald and other important personages, Hugh set out for Rome to appeal to the pope.[1]

Another nephew of the king and Bishop Henry was also affected by this series of deaths. It will be remembered that after Eugenius III, at the insistence of Bernard of Clairvaux, had deposed William as archbishop of York, William had retired to Winchester and lived under his uncle's protection. When he learned of the deaths of his two opponents he went to Rome, 'not to ask for justice but humbly to beg for mercy', as William of Newburgh puts it. The situation was clarified by the death of Henry Murdac, news of which reached Rome shortly after William's arrival.

The two cousins found the new pope, Anastasius IV, to be of an entirely different character from his predecessor. He confirmed Hugh's election and consecrated him bishop on 20 December 1153, and he restored William to his archbishopric and gave him the pallium, which William had never succeeded in obtaining, some thirteen years after his election as archbishop of York. The archbishop spent Easter 1154 in Winchester and then went to York to take possession of his see. Robert, dean of York, and Osbert, the archdeacon, tried to bar him from his cathedral and foolishly appealed to Archbishop Theobald as papal legate to reverse the pope's decision, but the clergy and people of York welcomed their archbishop with enthusiasm. Shortly after celebrating Mass on 1 June, William fell ill and died a week later. Immediately rumours began to fly that he had been poisoned by means of the chalice he had used at his last Mass.[2]

After Duke Henry left England, Stephen made a number of royal progresses through the country, 'showing himself like a

---

[1] G.S.,, p. 142; Geoffrey of Coldingham: *Liber de Statu Ecclesiae Dunelmensis* in *Historiae Dunelmensis Scriptores Tres*, ed. James Raine (Surtees Society, Vol. IX, 1939), p. 4; John of Hexham, Vol. II, pp. 328–30.

[2] William of Newburgh, Vol. I, pp. 79–80; Knowles: *The Case of St. William of York*, pp. 91–2.

*o

new king' and being received wherever he went with great honour and respect. One of the objects of the progress appears to have been an enquiry into the unauthorised castles, for William of Newburgh says that these dens of thieves were burned in his presence and melted away like wax before a flame. At Drax, near Selby, in Yorkshire, however, Philip of Coleville attempted to hold out against him. Stephen raised an army from the surrounding countryside and quickly captured the castle late in the summer.

The king held his court at London near Michaelmas, 29 September 1154. William of Newburgh says that there were two subjects to be discussed with the bishops and nobles: the affairs of the kingdom and the vacancy at York caused by Archbishop William's death. He further says that Archbishop Theobald, with the king's connivance, engineered the election of his archdeacon, Roger of Pont l'Evèque, and that Robert, the dean, and Osbert, the archdeacon of York, forced the chapter to elect him. To succeed Roger as archdeacon of Canterbury Theobald named one of his clerks, Thomas of London, later known as Thomas Becket.[1]

In the presence of the king and his council, one of Archbishop William's clerks accused Osbert of having murdered the archbishop by poisoning the chalice at Mass. Although Osbert denied the charge, he never succeeded in clearing himself, and he later became a layman. Miracles were soon reported at William's tomb, and in 1227 he was canonised.[2]

After Roger's consecration as archbishop of York on 10 October by Archbishop Theobald, Stephen dismissed the council and went to Dover for another meeting with Count Thierry. Shortly thereafter he fell suddenly and violently ill 'of a chronic flux of haemorrhoids' and died on 25 October 1154. He was buried beside his wife and son in the abbey he and Matilda had founded at Faversham.[3]

Duke Henry sailed from Barfleur on 7 December and was crowned in Westminster Abbey on 19 December 1154 by

---

[1] William of Newburgh, Vol. I, pp. 81-2, 94-5; Gervase of Canterbury, Vol. I, p. 159; Saltman: *Theobald, Archbishop of Canterbury*, pp. 122-3.
[2] *The Letters of John of Salisbury*, ed. Brooke, pp. 26-7; Knowles: *The Case of St. William of York*, pp. 92-4.
[3] William of Newburgh, Vol. I, p. 95; Gervase of Canterbury, Vol. I, pp. 158-9.

Archbishop Theobald, who is credited with having maintained the peace during the interval.[1]

Thus Stephen closed a laborious and unhappy reign of almost nineteen years, in the words of Henry of Huntingdon,[2] and the verdict of history has not been kind to him. His first and greatest mistake, the root of all his later troubles, is commonly held to be his having claimed the crown in the first place. Yet it should be realised that to the men of his time he had a legitimate title, as is shown by the fact that he met with almost no opposition when he claimed the throne, and that by virtue of his coronation he became in very truth king of England, no matter what men might think of his hereditary qualifications for that title.

Before condemning Stephen out of hand, one should consider the alternatives to his rule and what the results of those alternatives might have been, for the men of his time were faced by a choice not between Stephen and some ideal king but between Stephen and the few other people who might be considered to have a claim to the crown. The first and most obvious alternative was the Empress Matilda, and a more disastrous one could hardly be imagined, as the men of her time realised. She could not have ruled in her own right, for that would have been contrary to all the traditions of the time, and if she had attempted to do so the events of the brief period when she was lady of England showed how unfit she was for such a task. The practical result of recognising her claim or that of her infant son would have been to install her husband, Geoffrey of Anjou, as ruler of England, assuming that he would be willing to take on a job in which he did not show the slightest interest, and the Anglo-Norman barons, who regarded Anjou as their traditional foe, would never have tolerated that. Geoffrey, like almost everyone else, found his wife unbearable, and the joint rule of Geoffrey and Matilda, while it might have provided satirists with some notable material, would certainly have wrecked England.

The second alternative was Count Theobald, whose title was even clearer than his brother's since he was the elder. There is no indication that he could have managed affairs any better than his brother did, and at least Stephen knew England well and was popular there, whereas Theobald did not know the country at all.

[1] Gervase of Canterbury, Vol. I, p. 159.   [2] Henry of Huntingdon, p. 291.

The only other possible claimant was Robert, earl of Gloucester, but his illegitimacy ruled him out from the start, so that no one even proposed him. His grandfather, it is true, had been a bastard also, but for all his hereditary claims William had ruled England by right of conquest, and Robert was certainly not the man to follow in William's footsteps and acquire England by force of arms. He was not so capable a military leader as Stephen and probably would have had even less success in dealing with rebellious barons.

Stephen, in other words, made a better king than anyone else could have done who had a clear title to the crown. For nineteen years he was almost constantly occupied either in overcoming the efforts of his Angevin opponents to unseat him or in resisting the attempts of rebel barons to defy his authority, and often he had to face them both together. And yet, harassed by this almost unremitting opposition, Stephen succeeded in holding on to his crown and in overcoming all his opponents save one, and to that one he ceded the succession of his own free will and not because he was defeated and forced to do so.

Stephen's reign may have been a necessary, though painful, step in the political development of the country. The rule of Henry I had been increasingly oppressive, his centralisation of the government too advanced for the structure of society at the time to bear, and his financial exactions too unscrupulous for his victims to endure indefinitely. If Stephen had continued his uncle's policies of ruling with an iron hand, the country would probably have been torn asunder by revolts of which those of Geoffrey de Mandeville and Ranulf of Chester were only samples.

On the other hand, if Stephen had been as weak and ineffectual as he is often painted, he could not have kept, as he undeniably did, the loyalty and support of a majority of his barons and he could not have retained control of the greater part of the country, including the richest areas and all the larger towns save Bristol. The country would have lapsed into anarchy, and the central government would have disappeared completely.

As it was, Stephen was weak enough to allow his authority to be challenged and yet strong enough to meet those challenges and preserve his authority. His reign provided a breathing-space between the reigns of Henry I and Henry II during which his men first revolted against a central government and then, dismayed by the results of their revolts, came to see the necessity for a strong central government and in some cases to welcome it. Stephen of course deserves no credit for having provided this breathing-space and certainly did not do so consciously, but one should perhaps bear it in mind in attempting to assess his reign.

Part of Stephen's troubles arose from his own character and part of them from circumstances over which he had no control and that would have confronted anyone who became king of England at that time. He was a pleasant, easy-going man who won a host of friends, both amongst the nobles of his uncle's court and amongst the leading men of London, during the period when he was the king's favourite nephew, and the chroniclers of the time all speak of his easy, friendly manners and his charm. He no doubt began his reign with the intention of preserving friendly relations with his barons, and it seems evident that he was determined not to model himself on his stern, harsh uncle in his dealing with them. In his easy-going way he allowed Robert of Gloucester to renounce his fealty and the Empress Matilda to establish herself in England, and he seems not to have taken them seriously till their revolt was well organised and under way, whereas Henry I, one may be sure, would have visited the rebels immediately with the direst punishment in his power. Over and over again in his dealings with the rebels Stephen failed to follow up his victories by those extremities of harsh punishment that alone would have put an end to their activities. He was by no means lacking in courage or in military skill; he lacked ruthlessness, the essential characteristic for a successful king of medieval England, and therein lay the root of his failure.

It was his misfortune to come to the throne at a time when such men as Ranulf of Chester, Hugh Bigod, and Geoffrey de Mandeville were flourishing. These men were rebels against any authority, no matter whose, and Stephen was forced to devote a considerable part of his time and energy to holding them in check. They were determined on their own aggrandisement and infinitely resourceful in pursuing it. Death removed two of them during Stephen's reign, but Hugh Bigod rebelled just as violently against Stephen's successor as he had against Stephen. Of the disorders and civil wars during Stephen's reign, half of the trouble came from the Angevin party in the west of England, disputing the succession to the crown, and the other half from such men as Earl Ranulf, who disputed the very concept of orderly government.

While the disorders were, in the end, instructive to the English nobles in that they showed them that orderly government was in the long run to their own best interests, the nobles, who after all were were only a minute fraction of the population of England, learned their lesson at a dreadful cost to the common people. Every chronicler, without exception, paints an appalling picture of the misery that prevailed during Stephen's reign, and the graphic account in the English Chronicle is only the most vivid of a whole series. The type of warfare that was practised during this period, as had already been pointed out, whilst it was economical of the lives of knights, inflicted untold suffering upon the common people of the area in which it took place. The first step in laying siege to a castle was to reduce the surrounding countryside to a desert, with the object of starving the garrison of the castle into submission. Long before the garrison of a well-stocked castle would begin to feel any discomfort, however, the peasants of the neighbourhood would probably have died of starvation. If the castle were in the midst of a town, the town would be sacked and plundered and often burned to the ground.

In addition to the operations of the king and the rebels against each other, individual barons seized the opportunity afforded by the king's troubles elsewhere to wage private wars against their enemies. Although most of them went unrecorded, these private wars inflicted just as much suffering as the official ones.[1]

Whilst it would be incorrect to say that the central government ceased to function in the areas that remained under Stephen's control, it was certainly weakened by the troubled conditions of the time, and the general relaxing of the central administration afforded lawless men an opportunity to indulge in such conduct as is recorded in the complaints of all the chroniclers.

Faced by such difficulties, Stephen's whole attention was necessarily centred on fighting the rebels and holding on to his crown, and that he succeeded in doing this is evidence of his resourcefulness, his courage, and his military ability. It is impossible to guess what sort of king he would have made if he had been able to reign in peace, but one may venture the opinion

[1] See the examples recorded in Stenton: *The First Century of English Feudalism*, pp. 244–5.

that he would have made no important contribution to the development of English institutions. In spite of his having received his training in the court of Henry I, there is no indication that he understood, much less shared, his uncle's interest in the details of orderly administration, in the extension of the influence and jurisdiction of the king's justices, in the gradual supplanting of local magnates in the administration of the counties by officials responsible only to the king, and in the development of the highly efficient work of the Exchequer in providing England with the most sophisticated system of financial accounting in Europe. There were, after all, some fairly long stretches of peace during his reign, and some parts of the country, particularly in the south-east, were little affected by the war, and yet during those times and in those areas there is no evidence that he did anything more than preserve as best he could the existing state of things.

Stephen, in spite of every advantage of birth, education, and the example of his uncle, simply was not a big enough man to be king of England in 1135. Neither was anyone else.

BIBLIOGRAPHY

Ailred of Rievaulx: *Relatio de Standardo,* ed. Richard Howlett, in *Chronicles of the Reigns of Stephen, Henry II, and Richard I* (Rolls Series 82, 4 vols., 1884-9), Vol. III.

Annals of Margam, in *Annales Monastici,* ed. H. R. Luard (Rolls Series 36, 5 vols., 1864-9), Vol. I.

Annals of Winchester, in *Annales Monastici,* Vol. II.

Arbois de Jubainville, H. d': *Histoire des ducs et des comtes de Champagne* (7 vols., Paris, 1859-66).

Beeler, John: *Warfare in England, 1066-1189* (Ithaca, N.Y., 1966).

Bernard of Clairvaux: *Epistolae,* in J. P. Migne, *Patrologia Latina,* Vol. CLXXXII.

Brooke, Z. N., *The English Church and the Papacy from the Conquest to the Reign of John* (Cambridge, 1932; reprinted 1968).

Brooke, Z. N., and Brooke, C. N. L.: 'Henry II, Duke of Normandy and Aquitaine', *English Historical Review,* LXI (January 1946).

Chronicon Abbatiae Rameseiensis, ed. W. Duncan Macray (Rolls Series 83, 1886).

Corbett, William John: 'England, 1087-1154', *The Cambridge Medieval History,* Vol. V.

Cronne, H. A.: 'Ranulf de Gernons, Earl of Chester, 1129-1153', *Transactions of the Royal Historical Society,* 4th Ser., Vol. XX.

Cronne, H. A. and Davis, R. H. C. (eds. in continuation of the work of the late H. W. C. Davis): *Regesta Regum Anglo-Normannorum, 1066-1154.* Vol. III, *Regesta Regis Stephani ac Mathildis Imperatricis ac Gaufridi et Henrici Ducum Normannorum, 1135-1154* (Oxford, 1968).

David, Charles Wendell: *Robert Curthose, Duke of Normandy* (Cambridge, Mass., 1920).

Davis, H. W. C.: 'The Anarchy of Stephen's Reign', *English Historical Review,* XVIII (October 1903).

— 'Henry of Blois and Brian FitzCount', *English Historical Review,* XXV (April 1910).

— 'Some Documents of the Anarchy', in *Essays in History Presented to Reginald Lane Poole* (Oxford, 1927).

Davis, R. H. C.: 'The Authorship of the *Gesta Stephani*', *English Historical Review,* LXXVI (April 1962).

— 'Geoffrey de Mandeville Reconsidered', *English Historical Review,* LXXIX (April 1964).

Davis, R. H. C.: *King Stephen* (London, 1967).
— 'King Stephen and the Earl of Chester Revised', *English Historical Review*, LXXV (October 1960).
— 'What Happened in Stephen's Reign, 1135-54', *History*, XLIX (February 1964).
Dugdale, William: *Monasticon Anglicanum*, rev. by John Caley *et al*. (6 vols. in 8, London, 1817-30).
Florence of Worcester: *Chronicon ex Chronicis and Its Continuations*, ed. B. Thorpe (2 vols., London, 1848-9).
Foster, C. W.: *The Registrum Antiquissimum of the Cathedral Church of Lincoln*, Vol. I (Publications of the Lincoln Record Society, Vol. XXVII, Lincoln, 1931).
Fulcher of Chartres: *Gesta Francorum Iherusalem Peregrinantium*, in *R.H.C.*, Vol. III.
Geoffrey of Coldingham: *Liber de Statu Ecclesiae Dunelmensis* in *Historiae Dunelmensis Scriptores Tres*, ed. James Raine (Surtees Society, Vol. IX, 1939).
Gervase of Canterbury: *Historical Works*, ed. William Stubbs (2 vols., Rolls Series 73, 1879-80).
Gesta Stephani, ed. K. R. Potter (Edinburgh, 1955).
Gilbert Foliot, Abbot of Gloucester (1139-48), Bishop of Hereford (1148-63) and London (1163-87), The Letters and Charters of, ed. Z. N. Brooke, Adrian Morey, and C. N. L. Brooke (Cambridge, 1967).
Hagenmeyer, H.: *Die Kreuzzugsbriefe aus den Jahren 1088-1100* (Innsbruck, 1902).
Haskins, Charles Homer: *Norman Institutions* (Cambridge, Mass., 1918).
Henry of Huntingdon: *Historia Anglorum*, ed. Thomas Arnold (Rolls Series 74, 1879).
Historia Gaufridi Ducis Normannorum et Comitis Andegavorum, ed. Louis Halphen and René Poupardin (Collection des textes pour l'étude de l'histoire, Vol. XLVIII, Paris, 1913).
Hollister, C. Warren: *The Military Organization of Norman England* (Oxford, 1965).
Howell, Margaret: *Regalian Right in Medieval England* (London, 1962).
Hüffer, G.: *Der heilige Bernard von Clairvaux*, Vol. I, *Vorstudien* (Münster, 1886).
John of Hexham, in Vol. II of Simeon of Durham: *Historical Works*, ed. Thomas Arnold (2 vols., Rolls Series 75, 1882-5).
John of Salisbury: *Historia Pontificalis*, ed. Reginald L. Poole (Oxford, 1927); also ed. Marjorie Chibnall (Edinburgh, 1956).
John of Salisbury, The Letters of, ed. C. N. L. Brooke (Edinburgh, 1955).
John of Worcester: *Chronicle*, ed. J. R. H. Weaver (Oxford, 1908).

Knowles, Dom David: 'The Case of St. William of York', *Cambridge Historical Journal*, V (1936), No. 2, reprinted in *The Historian and Character* (Cambridge, 1963).
— *The Episcopal Colleagues of Archbishop Thomas Becket* (Cambridge, 1951).
— *The Monastic Order in England* (2d edn., Cambridge, 1963).
Lloyd, Sir John Edward: *A History of Wales* (2 vols., 3d edn., London, 1939).
Materials for the History of Thomas Becket, ed. J. C. Robertson *et al.* (7 vols., Rolls Series 67, 1875–85).
Memorials of the Abbey of St Mary of Fountains, Vol. I, ed. John Richard Walbran (Surtees Society, Vol. XLII, 1863).
Morey, Adrian, and Brooke, C. N. L.: *Gilbert Foliot and His Letters* (Cambridge, 1965).
Nicholl, Donald: *Thurstan, Archbishop of York, 1114–1140* (York, 1964)
Orderic Vitalis: *Historia Ecclesiastica*, ed. A. Le Prévost and L. Delisle (5 vols., Paris, 1838–55).
Peter Tudebod: *De Hierosolymitano Itinere*, in *R.H.C.*, Vol. III.
The Peterborough Chronicle, 1070–1154, ed. Cecily Clark (Oxford, 1958).
Poole, Austin Lane: *From Domesday Book to Magna Carta, 1087–1216* (2d edn., Oxford, 1956).
— 'Henry Plantagenet's Early Visits to England', *English Historical Review*, XLVII (July 1932).
Poole, Reginald Lane: 'The Appointment and Deprivation of St. William, Archbishop of York', *English Historical Review*, XLV (1930).
Prestwich, J. O.: 'War and Finance in the Anglo-Norman State', *T.R.H.S.*, 5th Series, Vol. IV (1954).
Radulf Cadomensi: *Gesta Tancredi in Expeditione Hierosolymitica*, in *R.H.C.*, Vol. III.
Ralph of Diceto: *Opera Historica*, ed. William Stubbs (2 vols., Rolls Series 68, 1876).
Raymond of Aguilers: *Historia Francorum Qui Ceperunt Ierusalem*, in *R.H.C.*, Vol. III.
Richard of Hexham: *Chronicle*, ed. Richard Howlett, in *Chronicles of the Reigns of Stephen*, etc, Vol. III.
Richardson, H. G., and Sayles, G. O.: *The Governance of Medieval England from the Conquest to Magna Carta* (Edinburgh, 1963).
Robert of Torigni: *Chronicle*, ed. Richard Howlett, in *Chronicles of the Reigns of Stephen*, etc, Vol. IV.
Round, John Horace: *Feudal England* (London, 1895).
— *Geoffrey de Mandeville* (London, 1892).

Round, John Horace: 'King Stephen and the Earl of Chester', *English Historical Review*, X (January 1895).
— *Studies in Peerage and Family History* (London, 1901).
Runciman, Sir Steven: *A History of the Crusades* (3 vols., Cambridge, 1951–4).
Saltman, Avrom: *Theobald, Archbishop of Canterbury* (London, 1956).
Stenton, Sir Frank: *The First Century of English Feudalism, 1066–1166* (2nd edn., Oxford, 1961).
Stevenson, William B.: 'The First Crusade', *Cambridge Medieval History*, Vol. V.
Stubbs, William: *The Constitutional History of England in Its Origin and Development* (3 vols., 6th edn., Oxford, 1897, reprinted 1967).
Voss, Lena: *Heinrich von Blois, Bischof von Winchester (1129–71)* (Berlin, 1932).
White, Geoffrey N.: 'The Career of Waleran, Count of Meulan and Earl of Worcester (1104–1166)', *T.R.H.S.*, 4th Series, Vol. XVII (1934).
— 'King Stephen's Earldoms', *T.R.H.S.*, 4th Series, Vol. XIII (1930).
William of Malmesbury: *De Gestis Regum Anglorum*, ed. William Stubbs (2 vols., Rolls Series 90, 1887–9).
— *Historia Novella*, ed. K. R. Potter (Edinburgh, 1955).
William of Newburgh: *Historia Rerum Anglicarum*, ed. Richard Howlett, in *Chronicles of the Reigns of Stephen*, etc., Vols. I and II.

INDEX

Abingdon, 127
Ada, countess of Huntingdon, 63, 88
Adela, countess of Blois and Chartres,
    1–2, 5–7, 18, 22, 52
Adelaide, countess of Aumale, 55
Adelise, wife of Baldwin of Redvers,
    35–6
Adeliza of Louvain, queen of England,
    12, 74–5, 88
Æthelwulf, bishop of Carlisle, 163, 165
Agnes de Sulli, 6
Alan 'Fergant', duke of Brittany, 74
Alan of Dinant, count of Brittany and
    earl of Richmond, 66, 71, 74n, 80,
    92–6, 105, 113, 122–3
Alberic, bishop of Ostia, 57, 59, 61, 63
Aldreth, 79
Alençon, 10, 18
Alexander, bishop of Lincoln, 40, 64–6,
    68, 70–1, 89, 98, 109, 179
Alexandretta, 4
Alexis, emperor, 1, 5
Alnwick, 26
Alost, siege of, 16
Anacletus, anti-pope, 59
Anastasius IV, pope, 201
Andover, 114
Anselm, abbot of St. Edmunds, 106–7
Anselm, archbishop of Canterbury, 60,
    62
Antioch, 2, 4–5
Argentan, 31, 41
Arnulf, archdeacon of Séez, 20, 62
Arques, 153, 183
Arundel, 74
Aubrey de Vere, 71–2

Baldwin I, king of Jerusalem, 6
Baldwin II, king of Jerusalem, 16
Baldwin fitz Gilbert, 80, 94–6, 122
Baldwin of Redvers, earl of Devon,
    35–6, 40, 49, 73, 85, 109, 113
Bamburgh, 63
Bampton, 35, 125–6
Barfleur, 11, 185, 202

Bath, 49–51, 84
— bishop of. See Robert of Lewes
Bayeux, 79
Bec, 71, 70
Bedford, 43, 45–6, 106, 148, 189, 192
Benedict, abbot of Whitby, 159
Bernard, abbot of Clairvaux, 158–9,
    161–3, 167, 191, 199, 201
Bernard, bishop of St. David's, 97–8, 109
Bernard of Baliol, 53
Beverley, 174, 200
Bohemond, prince of Antioch, 4–6
Brampton, 40
Brian fitz Count, 15, 28, 74–6, 98, 109,
    113, 115, 126–7, 131–3, 148, 182
Bridport, 176
Bristol, 47, 49–51, 74–6, 79–81, 97,
    99, 101, 114–15, 117, 128–9, 155,
    173, 186
Burtuna, 154
Burwell, 140
Bury St. Edmunds, 190
Bytham, 91

Caen, 24, 79, 125
Cadwaladr ap Gruffydd ap Cynan, 93
Calixtus II, pope, 12
Cambridge, 137
Canterbury, 22, 120–1, 164, 166, 168,
    170–1, 198–9
— archbishops of. See Anselm; Lan-
    franc; Theobald; William of Corbeil
Cardiff, 17
Carisbrooke, 38
Carlisle, 26, 55, 57, 59, 85, 87, 113,
    172–3
— bishop of. See Æthelwulf
Castle Cary, 51, 155
Celestine II, pope, 159–60, 178
Charles the Good, count of Flanders,
    16, 41
Chartres, 5–6
Chester, earls of, 86. See also Ranulf
    'aux Gernons'; Ranulf 'le Meschin';
    Richard

Chichester, 160
— bishop of. *See* Hilary
Christian, a clerk, 103
Cirencester, 97, 125, 127
Cluny, 7, 22, 60, 160
Constance, daughter of Louis VI, 68, 79, 135, 183
Constance, daughter of Philip I, 6
Constantinople, 1
Corfe, 73–4
Cornwall, earl of. *See* Reginald of Dunstanville
Coventry, 152
— bishop of. *See* Roger
Cricklade, 143, 145, 154
Cuthbert, prior of Guiseborough, 120

Danegeld, 25
Daniel, a monk, 79, 137–8
David, king of Scots, 15, 26–8, 32, 46, 52–3, 55, 57, 59, 63, 87, 103, 106, 110, 113, 115, 120, 132, 155, 172–3, 175, 188, 199
Derby, earls of, 56. *See also* Robert of Ferrers
Devizes, 65, 67, 78, 81–3, 105, 115, 123–4, 173, 175–6
Devon, earl of. *See* Baldwin of Redvers
Diffidatio, 48
Domfront, 31
Dorset, earl of. *See* William of Mohun
Dover, 21, 52, 55, 198, 202
Drax, 202
Dudley Castle, 51
Dunstable, 40, 198
Dunster, 73
Durham, 26, 63
— bishops of. *See* Hugh of Le Puiset; William of St.-Calais; William of Ste.-Barbe
Dursley Castle, 173

Earls, functions of, 55, 57
Edmund Ironside, king of England, 9
Edward the Confessor, king of England, 14, 24, 109
Egbert, king of West Saxons, 14
Eleanor, duchess of Aquitaine, 184–5
Élie, count of Maine, 12
Elizabeth, countess of Pembroke, 55
Ely, 79
— bishop of. *See* Nigel
Emma, daughter of Count Stephen, 91

Eremburga, countess of Anjou, 12
Ernulf, bishop of Rochester, 61
Ernulf de Mandeville, 121, 141–2
Ernulf of Hesding, 51
Essex, earl of. *See* Geoffrey de Mandeville
Eudes, count of Champagne, 55
Eugenius III, pope, 161–9, 177–80, 185, 191, 201
Eustace II, count of Boulogne, 9
Eustace III, count of Boulogne, 9
Eustace, son of King Stephen, 68, 79, 109, 111, 117, 173, 175–9, 183, 185, 187, 190–1, 193, 199–200
Évreux, 40
Exeter, 35, 38
— bishop of. *See* Robert Warelwast
Exmes, 31, 41

Falaise, 10, 19
Faringdon, 145–6
Faversham, 191, 202
Fontevraud, 12
Forests, 25, 33, 40
Framlingham, 170
Fulk, count of Anjou and king of Jerusalem, 9–10, 12, 16

Galclint Castle, 105
Geoffrey, archbishop of Rouen, 15
Geoffrey, archbishop of York, 90
Geoffrey, count of Anjou, 16–17, 20, 31, 39–42, 49, 74, 79, 103, 124–7, 153–4, 176, 181, 183–4, 203
Geoffrey, son of Geoffrey of Anjou, 17, 185
Geoffrey de Mandeville, earl of Essex, 29, 107–9, 111, 114, 121–2, 134–8, 140–2, 144–5, 204–5
Geoffrey de Mandeville II, 142
Geoffrey Halsalin, 53
Geoffrey of Boterel, 113
Geoffrey Talbot, 47, 50
Gervase, abbot of Westminster, 180
Gilbert Foliot, bishop of Hereford, 97, 133, 169, 171, 180
Gilbert of Clare, earl of Hertford, 93–5, 116, 122, 151–2
Gilbert of Clare, earl of Pembroke, 55, 122, 151–2
Gilbert of Lacy, 50
Gilbert 'the Universal', bishop of London, 106

Gilon de Sulli, 6

Glastonbury, 22

Gloucester, 47, 76–82, 85, 97, 111, 114–15, 173

— earls of. *See* Robert; William

Gregory VII, pope, 34, 101

Guignan Algaso, viscount of Exmes, 31

Guildford, 112

Gundreda, countess of Warwick, 188

Harptree, 51

Hawise, countess of Derby, 55

Hawise, countess of Lincoln, 85, 88

Hélias of Saint-Saëns, 10

Henry V, emperor, 13

Henry I, king of England, 1, 7, 9–24, 28–30, 33, 37, 39–40, 43, 62, 80, 85, 94, 100, 107–9, 132, 204, 207

Henry II, king of England: birth, 17; visits England (1142), 126–8; second visit (1147), 153–5; and election of Gilbert Foliot, 169; third visit (1149), 172–3, 176–7; defends Normandy, 183–4; marriage, 184–5; returns to England (1153), 186–9; meets Stephen at Wallingford, 189–90; invades Midlands, 191–2; recognised as Stephen's heir, 193–9; crowned king, 202–3

Henry, bishop of Winchester: youth, 7, 22; helps Stephen gain crown, 22–4, 34, 64; at siege of Exeter, 35–8, and of Bedford, 46; aspires to be archbishop, 59–61, 160–2, 167; condemns Stephen's treatment of Roger of Salisbury, 69–73; receives Matilda, 97–103, 106, 109, 111–12; at siege of Winchester, 113; negotiates for Stephen's release, 117–18; returns to Stephen's support, 118–20, 122; and Archbishop William of York, 120, 158–9, 162–3; at Battle of Wilton, 129–30; and Brian fitz Count, 131–3; suspended by pope, 167; and election of bishop of Lincoln, 179–80; negotiates with Duke Henry, 193–4, 196

Henry, count of Blois, 185

Henry, earl of Huntingdon and of Northumbria, 26, 28, 46, 53, 55, 59, 88

Henry Murdac, archbishop of York, 161–2, 164–5, 168, 174, 177–9, 199–201

Henry of Sulli, 28, 83, 90, 179

Henry of Tracy, 73, 155, 176

Herbert of Luci, 127

Herbert of Winchester, 91

Hereford, 47, 50, 78, 173

— bishops of. *See* Gilbert Foliot; Robert of Béthune

— earls of. *See* Miles of Gloucester; Roger

Hertford, earls of, 58. *See also* Gilbert of Clare

Hervey of Léon, earl of Wiltshire, 83, 105

Hilary, bishop of Chichester, 163–4, 166, 169–70

Hugh, abbot of St. Benet's Hulme, 180

Hugh, archbishop of Rouen, 19, 28, 34, 41, 72, 103

Hugh Bigod, 20–1, 24, 34, 62, 93–4, 138, 144, 170, 176–7, 190, 205

Hugh of Le Puiset, bishop of Durham, 163, 165, 178, 200–1

Hugh 'the Poor', 43–6, 106

Humphrey of Bohun, 77, 116

Huntingdon, earls of, 27. *See also* David; Simon of Senlis

Ilbert of Lacey, 52, 95

Imar, cardinal, 160–1

Ingelram of Sai, 24, 95

Innocent II, pope, 19–21, 29–30, 33, 57, 59, 61, 63–4, 91, 107, 118, 157–9, 161–2, 178, 180

Ipswich, 191

Isabel, daughter of William of Warenne, 193

Isle of Portland, 127

Isle of Wight, 38

Ivo, bishop of Chartres, 6

Jeanne, wife of William Clito, 12

Jeremiah, prior of Christ Church, 61

Jerusalem, 6

Jocelin, bishop of Salisbury, 169

John fitz Gilbert, 82

John Marshal, 114

John of Neuville, bishop of Séez, 84

Joppa, 6

Karbogha, emir, 5

La Hougue, 40
Lanfranc, archbishop of Canterbury, 60
Leicester, earls of, 44. *See also* Robert; Robert, count of Meulan
Le Mans, 16
Lincoln, 87–96, 149, 151, 175, 196
— bishops of. *See* Alexander; Robert of Chesney
— earls of. *See* William of Aubigny; William of Roumare
Lisieux, 10, 21, 40–1, 184
London, 13, 22, 49, 83, 102, 106–7, 110, 114, 136, 179, 192, 194, 196, 202
— bishops of. *See* Gilbert 'the Universal'; Richard of Belmeis; Robert 'of the Seal'
Louis VI, king of France, 9, 12–13, 16, 29, 41
Louis VII, king of France, 79, 84, 164, 183–5
Lucius II, pope, 160
Lucy, countess of Chester, 85–7
Ludgershall, 115
Lulworth, 127
Lupel, a clerk, 62
Lyons-la-Forêt, 19

Mabel, countess of Gloucester, 15, 116
Madog ap Maredudd, 93
Malcolm III, king of Scots, 9, 14
Malcolm IV, king of Scots, 188
Malmesbury, 65, 67, 77, 81, 143, 145, 186–8, 192
Marcigny-sur-Loire, 7, 52
Margaret, queen of Scots, 14
Marlborough, 82, 173, 175
Mary, countess of Boulogne, 9
Mary, daughter of King Stephen, 83
Matilda the Empress: recognised as father's heir, 13–15; second marriage, 16–17; her claim to the crown, 20–1, 23, 29–31, 48–9, 61–2, 203; lands in England, 74–6; received at Winchester, 97–102; acts as Lady of England, 103–6; goes to Westminster, 106–10; flees to Oxford, 111; besieges Winchester, 112–15; summons Count Geoffrey, 123–4; besieged at Oxford, 126–8; dependence upon Miles of Gloucester, 142; negotiates for peace, 148–9; refuses to help Henry, 154; leaves England, 155–6

Matilda, queen of England, wife of Henry I, 9, 14, 62
Matilda of Boulogne, queen of England, 9, 14, 27–8, 52, 55, 59, 63, 79, 84, 88, 103, 109–13, 115, 117, 120–3, 135, 138, 141, 166, 168, 170, 191, 199
Matilda, queen of Scots, 26
Matilda, countess of Chester, 11, 85, 88
Matilda, countess of Perche, 11
Matilda, daughter of Fulk of Anjou, 10, 12
Matilda, daughter of Stephen, 43, 83
Matilda of Ramsbury, 67
Matthew, Master, 128
Melisende, daughter of Baldwin II, 16
Mildenhall, 141
Miles, bishop of Térouanne, 170
Miles of Beauchamp, 45–6, 106
Miles of Gloucester, earl of Hereford, 25, 28, 51, 75–8, 80, 82–3, 90, 98, 109, 111, 113, 115, 129, 142

Neufbourg, 21
Neufmarché, 185
Newark, 65, 68
Newcastle-upon-Tyne, 26, 46, 63
Nicholas, bishop of Cambrai, 170
Nicholas, prior of Brinkburn, 200
Nigel, bishop of Ely, 64, 67–8, 79–80, 97–8, 109
Norham, 26
Northallerton, 54
Northampton, 17, 47, 123, 149
— earl of. *See* Simon of Senlis
Northumbria, earls of, 27. *See also* Henry; Waltheof
Norwich, 34
— bishop of. *See* William
Nottingham, 63, 84–5, 106, 192

Odo, bishop of Bayeux, 71
Orkneys, bishop of. *See* Ralph Nowel
Osbert, archdeacon of York, 201–2
Osbert Eight-Pence, 132
Otto, Knight Templar, 196
Oxford, 25, 32–3, 65–8, 71, 99, 106, 111–12, 123, 126–8, 145–6, 173, 189, 196, 198

Paschal II, pope, 5–6, 62
Payne of Beauchamp, 46
Payne son of John, 24–5, 28

Pembroke, earls of, 58. *See also* Gilbert of Clare

Peter, archbishop of Bourges, 164

Pevensey, 153

Pharamus of Boulogne, 110, 122

Philip, bishop of Châlons, 7

Philip, count of Ypres, 41

Philip, son of Robert, earl of Gloucester, 145, 147–8

Philip of Coleville, 202

Philip of Harcourt, bishop of Bayeux, 83

Philomelium, 5

Pleshy, 136

Plympton, 35

Pontefract, 90

Radcot, 125

Ralph Lovel, 51

Ralph Nowel, bishop of the Orkneys, 53–4, 159

Ralph Painel, 51, 84

Ramleh, 6, 96

Ramsey, 137–9, 141

Ranulf 'aux Gernons', earl of Chester, 28, 85–91, 93–6, 105, 113, 119, 143, 146–52, 156, 172–3, 175–7, 192, 199, 204–6

Ranulf 'le Meschin', earl of Chester, 85–7

Reading, 19, 24–5, 99, 107

Reginald of Dunstanville, earl of Cornwall, 28, 49, 80, 105, 113, 148, 183

Rheims, 165–6

Richard, abbot of Fountains, 61, 120

Richard, earl of Chester, 11, 85

Richard, son of Henry I, 11

Richard fitz Urse, 95–6

Richard of Belmeis, bishop of London, 181

Richard of Curcy, 52

Richard of Luci, 122

Richmond, 163

— earl of. *See* Alan of Dinant

Ripon, 165

Robert, abbot of Winchcombe, 47

Robert, count of Flanders, 1

Robert, count of Mortain, 55

Robert, count of Perche, 184–5

Robert, dean of York, 201–2

Robert, earl of Gloucester: swears oath to Matilda, 15; at father's death, 19, 21; swears fealty to Stephen, 30–4; in Normandy (1137), 41; defies Stephen, 48–9, 65; lands in England, 74–7; at Marlborough (1140), 82; takes Nottingham, 84–5; at Battle of Lincoln, 90–5; swears fealty to Matilda, 98, 106; at Westminster with her, 109–10; at siege of Winchester, 112–13; captured and imprisoned, 115–17; released, 117; acts as envoy to Count Geoffrey, 123–7; at Battle of Wilton, 129; rules in West, 133–4; relieves Tetbury, 143; at Faringdon, 145–6; declines to help Henry, 154; dies, 155

Robert, earl of Leicester, 19, 43, 55, 66, 181, 187–8, 192

Robert, prior of Bermondsey, 196

Robert Curthose, duke of Normandy, 1, 7, 10–12, 14, 17

Robert fitz Edith, 113–14

Robert fitz Hubert, 77, 81–3

Robert Hoset, 50

Robert of Bampton, 34–5, 40, 73

Robert of Beauchamp, 45

Robert of Beaumont, count of Meulan and earl of Leicester, 43, 188

Robert of Bellême, 10

Robert of Béthune, bishop of Hereford, 98, 109, 142, 166

Robert of Bruce, 52–3

Robert of Chesney, bishop of Lincoln, 180

Robert of Ferrers, earl of Derby, 52–3, 55, 122, 188

Robert of Ferrers II, earl of Derby, 188, 192

Robert of Gant, 163

Robert of Lewes, bishop of Bath, 29, 50, 98

Robert of Oilly, 99, 113

Robert of Stuteville, 52

Robert 'of the Seal', bishop of London, 107, 109, 169–70, 180

Robert son of Hamon, 15

Robert son of Hildebrand, 129–30

Robert Warelwast, bishop of Exeter, 47, 61

Rochester, 115–17

— bishop of. *See* Ernulf

Roger, king of Sicily, 162

Roger, bishop of Coventry, 61–63

Roger, bishop of Salisbury, 14–15, 23–4, 39, 57, 64–71, 77–8, 83–4

Roger, earl of Hereford, 143–4, 154–5, 172–3, 176–7, 182–3
Roger, son of Robert, earl of Gloucester, 128
Roger fitz Gerald of Roumare, 85
Roger of Beaumont, earl of Warwick, 28, 84, 113, 188
Roger of Mowbray, 26, 52
Roger of Pont l'Evèque, archbishop of York, 202
Roger the Chancellor, 64, 67, 83
Rotrou, count of Perche, 11, 19
Rouen, 16–17, 24, 153

Saffron Walden, 136, 144–5
St. Albans, 106–136
St. David's, bishop of. *See* Bernard
St. Omer, 168, 170
Salisbury, 39, 65, 67, 78, 173, 175
— bishops of. *See* Jocelin; Roger
Séez, 31, 184
Severin, abbot of St. Mary's, York, 159
Sherborne, 65, 67, 129
Shrewsbury, 51, 55, 75
Sibyl, daughter of Fulk of Anjou, 12, 16
Silvester, abbot of St. Augustine's, 180
Simon, bishop of Worcester, 61
Simon of Beachamp, 43
Simon of Senlis, earl of Northampton, 93–4, 104, 122
Sleaford, 65, 68
Somerset, earl of. *See* William of Mohun
South Cerney, 77–8
Southampton, 38
Stamford, 138, 147, 191–2
Stephen, king of England: parentage, 1; birth, 7; marriage and early life, 9–11; swears oath to Matilda, 15; character, 11, 38, 76–7, 156; claims crown (1135), 20–3; crowned, 23–4; at Reading (1136), 24–5; promises at Oxford, 25; meets King David, 26–7; Easter court 1136, 27–9; recognised by pope, 29–30, 33, 61–3; Oxford Charter, 32–4, 40; and Baldwin of Redvers, 35–9, 73; visits Normandy (1137), 40–2; besieges Bedford, 43–6; invades Scotland (1138), 46–7; receives Earl Robert's *diffidatio*, 48–9; reconnoitres Bristol, 50–1; creates earls, 55–7; and

election of Archbishop Theobald, 60–1; proceeds against Roger of Salisbury (1139), 64–73, 78; and landing of Matilda, 74–5; in Isle of Ely and South West, 79–84; visits Ranulf of Chester, 85–8; at Battle of Lincoln (1141), 89–96; imprisoned at Bristol, 97, 99, 101, 116; released, 117–18; second crowning, 120–2; visits Yorkshire (1142), 123; besieges Oxford, 125–8; defeated at Wilton, 128–9; overcomes Geoffrey de Mandeville (1143), 134–42; captures Faringdon (1145), 146; subdues Ranulf of Chester, 146–53; 175–6; helps Henry (1147), 154–5; and election of Archbishop William of York, 156–8, 164–5; quarrels with Archbishop Theobald, 165–71, 179; repels Scots (1149), 173–4; attempts to secure Eustace's succession, 177–9; and episcopal elections, 180–1; declines battle at Malmesbury (1153), 186–8, and at Wallingford, 189–90; recognises Henry as his heir, 194–8; dies, 202; assessment of his reign, 203–7
Stephen, count of Blois and Chartres, 1–7, 18, 22, 91, 96, 132
Stephen, count of Burgundy, 5–6
Stockbridge, 115
Surrey, earl of. *See* William of Warenne
Sussex, earl of. *See* William of Aubigny

Tetbury, 143–4
Theobald, archbishop of Canterbury, 60–1, 64, 70, 72, 84, 99, 101, 109, 113, 117, 120, 122, 132, 157, 159–60, 164–71, 178–80, 193–4, 196, 200–3
Theobald, count of Blois, 6, 10, 21, 29, 31, 39–40, 84, 103, 167, 180, 185, 203
Thierry of Alsace, count of Flanders, 41, 199, 202
Thirsk, 53
Thomas Becket, 166, 179, 202
Thurstan, archbishop of York, 28, 52–3, 61, 70, 90, 107
Tinchebrai, Battle of, 7, 9
Tours, 103
Trèves, 164

Trowbridge, 77
Turgis of Avranches, 144–5
Tutbury, 188, 192

Ulgar, bishop of Angers, 21, 62

Waldef, prior of Kirkham, 120
Walden Priory, 141
Waleran, count of Meulan and earl of
  Worcester, 19, 28, 43, 49, 55, 65–6,
  75, 83, 93–5, 104, 181–2, 188
Walkelin Maminot, 52
Wallingford, 75–8, 126–8, 148, 182–3,
  189–90, 192
Walter, abbot of Ramsey, 137–8, 140–1
Walter Espec, 52, 54
Walter of Gant, 52
Walter of London, 91, 120
Walter of Pinkney, 145
Waltheof, earl of Northumbria, 26
Walton, 141
Wareham, 73, 125, 127–8, 154, 186
Wark, 26
Warwick, 192
— earls of, 44. *See also* Roger of
  Beaumont
Weobly, 47
Westminster, 24, 28, 59, 106, 110, 119
Wheldrake, 174
Wherwell, 98, 114
White Ship, 11–12
William I, king of England, 1–2, 7, 9,
  12, 14, 26, 33, 40, 48, 55, 71, 154,
  157, 204
William II, king of England, 7, 33, 40,
  71, 142
William, abbot of Rievalux, 120
William, archbishop of York, 90–1,
  120, 158–9, 161–4, 201–2,
William, bishop of Norwich, 166, 170
William, castellan of Salisbury, 129
William, count of Mortain, 9
William, earl of Gloucester, 81–2, 125,
  155, 176–7
William, son of Geoffrey of Anjou, 17
William, son of Henry II, 191
William, son of King Stephen, 193–7,
  199
William Clito, 10–14, 16, 41
William de Sulli, 6, 180
William fitz Gilbert, 109
William fitz Richard, 80
William Martel, 122, 129
William of Aubigny, earl of Lincoln or

Sussex, 74, 88, 105, 122, 189
William of Aumale, earl of York, 52,
  55, 91, 93–6, 120, 122–3, 143, 158,
  163, 165
William of Beauchamp, 182
William of Cahagnes, 96
William of Chamai, 146
William of Corbeil, archbishop of
  Canterbury, 15, 20, 23–4, 28, 30, 33,
  59, 62
William of Dover, 143, 145
William of Eu, 163–4
William of Fossard, 52
William of Mohun, earl of Dorset or
  Somerset, 73, 109, 113
William of Percy, 52
William of Pont de l'Arche, 22–4, 112,
  129–30, 132
William of Roumare, earl of Lincoln,
  85–9
William of St.-Calais, bishop of Dur-
  ham, 71
William of Ste.-Barbe, bishop of
  Durham, 158–9, 161–3, 165, 199–200
William of Salisbury, 116
William of Saye, 138
William of Warenne, earl of Surrey,
  19, 28, 63, 93–5, 104, 115, 122, 153,
  188, 193
William of Ypres, 41–2, 49, 67, 77,
  71, 92, 95–6, 110, 113–16, 122, 168, 170
William Paganel, 106, 192
William Peverel, 53, 106, 192, 199
William son of Alan, 51
William son of John, 51
William the Atheling, 10–12, 15
Wilton, 99, 128–9
Wiltshire, earl of. *See* Hervey of Léon
Winchcomb, 78, 144
Winchester, 22, 70–1, 73, 83, 98–101,
  111–15, 117, 129, 160, 167, 194, 201
— bishop of. *See* Henry
Windsor, 196
Wissant, 21
Worcester, 78, 181–3
— bishop of. *See* Simon
— earl of. *See* Waleran

York, 53, 123, 165, 173–4, 201
— archbishops of. *See* Geoffrey;
  Henry Murdac; Roger of Pont
  l'Evêque; Thurstan; William
— earl of. *See* William of Aumale

DATE DUE

OCT 2 '76			

DEMCO 38-297